Reclaiming Haiti's Futures

Critical Caribbean Studies

Series Editors
Yolanda Martínez-San Miguel,
Carter Mathes, and Kathleen López

Editorial Board: Carlos U. Decena, Rutgers University; Alex Dupuy, Wesleyan University; Aisha Khan, New York University; April J. Mayes, Pomona College; Patricia Mohammed, University of West Indies; Martin Munro, Florida State University; F. Nick Nesbitt, Princeton University; Michelle Stephens, Rutgers University; Deborah Thomas, University of Pennsylvania; and Lanny Thompson, University of Puerto Rico

Focused particularly in the twentieth and twenty-first centuries, although attentive to the context of earlier eras, this series encourages interdisciplinary approaches and methods and is open to scholarship in a variety of areas, including anthropology, cultural studies, diaspora and transnational studies, environmental studies, gender and sexuality studies, history, and sociology. The series pays particular attention to the four main research clusters of Critical Caribbean Studies at Rutgers University, where the coeditors serve as members of the executive board: Caribbean Critical Studies Theory and the Disciplines; Archipelagic Studies and Creolization; Caribbean Aesthetics, Poetics, and Politics; and Caribbean Colonialities.

For a complete list of titles in the series, please see the last page of the book.

Reclaiming Haiti's Futures

Returned Intellectuals, Placemaking, and Radical Imagination

DARLÈNE ELIZABETH DUBUISSON

RUTGERS UNIVERSITY PRESS
NEW BRUNSWICK, CAMDEN, AND NEWARK, NEW JERSEY
LONDON AND OXFORD

Rutgers University Press is a department of Rutgers, The State University of New Jersey, one of the leading public research universities in the nation. By publishing worldwide, it furthers the University's mission of dedication to excellence in teaching, scholarship, research, and clinical care.

Library of Congress Cataloging-in-Publication Data

Names: Dubuisson, Darlène Elizabeth, author.
Title: Reclaiming Haiti's futures : returned intellectuals, placemaking, and radical imagination / Darlène Elizabeth Dubuisson.
Description: New Brunswick, New Jersey: Rutgers University Press, [2025] | Series: Critical Caribbean studies | Includes bibliographical references and index.
Identifiers: LCCN 2024016204 | ISBN 9781978837393 (paperback) | ISBN 9781978837409 (hardcover) | ISBN 9781978837416 (epub) | ISBN 9781978837423 (pdf)
Subjects: LCSH: Social change—Haiti—History—20th century. | Social change—Haiti—History—21st century. | Return migrants—Haiti. | Haitian diaspora—History—20th century. | Haitian diaspora—History—21st century. | Haiti—History—20th century. | Haiti—History—21st century.
Classification: LCC HN213.5 .D83 2025 | DDC 303.4097294—dc23/eng/20240709
LC record available at https://lccn.loc.gov/2024016204

A British Cataloging-in-Publication record for this book is available from the British Library.

Copyright © 2025 by Darlène Elizabeth Dubuisson

All rights reserved

No part of this book may be reproduced or utilized in any form or by any means, electronic or mechanical, or by any information storage and retrieval system, without written permission from the publisher. Please contact Rutgers University Press, 106 Somerset Street, New Brunswick, NJ 08901. The only exception to this prohibition is "fair use" as defined by U.S. copyright law.

References to internet websites (URLs) were accurate at the time of writing. Neither the author nor Rutgers University Press is responsible for URLs that may have expired or changed since the manuscript was prepared.

♾ The paper used in this publication meets the requirements of the American National Standard for Information Sciences—Permanence of Paper for Printed Library Materials, ANSI Z39.48-1992.

rutgersuniversitypress.org

For Kingston and Nthando

Contents

Preface   ix
Note on the Text   xv
Abbreviations   xvii
Chronology   xix

Introduction: Homing: A Futural Orientation   1

PART I
Fractures

1   Colonial Ruptures in the Caribbean and the
Displacement of Haitian Intellectuals   23

2   Internal Displacements: Tracing the Generational
Aspects of Exile and Diasporic Homecomings   51

3   The "Crisis Factory": Improvising Place in the (State)
University of Haiti   78

PART II
Sutures

4   *Rasanblaj*: Assembly beyond Coloniality's
Fractures   101

5   Imagining Emancipatory Caribbean Futures   126

Coda: Reclaiming Haiti's Futures: A Call for
Planetary Suturing and Repair   143

Acknowledgments 149
Notes 153
References 163
Index 187

Preface

In an essay about her journey to rejoin her Haitian roots after the 2010 quake, U.S.-based Haitian educator, scholar, and spiritual healer Charlene Désir (2011, 278) writes: "[T]he January 12, 2010, earthquake was a profound wound for the people of Haiti, but only the most recent one. For the Haitian diaspora, however—and particularly for Haitian academics—it raised a new set of complexities: what is our role and what is our responsibility in response to post-earthquake needs?" As a member of the Haitian *dyaspora* (diaspora), this question, which formed in my spirit long before I read it, would lead me to pursue doctoral research on the engagement of Haitian intellectuals and academics in social transformation.

This book, then, started as a doctoral dissertation, which I undertook in the joint applied anthropology program at Columbia University under the initial supervision of Dr. George Clement Bond. I worked with Dr. Bond during my master's and pursued a doctorate in the joint program, mainly to continue our work together. Dr. Bond was a London School of Economics–trained social anthropologist who studied social change and the intellectual productions of thinkers and political leaders across Africa and the African diaspora. In the edited volume, *The Second Generation of African American Pioneers in Anthropology*, Black American biocultural anthropologist Rachel Watkins (2018, 41–42) notes the following concerning Dr. Bond's work:

> His work offered important critiques of dominant approaches to research on Africa that reified the continent as the place where the "savage in modernity" could be found. In addition to seeking to write Africa and Africans into modern history, Bond aimed to represent the voices of Africans as participants in and producers of their own history before, during, and after colonialism. . . . Bond's work demonstrates that African American vindicationist intellectual

projects involve more than countering narratives that cast Africans and their descendants in a negative light. Rather, Bond asserts that approaches to the study of Africa that counter its positioning as peripheral to the modern world are a critical part of refining method and theory in the social sciences.

Dr. Bond's upbringing in an esteemed family of Black intellectuals and activists informed his intellectual proclivities and research interests (Watkins 2018). Dr. Bond's grandfather, "James M. Bond, who was a two-year-old enslaved child when the Civil War began, became a Congregational minister with a superior education he earned at Berea and Oberlin colleges, receiving a Bachelor of Divinity in 1896 from the latter and thus establishing superior education and very high achievements as family markers" (Rowell 2015, xiv). Born in 1936, Dr. George Bond "spent periods of his childhood in Haiti, Liberia, and Afghanistan as well as the American South as a result of his father's various posts. J. Max Bond Sr. was a notable educator with a doctorate in sociology from the University of Southern California" (Watkins 2018, 143). J. Max Bond Sr. also served as the president of the University in Liberia in the 1950s (Williams 1971). Dr. George Bond's mother, Ruth Clement Bond, "was also an educator and civic leader born into a prominent black family. Ruth received bachelor's and master's degrees in English literature from Northwestern University. She is also known for her work on a quilting project with the wives of men building dams for the Tennessee Valley Authority. During this time, she designed what is thought to be the first 'black power quilt'" (Watkins 2018, 143). Dr. Bond's cousin, Horace Julian Bond, was a notable African American civil rights movement leader, politician, and professor. His late brother, J. Max Bond Jr., was an internationally acclaimed architect; his sister, Jane Bond, is an accomplished historian and professor emerita at Baruch College (Rowell 2015).

I remember my first interaction with Dr. George Bond. He addressed me in Haitian *Kreyòl* and genuinely sought to connect his biography with mine. As a first-generation Haitian American raised in a working-class, single-parent household, the only one in my family to pursue graduate education, I assumed a chasm between us. But Dr. Bond treated me like his intellectual progeny, colleague, and friend. As his PhD advisee, I led master's seminars and graded student papers alongside him. I also recall the thought-provoking conversations in his office on the third floor of Grace Dodge Hall: hundreds of books and dozens of yellow legal pads filled with the copious notes he had taken over the decades lined his office walls, reflecting what I imagined to be the wealth of his academic knowledge. Dr. Bond passed away in the second year of my doctoral studies, leaving me without a dedicated mentor in the program. The pain of this experience still lingers.

But, looking back, I realize that Dr. Bond did continue to guide me. For instance, when others sometimes challenged my decision to work with Haitian

PREFACE   xi

scholars as opposed to a more "subaltern group," I recalled Dr. Bond's conten-
tion that if we were to understand the (post)colonial moment, it was essential to
grapple with how postcolonial "elites" sought to create new worlds and reclaim
their sovereignty through radical thought and action—even if they had fallen
short of or betrayed their goals. And when I wondered whether engaging in ethnographic research in my ethnic homeland undercut my so-called credibility as
an anthropologist, I remembered Dr. Bond's assertion that "at-home" ethnography was rooted in a long tradition of Black, particularly Black feminist,
ethnography that sought to decolonize the discipline through self-reflexive
and engaged methodologies (see Harrison 1991; Harrison and Harrison 1999;
Harrison, Johnson-Simon, and Williams 2018; McClaurin 2001). So, with
Dr. Bond as my guide, I undertook what I saw as one of my responsibilities in
national rebuilding: illuminating the radical and even contradictory thoughts
and actions of Haitian scholars who had returned home to participate in the
transformation of Haiti after a crisis and, in the process, work toward constituting belonging for themselves and others.

———

Engaging in ethnography at home or in one's ethnic homeland carries certain
advantages and challenges. I recall Barnard-Columbia-trained cultural anthropologist Zora Neale Hurston's return to her all-Black hometown of Eatonville,
Florida, to undertake research for *Mules and Men* (1935). The pathbreaking book
effectively merges autoethnography and Eatonville residents' recounting of African American folktales, making it one of the first native and multivocal ethnographies. In the book's introduction, Hurston (1935/2009, 2) writes: "I hurried
back to Eatonville because I knew that the town was full of material and that I
could get it without hurt, harm or danger." In this passage, Hurston is less
undermining the inherent risks of all ethnographic fieldwork and more pointing
to her belief that her positionality allowed her a unique entry point and greater
access and trust within the community under study. In an article about Hurston's
ethnographic approach, Black feminist anthropologist Gwendolyn Mikell (1982,
219) writes: "Hurston approached the study of black people with an assumption
that the best researcher was one who had an element of commonality with the
people being studied. She thought that one had to 'feel the material,' 'be of the
group.' Only by entering into the heads of the participants, viewing the culture
through their eyes, and describing it in their terms, would one obtain an accurate picture of their cultural reality." Hurston's perspective thus countered then
(and I would argue, still now) prevailing disciplinary conventions that required
"anthropologists to study 'other' cultures, cultures that are not her own, that are
either faraway or close exotic or primitive cultures" (Nwankwo 2003, 51).[1]

    Still, Hurston experienced dilemmas and perpetuated contradictions nego-
tiating her assumed status as an "insider" and her ascribed role as a translator

xii   PREFACE

for her community to the academy.[2] When Hurston returned to Eatonville for fieldwork, she engaged in initiation ceremonies with "hoodoo doctors," emphasizing "her investment in constructing herself as an insider" (Nwankwo 2003, 57). Literary scholar Ifeoma Nwankwo (2003, 57) posits that Hurston's discomfort with being seen as an outsider was informed by her anthropological training and positioning as a token in the academy. Nwankwo (2003, 57) writes: "Part of Hurston's attitude is certainly attributable to her white advisor's (Franz Boas) and her white patron's (Charlotte Osgood Mason) valuation of her as an insider who can tap into and write about blackness in a way that they cannot. For them, she is and must be authentically black and therefore able to automatically know and understand black communities everywhere." The reality was, however, that Hurston's assumed "insider" status did not allow her comfort within or knowledge of "black communities everywhere." Although Hurston sought to bring an "insider" perspective to her research in the Caribbean, she failed to appreciate the region on its own terms and within its own logics, theorizations, and realities.

In her ethnography, *Tell My Horse: Voodoo and Life in Haiti and Jamaica*, published in 1938, "just four years after the end of the U.S. Occupation of Haiti [1915–1934] and during a relative explosion of scholarly and artistic interest in that republic" (Nwankwo 2003, 63), Hurston reproduced U.S. imperialist illogics of intervention despite her best intentions. While Hurston's *Mules and Men* points to "familiarity" as an impetus for research, her work in the Caribbean brings into sharp relief the tensions that arose "when [the] driving force of familiarity [was] not available to her" (Nwankwo 2003, 51). Despite being a racial "insider,"[3] Hurston was a national "outsider" who fostered U.S. imperialist attitudes toward the Caribbean. An apologist for the U.S. Occupation of Haiti and trained within the exoticizing gaze of anthropology (Nwankwo 2003; Owens 2023; Trefzer 2000),[4] Hurston represented the Caribbean through an imperialist lens obscured and legitimated by her racial identity. In the case of Haiti, though she sought to provide an authentic view of *Vodou* (Voodoo in her text), she participated in the demonization of the life-affirming Afro-syncretic religion, furthering Euro-American perversions of the religion as a devil-worshipping cult.[5] In her essay, "Possessing the Self: Caribbean Identities in Zora Neale Hurston's *Tell My Horse*," literary scholar Annette Trefzer (2000) highlights the tensions and contradictions inherent in *Tell My Horse*. Trefzer (2000, 299) writes:

> Hurston seems caught between defending the U.S. imperial "possession" of Haiti and simultaneously critiquing it by highlighting spiritual possession of Haitian voodoo [*sic*] rituals as a strategy of resistance to colonial politics. The resulting tension between an imperial nationalism articulated explicitly within the political context of American occupation and the cultural, anthropological discourse of Hurston's observations on voodoo [*sic*] leads to an unresolved dialectic in *Tell My Horse*. This contradiction is instructive, how-

PREFACE xiii

ever, because it reveals the construction of a national "Other" as an intensely complex and always ambiguous task which ultimately mirrors the culture and politics of the ethnographer more than that of her subjects.

Hurston's shortcomings as a pioneering native anthropologist taught me to be careful of claims of "insider" knowledge and to continually interrogate how my U.S. citizenship and anthropological training in the United States informed how I viewed and experienced my ethnic homeland and related to those with whom I worked. Familiarity could not be my driving force, nor could strangeness.

Since Hurston, Black ethnographers studying Black people at home and abroad (e.g., Bolles 2022; Bond 1976; Bonilla 2015; 2019; Carter 2010; Cox 2015; Gwaltney 1993; McClaurin 1996; Mullings 1996, Simmons 2009; Ulysse 2007) have theorized and worked through the tensions of what Afro-Dominican anthropologist Kimberly Simmons (2001) called "sameness and difference," demonstrating that engaging in research at home or with one's racial kin must include rigorous interrogations of what it means and looks like to navigate being an outsider within/insider without.[6] In this book, I follow in the footsteps of Black—particularly Black feminist—anthropologists who have bravely traversed the contradictions, challenges, and responsibilities of theorizing on the margins of the academy and from the experiences and perspectives of Black people.

Like many Black ethnographers before me, this book required my homecoming. I returned to Haiti in 2013, 2016, and 2017 to pursue ethnographic research on Haitian returned scholars. But my most recent homecoming in 2017 for prolonged fieldwork felt markedly different than previous ones because I would be navigating life in Haiti as a caretaker and would, for the first time, go without the buffer provided by staying with family. In fall 2017, I moved into a 3.5-bedroom apartment in a mixed-income *Pòtoprens* (Port-au-Prince) neighborhood with my then three-year-old son. I also took a position as a visiting professor at the State University of Haiti (UEH). Within a few months, I would learn the daily rhythms of the neighborhood: the near-hourly crow of roosters; the nightly smell of burning rubbish; the early-morning sing-song of *machann* (street vendors) selling freshly baked bread, avocados, and bananas; the staccato voices of the couple in the makeshift home next door who used cajoling and threats to teach their children the French alphabet; and the youth who sat under streetlamps at dusk to memorize lessons from textbooks or photocopies. I would also come to befriend two women who had returned post-2010: one helped me navigate childcare, and the other ran a grocery delivery service, which I used to mitigate time-consuming trips to open-air markets downtown or high-end supermarkets in *Petyonvil* (Pétionville). Cooking under candlelight during blackouts, lugging gallons of drinking water uphill to the apartment, haggling with machann, hanging out with friends and colleagues at cafés and bars, navigating through dense traffic on the back of moto-taxis to get to work, and teaching at a university emerging from a roughly two-year crisis all helped me better understand the everyday (albeit class-specific) aspects of life in Haiti.

Nonetheless, I knew the stakes were different for me than for the returned scholars I worked with. Returning from countries such as France, Canada, the United States, Belgium, Mexico, and Brazil, these scholars were a diffuse and diverse group of men and women. Indeed, many Haitians with advanced graduate degrees and doctorates have studied and lived abroad. The returned scholars I worked with had generally come home after the 1986 overthrow of the Haitian dictator Jean-Claude Duvalier to participate in the country's democratic transition through political leadership and activism or after the 2010 earthquake to partake in postearthquake reconstruction through public higher-education reform. How could I draw from my experiences to better understand theirs while considering what separated us? With this question in mind, I navigated fieldwork attempting to attune to *"sameness and difference"* (Simmons 2001) or how my gendered, diasporic, and generational identity informed my interactions and relationships with my homeland and those with whom I worked.

Based on ethnographic fieldwork in metropolitan Pòtoprens between 2013 and 2018, *Reclaiming Haiti's Futures: Returned Intellectuals, Placemaking, and Radical Imagination* is a *self*-reflexive, *multivocal* ethnography that illuminates how two generations of Haitian returned intellectuals envisioned and sought to enact new worlds after crisis. An ethnography of the future, this book pursues fundamental anthropological questions of home, belonging, and emplacement. These concerns are ever more relevant amid political, socioeconomic, and ecological crises displacing and enclosing the prospects of many, especially those living in (post)colonial (outer) peripheries like Haiti (see Fatton 2014).

Note on the Text

In this book, my decisions around whether or not to use pseudonyms are guided by my commitments to those with whom I worked and concerns of style and consistency. Some of the scholars with whom I worked desired anonymity, but most (specifically, figures known to the Haitian public) expected to be named. For consistency's sake, I use pseudonyms for all interlocutors except for known and emergent public figures who have aspects of their life stories in the public domain and who permitted me to name them. I demarcate a real name by including a surname the first time the name appears in the text.

I do not give a pseudonym to the university where most of my fieldwork occurred. Given that only one state university exists in Haiti, using a pseudonym would be futile. Doing so would have also gone against my commitment to provide a transparent analysis of the university's policies and procedures as they reflected a tense relationship with the state and inequalities within the global knowledge economy and neoliberal university system. I also name non-university sites where I undertook fieldwork (unless doing so would reveal the identities of pseudonymized interlocutors) because these sites merit greater visibility in a global knowledge economy that fails to appreciate the intellectual and artistic innovation that occurs in places like Haiti.

Finally, I engage a "politics of citation" (Delgado 1984) by referencing and thinking with the works of the scholars I worked with in Haiti. These scholars are writers and theorists who write primarily in French, and some in English and Kreyòl. I cite excerpts in the original language and follow Kreyòl or French passages with English translations. Unless another translator is noted, the translations, and any errors within them, are my own.

Abbreviations

CARICOM	Caribbean Community and Common Market
CE	Conseil Exécutif (Executive Board)
CNG	Conseil National de Gouvernement (National Council of Government)
CU	Conseil de l'Université (University Council)
CUEH	Le Conseil de l'Université d'État d'Haïti (Council of the State University of Haiti)
ENS	École Normale Supérieure (School of Education)
FASCH	Faculté des Sciences Humaines (Faculty of Human Sciences)
FE	Faculté d'Ethnologie (Faculty of Ethnology)
HSA	Haitian Studies Association
IDB	Inter-American Development Bank
IERAH	Institut d'Études et de Recherches Africaines (Institute of African Studies and Research)
INURED	Interuniversity Institute for Research and Development
KONAKOM	Komite Nasyonal Kongres Oganizasyons Demokratik (National Committee of the Congress of Democratic Organizations)
MENFP	Le Ministère de l'Education Nationale et de la Formation Professionnelle (Ministry of National Education and Vocational Training, or simply "Ministry of National Education")

MENJS	Ministère de l'Education Nationale de la Jeunesse et des Sports (Ministry of National Youth and Sports Education)
MINUSTAH	Mission des Nations Unies pour la Stabilisation en Haïti (United Nations Stabilization Mission in Haiti)
NACLA	North American Congress on Latin America
UEH	Université d'État d'Haïti (State University of Haiti)

Chronology

cir. 5000 B.C.E.	Ayiti was home to the first Ayitians.
1492	Christopher Columbus came upon the island in 1492; he renamed it Hispaniola and set up a small outpost on its northern coast.
1501	The first enslaved Africans arrive in Hispaniola.
1685	King Louis XIV issued the edict that would become the *Code Noir* (Black Codes).
1697	The Spanish legally ceded the island's western half to the French with the Treaty of Ryswick. The French translated the Spanish name to Saint-Domingue (the current-day Republic of Haiti).
1791–1804	The Haitian Revolution, a collective of successful slave revolts and rebellions, led to the overthrow of French colonialism in Saint-Domingue.
1805	Revolutionary hero Jean-Jacques Dessalines, named Emperor of Haiti, ratified Haiti's first constitution as a free country.
1806–1820	Haiti divided into two, the Kingdom of Haiti in the north, ruled by Henri Christophe (or Henri I), and Alexandre Pètion's republic in the south, which centered around Port-au-Prince.
1820	President Jean-Pierre Boyer reunited Haiti.
1820–1823	Haiti's Schools of Medicine and Law were established.

1825	King Charles X declared that France would recognize Haitian independence for the price of 150 million francs.
1826	Boyer implemented the infamous Code Rural, establishing state control over agricultural production.
1885	Anténor Firmin published *De l'égalité des races Humaines (Anthropologie positive)*.
1915	The start of the U.S. miliary Occupation of Haiti.
1927	Jean Price-Mars led the formation of *indigéniste*—a literary movement predicated on Haitian indigénisme or the culture of the Haitian peasantry.
1928	Jean Price-Mars published *Ainsi parla l'oncle: Essais d'ethnographie.*
1929	A widespread anti-U.S. Occupation protest, the Damien revolt, erupted throughout Haiti.
1934	U.S. troops withdrew from the country. Haitian communists formed the Parti Communiste Haïtien (PCH). A group of Haitian feminists formed the Ligue féminine d'action sociale (Feminine League for Social Action).
1944	The establishment of the University of Haiti.
1946	A revolution successfully toppled the Élie Lescot's fascist dictatorship and ushered in a new era of Haitian politics where control shifted from *milat* to Black political elites.
1957	François Duvalier became president of Haiti.
1959	François Duvalier established the Tontons Macoutes or "bogeyman" (literally: "Uncle Gunnysack"), who persecuted intellectual and political dissents. Intellectuals and other professionals began fleeing the country.
1960/61	François Duvalier restructured the University of Haiti into the State University of Haiti.
1964	François declared himself "president for life."
1971	François amended the country's constitution to allow the president to choose his successor. François chose his nineteen-year-old son, Jean-Claude.
April 1971	Following his father's death, Jean-Claude Duvalier declared himself president for life.
1986	The fall of the 1986 Duvalier dictatorship. Intellectual exiles began returning to Haiti.

CHRONOLOGY

1987	Haiti adopted a new constitution to pave the way for democratic transition.
December 1990	Jean-Bertrand Aristide was elected president in a free democratic election.
September 1991	A military coup ousted Aristide.
1994–1995	Aristide was restored to the presidency to finish out his term.
1996–2001	René Préval's, a member of Aristide's Lavalas coalition, served first term as Haitian president.
1997	The State University of Haiti's Provisional Council and the state's Ministry of Education adopted the *Dispositions Transitoires* (Transitional Arrangements) giving the university more control over its leadership.
2001–2004	Aristide served second presidential term.
2004	A military coup ousted Aristide.
	"The UN Secretary-General recommends the creation of a multidimensional stabilization operation to assist with the situation in Haiti. The operation is called the United Nations Stabilization Mission in Haiti (MINUSTAH)."[1]
2006–2011	René Préval served second term as Haitian president.
January 12, 2010	A 7.0-magnitude earthquake struck fifteen miles west of Haiti, destroying most of the capital of Port-au-Prince, killing roughly 300,000 people, and leaving over two million without homes.
Post-2010	Members of Haiti's academic diaspora returned to assist postearthquake recovery through higher education reform.
October 2010	United Nations so-called peacekeeping forces introduced cholera to Haiti as many Haitians remained houseless in the wake of the 2010 earthquake. By September 2022, the "outbreak resulted in >820,000 cases and approximately 10,000 deaths (1,2). Nearly 12 years after the outbreak began, Haiti was declared cholera-free on February 4, 2022, after 3 years without a confirmed case."[2]
2011–2016	Michel Martelly served as Haitian president.
2016–2018	A university-wide crisis emerged at the State University of Haiti.

January 3, 2017	Jovenel Moïse, of Martelly's Tet Kale Party, was declared the new president of Haiti.
October 2017	MINUSTAH troops left Haiti.
Summer 2018	*Peyi lòk* ("country lockdown") began in protest of rising fuel prices, state corruption, and state-sanctioned violence.

Reclaiming Haiti's Futures

Introduction

HOMING: A FUTURAL ORIENTATION

A homing instinct.

I recall exactly where I was when I heard: in the bedroom of my old apartment in Boston, Massachusetts. And, if I concentrate, I can almost conjure the strange mix of emotions that grew from the pit of my belly to the base of my throat: confusion, denial, powerlessness, a weighted groundlessness. It was as if the *goudougoudou* (a Haitian onomatopoeia for the 2010 earthquake: the sound of the shaking earth) reverberated outward, creating fissures that reached far and wide across the Haitian *dyaspora* (diaspora).[1] Over the next few days and weeks, despite failed attempts to contact family and the increasing death toll, an intense feeling of hope and possibility overtook me, fueling a desire to grow wings somehow and "fly" back home.

Although I was born and raised in the United States, my earliest memories are of Haiti, where I lived with a maternal aunt between the ages of three and maybe four or five. The Haiti of my early childhood was colorful and fragrant. I remember plentiful mango and *kenèp* (Spanish lime) trees; handmade floral dresses and matching hair ribbons; roaming chickens with golden-flecked feathers; chatty neighbors and mischievous friends; and the mixed aromas of coffee, padded earth, and burning charcoal that clung to everything.

When I returned eighteen years later, in 2007, for a family trip, I found an occupied country still emerging from the *kriz* (crisis) surrounding the 2004 coup that deposed President Jean-Bertrand Aristide.[2] Plastics and other non-biodegradable materials littered downtown *Pòtoprens* (Port-au-Prince), second-hand clothes donated from abroad (*rad pèpè* in Kreyòl) lined the sidewalks, and the lush fruit-bearing trees that I remembered were fewer and nonexistent in some neighborhoods.[3] In short, the Haiti of my childhood seemed illusory. Still, some things remained as I had placed them: the embracing and grounding aromas, for one.

During this trip, I recognized a particular attachment and obligation toward Haiti—an orientation no doubt rooted in my growing identification as a dyaspora.[4] This homeward orientation intensified after the 2010 earthquake, propelling my eventual, although temporary, returns in 2013, 2016, and 2017 to engage in postearthquake recovery through ethnographic research.

My return was not unique.

At pivotal points in Haiti's history, various Haitian scholars living abroad returned home after a crisis in attempts to participate in birthing new horizons of possibilities—as if responding to the same sort of homing instinct I experienced. But unlike me, many of these scholars had been born and raised in Haiti and came back indefinitely. Two critical moments of such returns were surrounding the fall of the twenty-nine-year Duvalier dictatorship (1957–1986) and years after the 2010 earthquake. Despite a near quarter century separating their returns, those who returned to stay around these two periods would face overlapping societal fractures that would shape their reintegration and simultaneous efforts to participate in bringing about new futures in Haiti.

Returning Home to Build "Nests"

There is a Haitian proverb that I love: "Piti piti zwazo fè nich li" (Little by little, the bird builds its nest). Many Haitians use this proverb to refer to the small steps required to complete an enormous task. "Have patience," "step-by-step," "one day at a time," and so on. While the sentiment behind the adage is sound, I am more interested in its literal translation. I imagine a bird making her nest out of fragments: progressively weaving leaves, grass, and twigs, binding them with mud and her own saliva to create a place where she will lay her eggs and thus help ensure the future of her species. I think too about the innate instinct of birds and other animals to return home or to a place of origin after being displaced over long distances to build nests for their offspring.

Humans are also inclined to this sort of "homing." As biologist Bernd Heinrich (2014, xi) writes in *The Homing Instinct*, "For other animals and for us, home is a 'nest' where we live, where our young are reared. It is also the surrounding territory that supports us. 'Homing' is migrating to and identifying a suitable area for living and reproducing and making it fit our needs, and the orienting and ability to return to our own good place if we are displaced from it." For postcolonial Caribbean migrants displaced by political violence, socioeconomic disparity, and ecological disaster, leaving their home countries for former metropoles and present-day settler colonies and neocolonial empires is often seen as the best way to secure a better future for themselves and their families (see Crichlow 2012; Miller 2008; Sheller 2020; Werner 2015). Returning home to unsuitable conditions is rarely a choice, and voluntary permanent returns are

INTRODUCTION   3

usually only rendered conceivable when there is an opening for creating a livable future. This opening, I argue, may emerge after a crisis when it seems that another future is possible.

This book is, in essence, an ethnography of the future. Until recently, anthropology largely ignored the future due to what Arjun Appadurai (2013, 285) notes in *The Future as Cultural Fact* as the discipline's preoccupation with the "logic of reproduction, the force of custom, the dynamics of memory, the persistence of habitus, the glacial movement of the everyday, and the cunning of tradition in the social life of even the most modern movements and communities." As with other paradigm shifts in anthropology, the discipline turned toward studies of the future when a crisis demanded new approaches to understanding the human condition. Indeed, as anthropologists Rebecca Bryant and Daniel Knight (2019, 9) write in *The Anthropology of the Future*, the future emerged "as a developing field for anthropology in the 2000s when the 'war on terror' and global financial crisis and its aftershocks left many people around the world unable to anticipate the following day." Now a burgeoning field, the anthropology of the future covers myriad topics from the Anthropocene and climate change (e.g., Bauer and Bhan 2018) to biomedicine (Taussig et al. 2013) to outer space (Messeri 2016). As will become apparent in the following pages, my specific concerns in a study of the future center on coloniality: its proliferating crises and displacements and the spaces of possibilities existing in its contradictions.

In this book, I follow Bryant and Knight's (2019, 16) employment of "orientations" to "gain an ethnographic hold on the relationship between the future and action, including the act of imagining the future." Orientations describe a view of and feeling toward the future that informs action in the present. Like the past, the future exists in the present (Trouillot 1995). Or, as Bryant and Knight (2019, 16) posit: "The concept of the present *as present* derives from the future; . . . without a concept of futurity the present ceases to exist as such." The futural orientation of which I am concerned in this book is hope. Or, rather, the hope that emerges in the aftermath of a crisis. Crisis, here, describes a rupture and its resulting psychological, physical, and psychic dislocations, which create an inability to anticipate the future (Bryant and Knight 2019; Shevchenko 2008). Hope, for its part, "is a way of handling the indeterminacy of potentiality, of harnessing its remainders for momentum into a future that navigates the otherwise-than-actual. If the otherwise-than-actual always exists alongside the actual, hope is the affective result of trying to bring particular 'otherwises' into actuality" (Bryant and Knight 2019, 134). In the case of this book, this momentum (read: "homing") is toward the actualization of belonging, the otherwise of displacement. More specifically, I contend that "homing" or homecoming is about the potentiality of belonging. It is future-oriented, based on the possibility of constituting a livable place for oneself and others through social transformation.

4   INTRODUCTION

Throughout this book, I refer to Haiti's futures in the plural to gesture toward multiple belongings.

In the above vein, this book ethnographically traces the experiences of two generations of Haitian scholars who returned home to participate in social transformation. These two generations were locally referred to as *jenerasyon 86* (the 1986 generation)—intellectual exiles of the Duvalier dictatorship era—and the *jenn doktè* (literally, young doctorates)—the younger academics who returned after the 2010 earthquake. Jenerasyon 86 members include those who returned during an opening in the regime after François "Papa-Doc" Duvalier's death and the succession of his nineteen-year-old son Jean-Claude "Baby-Doc" Duvalier to the Haitian presidency (1971–1976) and those who came back after the 1986 overthrow of Jean-Claude Duvalier but before the inauguration of Jean-Bertrand Aristide to the presidency (1986–1991). Jenerasyon 86 members generally returned to participate in the country's democratic transition through political leadership and activism. As Carole, a former artist-activist and jenerasyon 86 member, told me: "When Duvalier fell, there was a wave of hope that things would change. I had to be there! I had to participate in the change!"

In contrast with jenerasyon 86, the later jenn doktè had generally emigrated around the tumultuous years of President Aristide's two nonconsecutive tenures (1994–1996, 2001–2004) to seek graduate education abroad. After the 2010 earthquake, the jenn doktè returned to partake in national reconstruction through public higher education reform. In the words of Pierre, a jenn doktè and professor at the State University of Haiti (UEH) who returned from Belgium in 2012: "I always said that if I went abroad for a doctorate, it would not be predicated on departure but return. [In Haiti] I studied at a university and department plagued with problems and aspired to return to contribute to the department, the university, [and] the country." Like jenerasyon 86 before them, the jenn doktè came home after a crisis that signaled both trauma and possible change.

This book, however, is less about what initiated the returns of jenerasyon 86 and the jenn doktè and more about what happened once they returned. After their displacement, how were these returnees able to identify and create their "own good place" in Haiti as intellectuals and academics? How were they received by local institutions, as well as by those who stayed? To what degree were they able to fulfill their ambitions to transform Haiti through political leadership and activism on the one hand and public higher education reform on the other?

In pursuing these questions, this book confronts prevailing notions of Haiti's "uninhabitability," or Haiti as "an uninhabitable place of transit and ongoing exile" (Munro 2007, 6).[5] This concept of uninhabitability goes hand in hand with prevalent ideas of *Black no futures*, meaning the "racialized temporality that conditions and shapes the way black spaces—the objects and people within them—are managed as places with no future on its own terms" (Solomon 2019, 85). Indeed, Appadurai (2013, 287) cautions that "the future is not

INTRODUCTION 5

just a technical fact or neutral space but is shot through with affect and with sensation." In other words, the future is felt and experienced differently across a fractured and unequal globalized world (see also Trouillot 2003). For instance, coloniality and its anti-Black illogic[6] have sought to foreclose and manage the futures of Black people existing in what Black feminist scholar Christina Sharpe (2016, 2) terms "the wake," defined as "the conceptual frame of and for living blackness in the diaspora in the still unfolding aftermaths of Atlantic chattel slavery." Continuing, Sharpe (2016, 15) adds, "Living in the wake on a global level means living the disastrous time and effects of continued marked migrations, Mediterranean and Caribbean disasters, trans-American and -African migration, structural adjustment imposed by the International Monetary Fund that continues imperialisms/colonialisms, and more." In the wake, coloniality and its anti-Black illogic have sought to reduce Black people and Black spaces to "bare life." Bare life, or *nuda vita*, as Italian philosopher Giorgio Agamben coined it, refers to the "conception of life in which the sheer biological fact of life is given priority over the way a life is lived" (Buchanan 2010, n.p.; see also Agamben 1995). Appropriating Agamben's "fantasies of bare life," Sibylle Fischer (2013) shows how Western representations of Haiti and Haitians diminish them to "bare life:" Haiti's Black, socioeconomically marginalized majority readily gets reduced "to their mere physical being, to their suffering, to their mortality" (Fischer 2013, 71), which in turn instantiates the idea that futures for and in Haiti are not possible outside of Western intervention. Such representations of Haiti and Haitians contribute to ongoing efforts to foreclose the futures of the first Black Republic, ensuring that it continues as what late Haitian anthropologist and theorist Michel-Rolph Trouillot (1990b, 5) called "the longest neocolonial experiment in the history of the West."

Conversely, this book follows Haitian literary scholar, UEH professor, and interlocutor Nadève Ménard's (2013) counter-concept, "inhabitability": Ménard's assertion that "Haiti is liveable in, and that individuals choose, and have always chosen, to leave, and also to stay" (Benedicty 2015, 106), or in the case of this book, return to stay. In her essay, "The Myth of the Exiled Writer," Ménard interrogates the centrality of exile in foreign analyses of Haitian literature. She writes: "The fact that exile is central to the most cited critical works on modern Haitian literature strikes me as a problem, one connected to broader issues such as the continued silencing of Haitian voices and the refusal to see the Haitian space as anything other than oppressive or empty" (Ménard 2013, 54). As someone surrounded and raised by writers and intellectuals living and producing in Haiti,[7] Ménard (2013, 57–58) asks:

> Couldn't we say that to continually deny that Haitian writers inhabit the Haitian space is in fact to deny them their right to participate in and belong to that space? The emphasis on exile for Haitian literature and writers serves

to establish the Haitian space as marginal. The continual insistence on exile as the dominant trope of Haitian literature plays into the idea of Haiti as unlivable. The underlying message is that Haiti is not worthy of these writers and their works. That it can neither produce nor nourish them. The successful Haitian writer has either escaped from Haiti or in rare cases triumphed in spite of it.

Ménard is one of the many Haitian writers and scholars with whom I worked who had chosen to return and live in Haiti, affirming the fact that Black spaces are not barren in and of themselves and that Black people have the right to live—even if "in the wake of slavery." To quote Christina Sharpe (2016, 130–131) once again, "Living as . . . we do in the wake of slavery, in spaces where we were never meant to survive, or have been punished for surviving and for daring to claim or make spaces of something like freedom, we yet reimagine and transform spaces for and practices of an ethics of care (as in repair, maintenance, attention), an ethics of seeing, and of being in the wake as consciousness." By drawing attention to how returned intellectuals worked toward and created inhabitability or future-oriented places of belonging in Haiti against processes of coloniality that have led others to leave, *Reclaiming Haiti's Futures* positions itself as an assertion of "Black futurity"—that is, Black people's right to and reclamation of livability through conscious efforts to "reimagine and transform" (Sharpe 2016, 131) the very spaces they inhabit (see also Butler 2021; Keeling 2019; Quashie 2021).

Based on multivocal (or multi-voiced) and multi-sited (or multi-local) ethnographic research, *Reclaiming Haiti's Futures* argues that extant fractures in Haiti and the Caribbean—the consequences of coloniality and its myriad manifestations—contributed to the displacement of jenerasyon 86 and the jenn doktè and simultaneous crises in the Haitian public university system. My central claim is that these returned scholars nonetheless worked toward and created inhabitability or future-oriented places of belonging within and beyond Haitian academe through improvisation (chapter 3), *rasanblaj* (a Haitian term invoking assembly, gathering, and compilation [Ulysse 2017]) (chapter 4), and radical imagination (chapter 5). I conclude that Haiti and the Caribbean, as "ex-centric" sites of theorization (Harrison 2016), allow an appreciation of how fractures have come to typify more and more aspects of life globally and insights into what we might do about it.

Caribbean Displacements

The Caribbean was born out of colonial displacements: the arrival of European imperialists in search of wealth, the violent dispossession of Native lands, the enslavement and genocide of Indigenous peoples, the forceful dislocation and

INTRODUCTION

enslavement of African peoples, the later compulsory migration of Asian indentured laborers (Khan 2001; Mintz 1986; Palmié 2006; Slocum 2006; Slocum and Thomas 2003). As Stuart Hall (2015, 18) aptly put it, "We must think of this emerging colonial space as constituting a distinctive 'third space'—a space of unsettledness, of conquest, of forced exile, of unhomeliness." However, Caribbean peoples would constitute something entirely original within this "third space"—a Creole culture made from different elements combined in unique and overlapping ways to create various Caribbean societies. An overly idyllic view of Caribbean formation or "creolization" obscures issues of power under colonial domination (Hall 2015). Although a site of creative world-making, the Caribbean had been conscripted into "coloniality."[8] Coloniality, here, defines a set of beliefs, behaviors, practices, and ways of being that normalize the knowledge systems and institutional and societal structures that uphold "colonial power" (Mignolo and Walsh 2018)—that is, "a social, economic, and political force blocking the path to freedom and self-determination of the colonized" (Scott 1999, 11). Coloniality remained in the Caribbean even with the formal abolishment of enslavement by the mid-1800s (see Kamugisha 2019). Therefore, the path to emplacement, to emancipatory futures, for the Caribbean requires an end to coloniality in all its manifestations.

The Caribbean's quest for complete emancipation included the unprecedented Haitian Revolution (1791–1804), a collection of successful slave rebellions, revolts, and revolutionary resistance that led to the overthrow of French colonial rule in Saint-Domingue (modern-day Haiti). In 1804, Haiti emerged as the first Black Republic, claiming its right to direct its own path. However, extant colonial powers would violently enclose Haiti's prospects through (neo)colonial and (neo)imperial measures, including the French indemnity, various embargoes, military occupations, et cetera (see Alexander 2022; Trouillot 1990b). The wresting away of Haiti's hard-won freedom prefigured what would occur in much of the Caribbean over a century and a half later.

In the post–World War II era (1945–1968), student- and intellectual-led anticolonial movements and popular resistance swept the Caribbean region and the world, contributing to the decolonization of much of the Caribbean through political liberation or incorporation. However, as Puerto Rican political anthropologist Yarimar Bonilla (2015) observes in *Non-Sovereign Futures*: incorporated islands like Martinique and Guadeloupe did not fit the legal definitions of independent states or formal colonies. Still, "for many Caribbean populations decolonization came with the hope of finally attaining the promises of freedom that had been held out since the moment of abolition" (Bonilla 2015, 14). Throughout the 1970s and early 1980s, various independent Caribbean governments experimented with alternative political models that deviated from the individualistic capitalism of Western Europe and the United States: for instance, democratic socialism in Jamaica, cooperative socialism in Guyana, and Marxist-Leninist-inspired socialism in Grenada (see Warwick 2022). However, by the mid-1980s, the political freedom of the independent Caribbean began to unravel "when new forces of capitalist globalization were rearranging the local/global articulation and with it, the field of sovereignty" (Scott 1999, 11).[9] In other words, the promises of the postcolonial moment began to retreat with the global reworking of coloniality.

Today, the Caribbean confronts "new waves of displacement" driven by overlapping crises (Sheller 2020, xix). More concretely, the convergence of new manifestations of coloniality—namely, capitalist globalization and neoliberalism—have devastated regional economies and fueled political instability and ecological vulnerability (Kamugisha 2019; Sheller 2020), stimulating unprecedented levels of extra-Caribbean migration, "with Guyana, Jamaica, and Haiti recording the largest net outflows in relative terms [2020 estimate]" (Jaupart 2023, 3). Against this backdrop of Caribbean displacement, this book attunes to the possibilities seized by Caribbean exiles and diasporic populations who returned home to reclaim emancipatory futures and, in the process, undo their displacement.

Exile and Diaspora Returns

"Exile" and "diaspora" describe two overlapping dimensions of displacement. Exile traditionally defines an individual forcibly expelled from their home country for political or punitive causes. More contemporary manifestations of exile may not include force or compulsion but an expression of discontent and disagreement with "hostile regimes or colonialism" by choosing (however constrained the choice) to leave (Hackl 2017, 55; see also Said 2000). Either way, exile relies on the "impossibility of return" (Hackl 2017, 58): home is a forbidden place of belonging and a reminder of nonbelonging elsewhere. Conversely, diaspora defines a group of geographically dispersed people who take root in a host country while maintaining ties to an often imaginary or mythic homeland (Clifford 1994; Gilroy 1994). Anthropologists have examined how diaspora populations foster imaginaries of a shared homeland through storytelling, nostalgia, and the memorialization of shared violence and suffering (e.g., Daniel 1997; Malkki 1995). Diaspora populations often persist because there is no home to which to return (Safran 1991), and even if a homeland does exist, returning may be read as potentially unsafe or traumatic. Indeed, "most accounts of diaspora have a geographically absent homeland or home region at the very core of the definition of a diaspora" (Olsson and King 2014, 256). Yet, despite exile's solitariness and diaspora's groupness, "ethnic groups can form a diaspora under collective banishment from their homeland and subsequently experience the prolonged condition of exile individually" (Hackl 2017, 60). For Caribbean peoples collectively exiled through enslavement, further expulsion from the Caribbean represents the merger of the two dimensions of displacement.

INTRODUCTION   9

In recent decades, social science research has brought attention to the growing phenomena of exiles and members of diasporic populations voluntarily
returning home, particularly during realized or potential positive social transformations in their homeland (e.g., Markowitz and Stefansson 2004; Olsson and
King 2014; Stack 1996; Tsuda 2009). Some scholars have placed particular
emphasis on those who return after a crisis, such as a civil war, autocratic rule,
or a natural/manufactured disaster, to partake in postconflict or postdisaster
recovery (e.g., Cela 2021; Chattoraj 2022, Eastmond 2006; Roniger et al. 2018;
Schwartz 2019). In the case of "emerging economy countries" (e.g., China, India,
and South Korea), governments have incentivized the returns of intellectuals and
academics to facilitate the transfer of knowledge and skills toward national development (e.g., Guo et al. 2003; Li et al. 2021; Mukherjee 2009). These varied
returns are motivated as much by the (potential) transformation of homelands
into more hospitable places as by the desire of exiles and members of diasporic
populations to undo their displacement. As historical sociologist Michaeline
Crichlow (2012, 119) contends, "fleeing and homing" is a way "displaced peoples
seek to morph given states. . . . [D]isplaced peoples seek to become something
otherwise by unsettling the experiences of the present's unhomeliness." However, while return "triggers associations and images of an 'event' . . . a permanent settlement which concludes the migratory cycles started by the returnee
and their ancestors" (Olsson and King 2014, 256), the returnee's quest for home,
for belonging, may continue even after they return (Olsson 2004).

Recent ethnographies on return migration challenge a "fixed image of closure," highlighting the "many practical problems and frustrating processes of
'reintegration,' including stressful encounters with a strange and sometimes hostile homeland society" (Olsson and King 2014, 256). These ethnographies reveal
how returning home may fundamentally reshape returnees' perception of and
relationship with the homeland and their sense of emplacement (e.g., Tsuda 2009;
Horst 2007; Ramji 2006). Even with these insights, the research must pay more
attention to homecoming's "generational" aspects. By generation, I do not simply mean biological age but also the socio-historical and political context of
return, "temporality" (see Scott 2014), and social positioning along the lines
such as color, class, gender, and so on, "location" (see Mannheim 1952/1972).
How do the experiences of returned migrants vary depending on temporality?
What role does social location play in returnees' ability to achieve emplacement?
This book approaches these questions by comparing the reintegration of two
generations of returned intellectuals and academics.

RETHINKING GEOGRAPHIES OF INTELLECTUAL LABOR

In the Caribbean and beyond, public intellectuals have come under suspicion
within a climate of "postcolonial malaise"—an environment defined by the

collective disappointment of postcolonial citizens with the unfinished project of decolonization and with the "intellectual-political generations" of the anti-colonial era who betrayed "their promises and principles once they grasped the reins of power within their hand" (Scott 2014, 158). Jamaican anthropologist and cultural critic David Scott (2014, 158) describes his experience of this malaise as a "generational apprehension," which "grows out of [his] experience of the collapse and seeming dead-end of the projects of political sovereignty, anti-imperialist self-determination, and socialist transformation that gave shape and point to the making of the Anglo-Creole Caribbean [he takes] to be [his] generation's inheritance." Of course, Western Europe and the United States led political campaigns to suppress and criminalize postcolonial and "third world" public intellectuals, as well as curtail the political sovereignty of postcolonial states, particularly those experimenting with socialist forms of governance. Nevertheless, within various postcolonial settings, more and more scholars have retreated from the formal political sphere to the more circumspect, while still political, domain of higher education (see Rajan 1997). As I will show in chapter 3, such was the case for members of jenerasyon 86.

In the late twentieth century, the decline of intellectuals in the public sphere corresponded with the rise of the "global knowledge economy" and the "neoliberal university." The knowledge economy refers to the "increased importance of knowledge, both know-how and information, and a well trained workforce that not only can apply know-how, but also is capable of analysis and decision making based on information" (Guruz 2011, 6–7). For its part, the neoliberal university describes the incorporation of academics and higher education institutions into the neoliberal logic of professionalization and marketization, which, in turn, undergirds the global knowledge economy (Olssen and Peters 2005; see also Shahjahan 2014). Both systems invariably privilege higher education institutions in former metropoles, neocolonial empires, and settler colonies (the Global North) while disadvantaging those in postcolonial states (the Global South).

More specifically, neoliberal market ideology has driven universities worldwide to compete for rankings and funding and to create "conformist academic subjects" through the imposition of an "academic audit culture" (Morrish 2020, 235). Audit culture, here, "refers to contexts in which the techniques and values of accountancy have become a central organizing principle in the governance and management of human conduct—and the new kinds of relationships, habits and practices that this is creating" (Shore 2008, 279). Academic audit culture uses surveillance and performance metrics technologies that monitor and measure scholarly productivity, such as publishing and acquiring grant funding (Strathern 2003). But, in the words of philosopher Ruth Barcan (2013, 94–95): "Academic audit culture measures proxies because it cannot measure the real thing: first, because so much of academic work deals with intangibles like understanding, meaning, and relationships . . . , and second,

INTRODUCTION

because only peers are in a position to judge scholarly content. Thus, many university auditing practices try to capture signs of productivity, like activity or busyness." This attention to productivity, in turn, undermines the culture of intellectual exchange and critique to which universities used to aspire and punishes engaged academics who openly speak against social injustices (see Schuller 2021b).

The global knowledge economy and neoliberal university system have compelled more and more postcolonial academics to invest in education in the Global North, some as a means of gaining "transnational cultural capital" to apply at home. Expanding on Pierre Bourdieu's concept of "cultural capital," meaning the accumulation of forms of knowledge, language, qualifications, and dispositions that provide social recognition and distinction, Martin Munk and others (2012) use transnational cultural capital to describe the phenomenon where individuals acquire familiarity with foreign cultures and institutions and foreign language skills to maintain or elevate their social status at home (see also Rizvi 2005; Wang 2020). However, as was the case with the jenn doktè (chapters 2 and 3), returned academics who receive education and training in the Global North may serve as conduits of academic audit culture, presenting a clash with local knowledge structures and practices.

In brief, the decline of scholars in the public domain and the preeminence of the global knowledge economy and the neoliberal university represent "contemporary crises of intellectual production [calling us] to attempt a rethinking of the geographies of intellectual labor" (Rajan 1997, 596). This book forwards this rethinking by mapping the experiences of returned Haitian scholars across three decades of unsettling changes in the global and local intellectual landscape. This book also reveals the "generational apprehension" (Scott 2014) of the jenn doktè toward jenerasyon 86 and how both groups of returnees navigated postcolonial disenchantment as they moved toward emplacement.

MULTIVOCAL ETHNOGRAPHY ACROSS MULTIPLE SITES

The topic of this book emerged during my initial dissertation field research in the summer of 2013. It was three years removed from the earthquake that had taken approximately 300,000 lives, displaced millions, and destroyed nearly 90 percent of the Haitian higher education institutions (INURED 2010). The failures of international recovery efforts were already apparent. Hundreds of thousands of internally displaced people (IDPs) still lived in makeshift camp settlements throughout the capital of Pòtoprens; debris removal and reconstruction were going slowly, and the cholera epidemic, brought to Haiti by U.N. so-called peacekeepers in the fall of 2010, continued to ravage the country. As predicted, despite billions in aid, the international humanitarian and development apparatus was not keeping its promise to help Haiti "build back better" (Schuller 2016).[10] In fact, much of the money was being funneled back to the international humanitarian and development actors, with minuscule amounts distributed to either the Haitian state or the Haitian people most affected by the quake (Ramachandran and Walz 2015; Schuller 2016).[11]

Given Haiti's long history of foreign-led development failures, many looked to the country's sizeable skilled diaspora as alternate development actors (Cela 2021; Wah 2013). Haitian academic diaspora members, in particular, were seen as strategically placed to contribute to postearthquake recovery and sustainable development by transferring knowledge and skills (Cela 2021). Within this perspective, the Canadian-based International Development Research Centre (IDRC) funded a cross-case study that examined, in part, the role of Haitian academic diaspora members in postdisaster recovery.[12] The Interuniversity Institute for Research and Development (INURED), an action-oriented think-tank located in the Pòtoprens neighborhood of Delmas, led the Haiti study. In 2011, INURED hired me as a research associate on the project. In this role, I surveyed Haitian scholars throughout the United States and Canada on their engagement in postearthquake recovery. I also interviewed U.S.-based Haitian academics working directly in Haitian higher education reform.

The project found that the Haitian diasporic academics who concentrated their efforts in the Haitian higher education sector saw its reconstruction as key to nation rebuilding (see Cela 2021). However, diaspora-led engagement in higher education typically consisted of short-term visits (usually a few weeks or months) and classroom-level interventions. Moreover, these interventions often met institutional barriers and resistance from academics in Haiti who critiqued diaspora-led interventions for not understanding the realities of Haitian higher education and yet seeking to impose Northern standards and so-called best practices (see also Cela 2016; 2021).

The tensions between Haitian academics from abroad and those in Haiti were palpable in my interviews with U.S.-based Haitian academics. I recall my interview with Rachelle, a U.S.-based Haitian academic and educator. For her, the diaspora had a "responsibility to be invested in Haiti's future and to act on that or to invest by bringing their skills to Haiti." She argued, however, that the diaspora members hoping to fulfill this responsibility faced a significant hurdle: relearning Haiti. Rachelle explained:

> Many people who left or returned after the earthquake assumed they knew Haitian culture or Haiti because they lived there twenty years ago or even ten years ago. I think this is a pretty common thing in immigration studies. A lot of literature shows that many people leave their [home] country, believing that it stays in the same condition that they left it, that it remains suspended, you know—*there*—without recognizing how the society has changed and how different historical events, broader culture, world politics and local politics, and so on, how those things change the country itself.

INTRODUCTION 13

Reflecting on her engagement in higher education reform in Haiti, Rachelle lamented what she saw as an atmosphere of competition that impeded collaboration between academic diaspora members and their homeland counterparts:

> It became apparent quickly that the Haitian [academic] partners were unwilling to face the realities of their situation's limitations, which became problematic. I understand it—I know it from the point of pride. Psychologically, it makes sense. . . . Haitians have been marginalized, and people assume they are not capable, and so on. So, I think one of the barriers was just a lot of resistance. Still, there is much politicking, and I think part of it is that the stage in Haiti is so small that many people are competing for a spot. I believe that many people want prestige and recognition for themselves, which is understandable, and it is the case in many other places. But when the stage is so small, it is much easier to see people knock each other off. Moreover, it creates a more competitive environment than is necessarily conducive [to change].

Rachelle indicates in the above quotation that the competition between Haitian academics from abroad and those in Haiti was situated within a more extensive system of inequalities that left one side frustrated and the other defensive. Although not a focus of the INURED study, I wanted to understand the perspectives of academics in Haiti navigating nation rebuilding and social transformation on the "so small" stage seemingly being encroached on by academic diaspora members. Thus, I decided to pursue my dissertation research on how academics in Haiti conceived of and participated in nation rebuilding. Unbeknownst to me then, this focus would reveal that many of the academics in Haiti who were resisting, or at least critical of, the apparent encroachment of Haitian academics from abroad were themselves returnees.

On a sweltering summer afternoon in June 2013, I sat with seventy-something-year-old Haitian sociologist and religion scholar, Laënnec Hurbon, in the living room of his home in the Pòtoprens metropolitan area. As I explained my research topic to him, he attentively listened while leaning back in a blue wicker chair. "I am interested in the role of local academics in nation rebuilding," I began. He slowly nodded, seemingly amused by the naiveté of my inquiry. Then, with the thoughtfulness of one who has spent a long career advising students, he suggested that I instead look at how academics' perception of Haiti changed from living abroad. "They may not like to admit it," he said as if revealing an open secret, "but many are returnees."

As I interviewed Haitian scholars that summer, I learned that many had lived abroad, some for decades, in Europe, the United States, or Latin America. Laënnec was himself a returnee. Born in Jacmel, a city in southern Haiti, he completed his undergraduate studies in Haiti before leaving for France in 1965 to pursue graduate education. Laënnec earned a doctorate in theology from the Institute Catholique de Paris in 1970 and a doctorate in sociology from the

University of Paris (Paris IV-Sorbonne) in 1976. Despite a successful academic career in France, Laënnec returned to Haiti after the fall of Duvalier and assumed professorships at the State University of Haiti (UEH) and Quisqueya University. The latter is a private institution he cofounded in 1987 (Joseph 2016). I was unprepared for this reality of return as the robust literature on Haitian migration and diaspora, which I had read in planning for fieldwork, concentrated on the unidirectional flow of movement and long-distance or short-term diaspora engagement.[13] I resolved to address this "gap in the literature," as it were, toward expanding scholarly understandings of Haitian migration and broader issues of Caribbean im/mobilities.[14] The core of my investigation centered on concerns of return, reintegration, and social transformation both before and after the 2010 earthquake. The multi-voiced dialogues in homes, offices, and cafés I began that summer with returnees around these concerns would lay the foundation of this multivocal and multi-sited (or multilocal) ethnography. In the words of ethnographer Martha Rodman (1992, 649): "Multivocality often involves multilocality. Polysemic places bespeak people's practices, their history, their conflicts, their accomplishments." In other words, to grasp returned scholars' myriad and overlapping perspectives and experiences, I would have to attend to how the diversity of their voices could not be disentangled from place as sites of contestation and co-creation.

Research for this book spanned over five years (2013–2018), with the bulk of ethnographic fieldwork occurring between October 2017 and May 2018. However, given my subsequent years of engagement with scholars and students in Haiti and the dyaspora through my work on the board of the Haitian Studies Association or HSA (2017–2021),[15] additional research for this book, and my positionality as a scholar and member of the Haitian dyaspora, I have yet to leave "the field"—if by "field" we mean a temporal space in which we are intensely asking questions, observing, participating, and formulating new understandings around a particular research topic (see Amit 2003).

The landscape of Haitian higher education within which I engaged in ethnographic fieldwork was a fractured terrain with grooves—some shallow, others deeper—connecting to the State University of Haiti (UEH), which comprised nineteen separate *fakilte* (schools) with loose institutional cohesion.[16] Before 2010, Haiti's higher education system included roughly 159 institutions divided into distinct public and private sectors:

> The former consisted of a small network of 14 public, government-run institutions of higher education (Instituts d'enseignement superieur, IES), including the State University of Haiti (Université d'État d'Haïti, or UEH). . . . Besides UEH, the public university sector also includes 13 IES either affiliated with or independent of UEH. In contrast, the private higher education sector consists

INTRODUCTION

of a vast array of 145 institutions of varying quality. Of the 145 private universities, 10 provide high-quality, accredited education; of the remaining 135 (often religious-based institutions), 67% (97) do not have permission to operate from the governmental Agency of Higher Education and Scientific Research (DESR). (INURED 2010, 4)

Some of the most prestigious public and private Haitian universities, including UEH, were members of the Regional Conference of Rectors and Presidents of Universities in the Caribbean or CORPUCA (INURED 2010, 4). As of 2019, CORPUCA included member universities from Haiti, the Dominican Republic, Cuba, Jamaica, Barbados, Trinidad and Tobago, and the French West Indies.[17] My role during ethnographic field research was that of an observant participator. "Unlike the participant observer, who tends to invent a new and somewhat transient role as a hang around, the observant participator is more likely to occupy and enact a preexisting role in the field. There are also important differences in passivity and proximity. Compared to participant observers, observant participators embrace a more active role in the field as they seek to minimize the distance between themselves and their empirical object" (Seim 2021, 3). As a postearthquake dyaspora returnee teaching at UEH (albeit temporarily), I was already implicated in what I sought to understand and could not stand outside my research as a participant observer. I thus moved as an observant participator across multiple sites.

According to anthropologist George E. Marcus (1995, 96), multi-sited ethnography not only "investigates and ethnographically constructs the lifeworlds of variously situated subjects" but "also ethnographically constructs aspects of the system itself through the associations and connections it suggests among sites" (see also Trouillot 2003). Employing this methodology allowed me to investigate interlocutors' "intellectual lifeworlds," so to speak. I accompanied interlocutors and worked with them as they moved across and between multiple locales of scholarly and artistic production throughout Pòtoprens, including UEH, private universities, and non-university settings. UEH was a node of academic and creative life in Haiti through the professional and social labor of UEH faculty, students, and alums. Thus, in addition to serving as a visiting professor at UEH Faculté d'Ethnologie (Fakilte Etnoloji or the School of Ethnology), I spent time at two other UEH fakilte—École Normale Supérieure (Lekòl Nòmal or the Teacher's College) and Faculté des Sciences Humaines (Syans Imen or the School of Human Sciences)—and led a semester-long research seminar for UEH professors. I also frequented scholarly and artistic gatherings at research institutes, cultural centers, intellectual salons, writing workshops, bookstores, and cafés. Through multi-sited observant participation, I was able to witness and experience how returned scholars worked to create inhabitability for themselves and others.

In addition to multi-sited observant participation, I undertook three types of interviews with various interlocutors: life history interviews with returned scholars; semi-structured interviews with UEH faculty, administrators, students, intellectuals, and artists, both those who had lived abroad and those who had not; and informal conversational interviews with non-academics. Formal interviews lasted from one to three hours and occurred primarily in Kreyòl with some intermixing of French or English.[18] As a temporarily returned academic dyaspora, I often served as a sounding board for senior scholars, peers, and students because I did not represent a threat of replacement or have institutional power or sway. To some, I was an open-eyed advisee; to others, a colleague and friend; and still others, a transient teacher with connections to the United States. Still, I had to navigate people's expectations of me and attempt to remain impartial when interlocutors sometimes blamed one group or another for strife within and beyond UEH. As I saw it, one of my jobs was to create dialogue between groups to move toward shared visions of the future. This book, in many ways, is a result of that labor.

I supplemented interviews with surveys and textual analysis. Foremost, I worked with a group of UEH students to survey the returnees I did not interview. The survey—administered across five UEH fakilte to 105 returned scholars—queried respondents' migration and professional history, academic production, and academic positions and affiliations. Additionally, I examined returned scholars' intellectual and artistic productions to gain an appreciation of their concerns and preoccupations. Finally, I analyzed official UEH documents to understand the inner workings of the university's legal and administrative structure. Survey and textual analysis revealed the rigor of intellectual and artistic production in Haiti despite material and institutional limitations (chapters 4 and 5) and how the global knowledge economy and neoliberalism (re)shaped higher education in Haiti (chapters 1 and 3).

Reclaiming Haiti's Futures is the culmination of multiple diverse voices, perspectives, and experiences, including my own. In the book, I present those with whom I worked as the co-intellectuals, mentors, and advisors they were in the field. Moreover, I draw on my earlier training in literature and poetry to illuminate the partial, dialogical, and affective nature of ethnographic fieldwork. Stylistically, I use lengthy excerpts from interviews to foreground interlocutors' voices and theorizations; present narratives in different literary modalities to re-enliven ethnographic moments; employ composite narrative to describe contested events; and intermix Kreyòl, French, and English to reflect the trilingual nature of my ethnographic field research. Through these varied devices and techniques, this book aims to create a textual space of assembly toward decolonial suturing.

INTRODUCTION

FRACTURES AND SUTURES: AN ORGANIZING STRUCTURE

I use the metaphors of fractures and sutures to structure this book. To quote feminist artist-anthropologist-activist Gina Athena Ulysse (2017, 69), echoing Rachel Beauvoir-Dominique: "We are living in times of deepest fracture and with fracture." Fractures conjure the image of breaking—the breaking of bones and earth, peoples and societies, spirits and psyches. Sudden bodily trauma, disease, or overuse may cause bones to break, resulting in displaced, non-displaced, simple, or compound fractures. Fractures are also associated with earthquakes. Massimo Cocco and others (2023) provide this technical and helpful description of earthquakes: "Earthquakes are caused by a shear rupture instability along a fault that undergoes a sudden displacement of the rocks on either side of the fault called slip. A fault is a zone of weakness with fractures between two hosting blocks (wall rocks), called the fault zone, which can move rapidly (~1 m/s), generating an earthquake, or slowly (up to 1 cm/year) in the form of nearly stable sliding and creep." (Un)natural disasters like earthquakes may bring into sharp relief the fault zones of our societies, as was the case with the 2010 Haitian earthquake. In *Failles* (*Faults*), award-winning Haitian Francophone writer and interlocutor Yanick Lahens (2010) evokes the aftermath of the January 12, 2010, earthquake to reflect on social cleavages in Haiti. Lahens points to what she sees as the foundational division in Haiti society: the fault line between the have-nots (*Bossales* or the Black economically poor majority) and the haves (*Creoles* "mulattos" or Black-skinned elite)—a fault line rooted in coloniality. She writes:

> I don't know of a greater historical and social fault line than that one in Haiti. It's the one that has been producing exclusion for two centuries. It cuts through all of us. Bossales as well as Creoles. It structures our way of being in the world. It shapes our imaginary, dictates our fantasies about skin color and class. It locks our society into two insurmountable molds: master and slave. Feeds our frustration. Nourishes our illusion. It silently crushes us as well. (Lahens 2020, 471)

In other words, societal fractures may result in spiritual and psyche fractures—fissures that foster illusions and an inability to reimagine the world otherwise.

Fractures are also sites of suturing or occasions for repair (meaning to mend or (re)assemble).[19] In medicine, sutures are vital for closing wounds and joining bones to promote healing. However, these sutures must stay in place long enough to restore total health. Or, to follow this metaphor in another direction: just as a flower may grow between cracks in cement, fractures present opportunities for something new to grow, but that which germinates between the breaks does not merge the two sides. Instead, it points to the systems that divide us. We must chisel away at the strata of the cracking concrete to build something new on the rich earth to which we all naturally belong. In short, the metaphors of fractures and sutures provide an apt visualization of coloniality's actual psychic, physical, and spiritual fissures—breaks that must be repaired and fault lines that must be attended to. The question remains: How do we build from instances of suturing toward systemic repair and multiple belongings?

I divide the book into two parts, reflecting the tension between fractures and sutures. Part I, "Fractures," consists of three interrelated chapters. Chapter 1 engages the longue durée of colonialism to tell the story of Haitian and Caribbean higher education and the formation and dispersal of Haitian intellectuals. Specifically, I center on scholars in an examination of the interplay between colonial oppression and collective resistance, presenting different historical moments as either fracturing or suturing.

Picking up where chapter 1 ends, chapter 2 explores the returns of jenerasyon 86 and the jenn doktè at two moments of hopeful social transformation in Haiti: post-Duvalier and postearthquake. I draw on a series of life history interviews to examine the generational aspects of homecoming or how temporality and location affected the returns and reintegration of jenerasyon 86 and the jenn doktè. First, I discuss how populism and the *dechoukaj* (political uprooting) contributed to the social displacement of jenerasyon 86 members who had returned to participate in Haiti's democratic transition. Subsequently, exile returnees generally withdrew from formal politics to constitute a domain for themselves in UEH. Next, I examine the returns of the jenn doktè to partake in public higher education reform in the context of the global knowledge economy and neoliberal university. I also outline the intergenerational struggles between jenerasyon 86 and the jenn doktè as the newer returnees struggled for a place at UEH. The chapter's central argument is twofold: (1) generation as temporality and social positioning created divergent and overlapping experiences of internal displacement for returnees and (2) the lack of intellectual friendship among returnees contributed to their initial inability to realize their aspirations of systemic change.

In chapter 3, I describe how the jenn doktè's struggle for a place at UEH contributed to the 2016–2018 crisis, which included campus closures and police occupations at two fakilte: UEH Faculté d'Ethnologie and Faculté des Sciences Humaines. I specifically examine the historical, structural, and embodied aspects of the 2016–2018 crisis at UEH to contextualize and disrupt a conventional notion of "Haitian perpetual crisis." First, I discuss the various approaches to crises in Haiti. I highlight anthropologist Greg Beckett's (2013, 2019) approach to *kriz* (embodied crisis) and employ the concepts of "articulation" and "embodied space" to forward a place-based understanding of kriz. Next, I examine the transnational processes that articulated UEH as a "crisis factory" by constituting it as a state/nonstate entity located in a United Nations–defined "yellow zone" (meaning a site of insecurity): the embodied space, thus instantiated, created affective uncertainty for individuals. In the final section, I use a composite narrative to retell the story of the 2016–2018 UEH crisis. I then trace kriz through the affective

INTRODUCTION 19

experiences and embodied practices of UEH students, professors, and administrators. My central claim in the chapter is that the 2016–2018 UEH crisis was a manifestation of the crisis factory articulation that geographically situated individuals incorporated and reified through a "habitus of improvisation." I conclude, however, by presenting collaborative improvisation as a possible means of realizing systemic change.

Part II, "Sutures," discusses scholars' strategies to form discrete places of belonging beyond coloniality's fractures. Chapter 4 examines physical spaces and chapter 5 textual and imaginative ones. Chapter 4 considers the sites of gathering that scholars created outside the university. Specifically, I survey four such sites: Soup at Sonson's (an intellectual salon), Vendredis Litteraires (a poetry night), Café Philo (televised philosophical debates), and La Pléiade (a bookstore). I argue that these spaces allowed instances of rasanblaj, decolonial assemblages that prefigured future "possibilities for other modalities and narratives" (Ulysse 2017, 69). In a gesture of decolonial assembly, I employ different literary modalities, namely, drama, poetry, and prose, to describe these instances of rasanblaj.

Chapter 5, "Imagining Emancipatory Caribbean Futures," centers on two postearthquake Haitian *revues* (journals): *Trois/Cent/Soixante* and *DO KRE I S*. *Trois/Cent/Soixante* offers a critique of globalization to envision a Haiti where plurality and mutuality thrive. Conversely, *DO KRE I S* challenges longstanding tropes of Haitian and Creole exceptionalism to position Haiti within a Creolophone world with its own internal vision. More centrally, I contend that *Trois/Cent/Soixante* and *DO KRE I S* are spaces of "Caribbean critique" (Nesbitt 2013) that interrogate present realities to imagine and enact emancipatory Caribbean and, thus, universal, futures.

I conclude the book with a reflection on contemporary Haitian and Caribbean displacements. I connect these displacements to others occurring throughout the globe. Then, extrapolating from interlocutors' placemaking strategies—improvisation, rasanblaj, and radical imagination—I offer collective means of moving beyond coloniality. Thus, more than a book about Haiti, the Caribbean, and even returned migrants, *Reclaiming Haiti's Futures* provides an analytical framework for understanding how people work beyond coloniality's fractures to envision and create future-oriented places of belonging.

———

Soon after the 2010 Haitian quake, U.S.-based Haitian literary scholar Nadège Clitandre (2011, 151–152) wrote that part of the challenging project of participating in rebuilding Haiti "has everything to do with creating alliances and exposing commonalities." She adds that "as scholars of Haitian Studies, part of our job is to foreground the Haitian intellectuals, writers, scholars, and artists who have dared to imagine Haiti bravely and link such imaginings to our own. How can we rebuild Haiti if we cannot imagine an empowering future for/with Haitians, one that can also be shared with the rest of the world?" (152). As with others across the Haitian dyaspora, I aspired to return home to partake in rebuilding Haiti after the earthquake. This book fulfills a small part of that aspiration. Stemming from my homing instinct, *Reclaiming Haiti's Futures: Returned Intellectuals, Placemaking, and Radical Imagination* not only foregrounds those who imagined and sought to actualize Haiti otherwise but also connects Haiti's futures to those of the wider Caribbean and the rest of the world.

PART I

Fractures

We are living in times of deepest fracture and with fracture.
       —*Gina Athena Ulysse,* Why Rasanblaj, Why Now?

CHAPTER 1

Colonial Ruptures in the Caribbean and the Displacement of Haitian Intellectuals

I myself do not think that the very many fractures of the modern world, including colonialism, have disappeared; rather, they have been complicated in the postmodern reconfigurations of modernity. Agency has not disappeared altogether either, as those fractures and the conflicts they breed are still very real. . . . On the other hand, it is also the case, I believe, that the concepts inherited from modernity are not sufficient to capture the realities of the contemporary world, and, to the extent that we are unable to see through earlier spatial and temporal mappings of the world, we may be unable also to capture the radical reorganization of power in the world, all the way to the psychic and physical remaking of what it means to be human. . . . Empire is one way to think our way through this difficulty. . . . Empire may be all-encompassing, but it also generates spaces within its very body in these contradictions, spaces that may hopefully produce not just chaos, but also new ways of thinking our way out of the burdens of not only the past but, more importantly, of the present.
—Arif Dirlik, Rethinking Colonialism: Globalization, Postcolonialism, and the Nation

By the early 1830s, Haiti boasted an army larger than that of imperial Britain but not a single university.
—Jean-Germain Gros, Haiti: The Political Economy and Sociology of Decay and Renewal

Where should one begin a story of exile and diasporic return? It is fitting, I believe, to start at the point of rupture that precipitated displacement. In the case of Haitian intellectuals, researchers often mark that moment as the 1957 ascension of François "Papa Doc" Duvalier to power. Indeed, François Duvalier's consolidation

23

of authority included the imprisonment and state-sanctioned murders of radical intellectuals and the curtailment of academic freedom through control of the University of Haiti. Duvalier-era repression thus led to the "massive displacement of the Haitian intelligentsia" (Prou 2009, 37), beginning a trend that would, by the twenty-first century, make Haiti the world's largest sender of skilled migrants by population size—with many of these migrants ending up in the Global North (Jadotte 2009; Shaw and Ratha 2007).

However, to define the Duvalier dictatorship as the rupture that caused the dislocation of Haiti's intellectuals would be to fall into "colonial geo-logics" (Yusoff 2018), which deny colonial legacies of violent dispossession and enslavement that create proliferating fractures to ensure the ongoing displacement of postcolonial subjects. To contend with how capitalist globalization and neoliberal processes—as contemporary drivers of coloniality—facilitate the *déplacement* of the functions of postcolonial states and the extraction or displacement of skilled laborers to the Global North, we must first reveal how colonial ruptures set in motion the fragmented globality and fractured localities we have inherited. In other words, where this story begins has epistemological and practical implications for the futures my interlocutors—as postcolonial Caribbean intellectuals—wished to reclaim and the present dilemmas they dared work through.

In this chapter, I engage the longue durée of colonialism to discuss the "fragmentary effects of its rupture" (Yusoff 2018, 64) on the Caribbean and Haiti specifically. Centering on the higher education sector as a site of intellectual formation, I reveal Haiti's postindependence efforts to develop the higher education sector and the role of French neocolonialism and United States imperialism in thwarting those efforts. I also analyze how intellectuals between the seventeenth and twentieth centuries either resisted or fostered coloniality as they took part in the projects and operations of the people or the state.[1] To construct this history, I engage a variety of texts written by both Haitian and non-Haitian scholars and historians, drawing extensively on Haitian historian Job B. Clément's 1979 companion essays, "History of Education in Haiti, 1804–1915 (Part 1)" and "(Part 2)," to discuss higher education in Haiti in the colonial and early postindependence periods. Echoing historian Marlene Daut in her tour de force *Awakening the Ashes: An Intellectual History of the Haitian Revolution*, the history that appears in this chapter "regards both acts and actes (deeds and discourse) as intellectual" (Daut 2023, xix). In other words, I read acts of liberatory transformation and actes that articulate a world beyond coloniality as interrelated forms of theoretical, imaginative, and actual worldmaking. Therefore, revolutionary resistance leaders like Boukman Dutty, Cécile Fatiman, Marie-Jeanne Lamartinière, and Sanite Bélair, and the various students, workers, and peasants who fought against U.S. imperialism are considered thinkers as much as "the revolutionaries turned statesmen, Louverture, Dessalines,

Christophe, and Pétion" (Daut 2023, xix), and the generations of intellectuals that formed in the nineteenth and twentieth centuries—scholar-activists like Anténor Firmin, Louis-Joseph Janvier, Jean Price-Mars, Madeleine Sylvain, and Jacques Roumain. While this chapter focuses specifically on Haiti, I also trace historical connections, as well as similarities and discontinuities with other sites in the Caribbean archipelago, allowing a comparative lens to appreciate how the Caribbean's diversity remains predicated on long histories of colonialism, whose divergent practices inform present-day structural and spatial-temporal realities. However, due to this chapter's limited space and vast scope, I can only touch on a fraction of the complexities of the periods and events I discuss.

I move this discussion forward both chronologically and dialectically: sequentially flowing from fracture to suture, I show how breaks are both sites of chaos and potentiality—potentiality, here, describes "the future's *capacity to become future*, or the future as virtuality in the present" (Bryant and Knight 2019, 107, emphasis in original). To put it another way, potentiality is the future-actual residing in the already unfolding present. Throughout Caribbean history, people have apprehended fractures as occasions for suturing and opportunities for calling the future into the present. However, since coloniality (not as the past but as that which holds the future hostage by limiting imaginative alternatives) had not been adequately dealt with, sutures reopened, revealing still-damaged tissue. This is not to say that the Caribbean cannot move beyond coloniality. Instead, echoing historian Arif Dirlik (2002), I suggest we continue to grapple with the effects of Empire and think/act outside its imaginative, discursive, and ontological limits so as not to insert its illogic in the new worlds we still wish to create.

COLONIAL RUPTURES

Ayiti (Haïti) was the earliest site of European imperialism in the Americas.[2] "Inhabited by humans since at least 5000 B.C.E., this Caribbean land was the site of the initial battles between Spanish colonizers and the existing occupants" (Daut 2023, 30). Soon after Christopher Columbus stumbled upon the island in 1492, he renamed it La Española (Hispaniola in English) and set up a small outpost on its northern coast. This outpost was the first European (un)settlement in the Americas. By the time Columbus returned, the Indigenous Ayitians had defeated all the settlers.[3] "The Spanish soon built a new settlement on the southeastern coast of the island, however, which they dubbed Santo Domingo, after the revered founder of the Dominican order" (Dubois 2012, 17).[4] The arrival of the Spanish to Ayiti—the "mountainous, *populated* land" (Daut 2023, 32)—was not intended to bring formal schooling nor any other pretense of so-called civilization to the Indigenous Ayitians (Clément 1979a). The Spanish sought to mine for gold and brutally enslaved Indigenous Ayitians to that end. Even Spanish attempts to convert the Indigenous to Christianity were a means for complete compliance (Clément 1979a, 151). By the mid-sixteenth century, disease, murder, war, and enslavement nearly eliminated Ayiti's estimated 500,000 to 700,000 inhabitants (Dubois 2012). And, to quote critical geographer Kathryn Yusoff (2018, 31) in *A Billion Black Anthropocenes or None*: "As Europeans invaded the [wider] Caribbean, deforming and decimating the indigenous 'Caribs,' they began to use the islands as an experimental archipelago in terms of both the social organization of categories of human *and* the ecological arrangements of flora and fauna. The invasion of Europeans in the Americas resulted in a massive genocide of the indigenous population, leading to a decline from 54 million people in the Americas in 1492 to approximately 6 million in 1650, a result of murder, enslavement, famine, and disease." As Yusoff (2018, xiii) asserts at the outset of her book, "Imperialism and ongoing (settler) colonialisms have been ending worlds for as long as they have been in existence." Indeed, the year 1492 marked the beginning of an end for the Indigenous peoples of the Caribbean and the greater Americas.

Considering the near decimation of the first Ayitians, the Spanish began enslaving and forcibly displacing African peoples, with the first captive Africans arriving on the island in 1501 after the "Spanish king and queen authorized Nicolás de Ovando, the governor of Ayiti (renamed by them Hispaniola), to transport African captives to the island for the purpose of chattel slavery" (Daut 2023, 50). Since the gold had been depleted, the Spanish forced enslaved African peoples to work on large coffee, cotton, sugar, and indigo plantations (Daut 2023; Mintz and Price 1985; Trouillot 1982). Intellectuals were among the enslaved. For instance, Clément (1979a) notes that some of the African captives were "Islamic blacks" who had received formal higher education at *Medersas*, Islamic universities founded in Sudan. "In fact, some of them were priests, writers, and educators" (Clément 1979a, 154; see also Sylvain-Bouchereau 1944). Additionally, other African peoples from groups and polities like the Kongo and Dahomey also arrived with skills and knowledge that would help them forge a new "Creole" culture in the crucible of the colonizer (see Casimir 2020; Casimir, Colon, and Koerner 2011; Clément 1979a; Trouillot 1995).

By the early 1600s, colonial Santo Domingo started to wane in importance for the Spanish, who were conquering massive territories on mainland America. The French, for their part, were extending their empire in the West Indies. In 1625, French buccaneers on the nearby island of Tortuga, operating under Bertrand d'Oregon's leadership, seized the western part of Santo Domingo. With the Treaty of Ryswick of 1697, the Spanish legally ceded the island's western half to the French. The French translated the Spanish name to Saint-Domingue (the current-day Republic of Haiti) (Dubois 2012). Like the Spanish, the French relied on enslaved African labor to cultivate sugarcane and other cash crops (Daut 2023; Mintz 1986; 1989; Obregón 2018). Saint-Domingue quickly became the most lucrative colony in the world: "By the late eighteenth century,

THE DISPLACEMENT OF HAITIAN INTELLECTUALS   27

it was the world's largest producer of sugar, exporting more of it than the colonies of Jamaica, Cuba, and Brazil combined," and it produced half of the world's coffee despite being roughly the size of Massachusetts (Dubois 2012, 19; see also Trouillot 1982). France's profit came at a devastating human cost: "anywhere from 25,000 to 40,000 [enslaved people] died each year due to punishments, work conditions, diseases, and suicide. Close to three million [enslaved people] were brought in total to grow and harvest Saint-Domingue's many crops" (Obregón 2018, 601). To put it simply, one cannot overstate the inhuman cruelty of enslavement in Saint-Domingue.[5]

In 1685, King Louis XIV issued the *Code Noir* (Black Code) to regularize the lives of the enslaved, whose treatment France had previously left up to the colonialists:

> This Code Noir was "an amazing mélange of religion and economics, humanitarianism and brutality;" it made no provision for the welfare of the [enslaved] except for a specific recommendation regarding religious instruction. This was found in Article II: "All the slaves in our islands will be baptized and instructed in the Catholic, Apostolic, and Roman religion."
>
> Despite the fact that no mention of formal education was made in the Code Noir, many of [the enslaved] began learning to read and to write with the help of a few humanitarian priests. This process of teaching and learning was conducted in secret and at night in the most remote areas of the forests. When caught, since every effort was made to keep the [enslaved] in the darkest ignorance, both teachers and students were punished. The priests were placed under house arrest, and the [enslaved] were sold at auction. (Clément 1979a, 154–155)

Issued first as an edict, the Code Noir "made slave status heritable through maternal lineage: 'Article XIII . . . if a male slave has married a free woman, their children, either male or female, shall be free as is their mother, regardless of their father's condition of slavery. And if the father is free and the mother a slave, the children shall also be slaves'" (cited in Daut 2023, 71). Curiously, the Code Noir also allowed manumission and protections for *gens de couleur*—"people of color" of African and European descent. Article IX of the Code Noir reads in part that an unmarried enslaver who enters "concubinage with his slave" should marry the said woman "according to the accepted rites of the Church. In this way, she shall be freed, the children becoming free and legitimate." Accordingly, Article LV states that "masters twenty years of age may free their slaves by any act toward the living or due to death, without having to give just cause for their actions, nor do they require parental advice as long as they are minors of 25 years of age." Finally, Article LVI contends that "the children declared to be sole legatees by their masters or named as executors of their will, or tutors of their children shall be held and considered freed slaves." These and other articles combined allowed enslavers to free the children they fathered through "monstrous intimacies" (Sharpe 2010), as well as give these children formal education and property, which often included land as well as enslaved people as so-called chattel. In effect, the Code Noir facilitated the formation of an educated, propertied, and free people of color.

By the 1700s, several private or religious schools existed in the Caribbean, but few higher education institutions. The institutions of higher education that did exist were racially exclusive schools founded by religious orders (Benjamin 1964). In his history of higher education in Latin America, Harold Benjamin (1964, 178) notes that between 1538 and 1624, "when there were only fifteen universities in all Europe, Spain established ten universities in her [*sic*] American colonies," with two of these universities founded in current-day Dominican Republic, one in 1538 and the other in 1558. Moreover, as education scholar Jocelyne Gacel-Ávila (2007, 401) notes: "Throughout Latin America 'royal and pontifical' universities—except for those in Brazil—were first created in the sixteenth century by the Spanish Crown and were meant to address a need to evangelize and provide higher education to the creoles' offspring, with a view to create a cultural link to the empire and to prepare civil servants for a colonial, civil, and ecclesiastic bureaucracy" (see also Green 2016). In the British West Indies, Codrington College—founded in Barbados in 1743 as a training school for Anglican priests—was the first and only institution of higher education in the British Caribbean Isles until 1921 (Braithwaite 1958; Cobley 2000). France, however, did not establish an institution of higher education in its most lucrative colony of Saint-Domingue. In general, the proliferation of public higher education institutions throughout the Caribbean would only begin between the late 1940s and 1980s, as formal colonialism was ending.

In Saint-Domingue, the absence of an institution of higher education in the colony compelled various elite colonists to send their sons of color to the metropole for higher education. Yet during the same time, "no public schools existed for Frenchmen or [enslaved people]. The white men could barely read and write (Saint-Méry 1797, 61). 'Toussaint Louverture learned to read and write when he was fifty years old. Jean Jacques Dessalines, the founder and first Chief of State, could not read or write' (Bellegarde 1936, 11)" (cited in Bernard 1989, 43). But despite their education, relative wealth, and parentage by white Frenchmen, the gens de couleur could not attain the same status as the white planter class since notions of white superiority were codified in language, practice, and law (Daut 2023; Trouillot 1982). According to Clément (1979a, 156–157), "The arrogance and ignorance of the planters pushed [the gens de couleur] as a group into an alliance with [the enslaved] and therefore provided educated leadership for the impending revolt." Of course, this is putting it too simply as the coalition between gens de couleur, free Blacks, and the enslaved would sometimes prove contentious (Trouillot 1995). Moreover, colonial-era class and color fissures would resurface in the postcolonial era.

SOLDERING BLACK FREEDOM DREAMS

On the evening of August 14, 1791, enslaved people gathered on a plantation near present-day Cap-Haïtien (a port city on Haiti's north coast) to plan a mass insurrection and remake the world as they knew it. Dutty Boukman, a Black enslaved man transported to Saint-Domingue from Jamaica, and Cécile Fatiman, believed to be the daughter of an enslaved African woman and white Corsican man, gathered a group of enslaved people for a religious Vodou ceremony in the woods at Bois Caïman or Bwa Kayiman ("Alligator Forest") to cement their freedom dreams (see Hurbon 1987; Trouillot 1977). A week later, in Acul, the enslaved revolted on several plantations (Dubois 2012). Like licks of fire rolling into a purifying inferno, the rebellion quickly spread throughout Saint-Domingue, setting into motion the Haitian Revolution (1791–1804). Although it occurred within the age of revolutions, the Haitian Revolution was a singular achievement, as it was the only one led by enslaved people (Trouillot 1995).

From 1791 until 1803, the enslaved, free Blacks, and gens de couleur entered an alliance that ultimately led to Haiti's independence. In 1794, this coalition brought slavery to an end in the colony and the entirety of the French Empire. Napoleon Bonaparte would, however, reinstate slavery in 1802, with the practice continuing until 1848 (Daut 2023; Schloss 2009). Even so, "the emancipation decreed in 1794 was a major step in the long, contorted journey that would ultimately lead to the elimination of slavery in the Americas" (Dubois 2004, 170). After abolishing slavery, Saint-Domingue remained a French colony under Toussaint Louverture as governor-general. Louverture was already free when he joined the insurrection in 1791, and he "had once warned the French that any attempt to bring slavery back to the colony was destined to fail" (Dubois 2004, 2; see also Laurent 1949). Despite his stance against enslavement, Louverture would vacillate between fighting for and against the French until he met a cruel and untimely death in 1803. Between 1801 and 1803, Napoleon Bonaparte's brother-in-law, General Charles Leclerc, led an infamous exposition to wrest Saint-Domingue from Louverture and reinstate slavery in the colony (Eddins 2021; Trouillot 1995). Under Napoleon's orders, Leclerc conspired with French general Jean-Baptiste Brunet to capture and send Louverture to Fort-de-Joux in France, where he was jailed, interrogated, and subsequently died in April 1803 (Daut 2023; Fagg 2022). Yet Louverture's death did not mean the end of the fight for liberation. Under the leadership of Jean-Jacques Dessalines (Louverture's former lieutenant), the people of Saint-Domingue overthrew the French army and ended over three hundred years of colonial rule in Saint-Domingue.

Despite being silenced in the historical record of the Haitian Revolution, women also played a significant role in the fight for independence. In his essay, "Rebelles with a Cause: Women in the Haitian War of Independence, 1802–04," Guadeloupean-born historian Philippe Girard (2009, 62–63) writes that "women . . . occasionally took a direct part in combat, or resorted to the channels specific to their group to make a unique contribution to the war of independence. Farm labourers [sic] acted as de facto quartermasters. Market women and courtesans used their access to French strongholds to work as spies for the rebellion." Some examples of revolutionary heroines include Marie-Jeanne Lamartinière, *a femme de couleur* who joined Louverture's army, and became Haiti's "symbol of the female soldier" (Boisvert 2001, 73). Another is Sanite Bélair—a maroon rebel leader—who headed a valent revolt in September 1802. She and her husband, Charles Bélair (Louverture's nephew), were consequently caught and executed (Boisvert 2001). In *The Black Jacobins*, C.L.R. James (1938/1989, 352) writes of Sanite and Charles Bélair's execution that they "died bravely, both of them, [Sanite] facing the firing-squad and refusing to have her eyes bound." As this latter example shows, female rebels of the Haitian Revolution "were not spared punishment at the hands of colonists because of their sex. Many were arrested and shown their courage even as they were about to be put to death" (Boisvert 2001, 73). Thus, while history books tend to elevate men as the bearers of liberation, women, too, fought and lost their lives in the struggle for freedom.

On May 20, 1805, Jean-Jacques Dessalines, named Emperor of Haiti, ratified Haiti's first constitution as a free country. This founding document reclaimed the Indigenous name Ayiti (Haïti) for the country (Art. 1), solidified in writing the abolishment of slavery (Art. 2), and proclaimed all Haitians "Black" (Art. 14). I cite these remarkable articles below:

> Article 1. By this document, the people living on the island formerly called Saint-Domingue agree to form a free and sovereign state, independent of all the other powers of the universe, under the name of the Haitian empire.
> Article 2. Slavery is abolished forever.
> Article 14. Because all distinctions of color among children of the same family must necessarily stop, Haitians will henceforth only be known generically as Blacks.[6]

African American historian Franklin W. Knight (2005, 394–395) outlines the human rights implications of these proclamations: "Intellectually, the ex-colonists gave themselves a new, if not entirely original name—Haitians—and defined all Haitians as "black," thereby striking a shattering psychological blow against the emerging intellectual traditions of an increasingly racist Europe and

North America that saw a hierarchical world eternally dominated by types representative of their European-derived somatic norm images. In Haiti all citizens were legally equal, regardless of color, race, or condition." By retrieving an Indigenous placename and redefining Blacks as humans and free citizens, Haiti effectively confounded "the ontological order of the West and the global order of colonialism" (Trouillot 1995, 89). Yet, from Haiti's independence onward, colonial powers would aim to undo Haiti's sovereignty and thus reestablish the global colonial order.

Haiti instilled fear among European colonialists while inspiring enslaved populations, free Blacks, and people of color throughout the Americas and beyond. In the Caribbean, colonialists dreaded that Haiti would lead a region-wide rebellion. For instance, Arnaud André Roberjot Lartigue, a Creole planter who fled Saint-Domingue in 1803 and held an administrative post in Dutch St. Thomas,

> perceived a general atmosphere of rebellion in the Caribbean and linked these events to what had recently happened in Saint Domingue. Each new rebellion had the potential to escalate the damage that had already been done to European colonialism and financial investment in the Caribbean. "The insurrections that have recently broken out in Surinam and Cayenne are events that force the increase of policing in all the colonies." Lartigue recognized the influence that events in one colony could have on the rest and encouraged the governors of St. Thomas, Martinique, and Guadeloupe to heighten security. (Gaffield 2015, 53–54)

Colonial governments throughout the Caribbean and broader Americas did heighten security and tried to silence talk of the Haitian Revolution. However, news of Haiti was on the lips and minds of many, shaping Black consciousness and stimulating plans of revolt and even emigration to Haiti.[7] According to William Alexander (2018, 123), "The Haitian Revolution . . . encouraged early black consciousness against the backdrop of the reinstitution of slavery in French colonies; and this reflected a growing Black Francophone community in the Atlantic involving France, the Caribbean, and Louisiana." Conversely, Cuban historian Ada Ferrer (2014, 5) finds evidence of Haiti's influence in the Spanish Caribbean. She observes how European colonialists feared that the enslaved in Havana, Cuba, were planning to mimic the Bois Caïman ceremony three weeks after the start of the Haitian Revolution. The Haitian Revolution also influenced free and enslaved Blacks in the United States. In her phenomenal work, *Fear of a Black Republic*, historian Leslie M. Alexander (2021, 218) notes how in the United States, an anonymous Black writer, referred to as "An Injured Man of Color," declared his "'unfeigned wish' that Haiti would unequivocally prove 'to the world, that an attempt to subvert [its] independence, and enslave [its] fellow-citizens, will terminate in the disgrace and the ruin of [its] adversaries.' Even more, he issued a courageous plea for Black solidarity across the Americas, reminding his Black readership that 'a united and valiant people' could overcome any obstacle, for as long as they remained united, they would be 'an unconquerable bulwark against an empire of treachery, violence and unrelenting ambition.'" Moreover, Denmark Vesey's 1822 revolt conspiracy in South Carolina and Nat Turner's 1831 rebellion in Virginia gained inspiration from the Haitian Revolution (see Egerton 2005; Horne 2015a; 2015b). Prominent free Black men Prince Saunders and Paul Cuffe of New England even pioneered a Haitian emigration movement in the early 1800s (L. M. Alexander 2021). In short, despite colonial attempts, Haiti emerged as a beacon of Black liberatory futures.

Postindependence Social and Political Cleavages

Refusing to legitimate a free Black Republic, Western Europe and the United States denied Haiti diplomatic recognition and enforced embargoes on the land; these sanctions, coupled with fears of re-enslavement and foreign invasion, compelled Haiti's leaders to adopt a defensive stance early on and thus postpone the development of public schooling and higher education (see Gros 2000). While Dessalines purportedly had plans to build "public schools in each of the six military districts" (Bernard 1989, 44), "a sense of general uneasiness was upon the whole population due to the eventual possibility of France to return to reestablish slavery. Therefore, the maintenance of the liberty of Haiti became the top priority of Dessalines at all costs" (Vincent and Lhérisson 1898, 8; cited in Bernard 1989, 44). Fears of outside threats also distracted Dessalines from dangers within his administration. In October 1806, members of Dessalines's administration, Alexandre Pétion and Henri Christophe, led the ambush and brutal assassination of Dessalines. They soon divided Haiti into the *milat* (Kreyòl term for light-skinned or biracial people)-controlled south, led by President Pétion, and the Black-controlled north led by Henri Christophe or King Henri I (Smith 2009; Trouillot 1995).[8] As such, Pétion and Christophe enshrined colonial-era color cleavages within Haiti's postindependence political structure.

From 1806 to about 1825, Haiti's leaders sought to develop the country's education sector. Between 1806 and 1820, Pétion and Christophe made "separate efforts at formal education. Henry Christophe . . . established several primary schools after the Lancastrian system and the Royal College, to which courses in surgery were added to the curriculum to form the beginning of the college of medicine. Alexandre Pétion, in his territory, established a school of health, a lycée—the Lycée Alexandre Pétion—and a Lancastrian school" (Clément 1979a, 165).[9] The development of Haiti's education sector continued in some measure under the leadership of the milat president Jean-Pierre Boyer (1818–1843), who

THE DISPLACEMENT OF HAITIAN INTELLECTUALS

reunited Haiti in 1820.[10] In 1823, Boyer requested that M. B. Inginac, the acting minister of public instruction, establish L'Académie D'Haïti (the Academy of Haiti) in Port-au-Prince. "It was supposed to include a school of medicine, a school of law, a school of literature, and a school of astronomy. The Colleges of Medicine and Law were established, but there is no information available on the Colleges of Letters and Astronomy" (Clément 1979b, 59). Within the first few years of national reunification under Boyer, the development of Haiti's education sector met a devastating blow: the French indemnity.

After over two decades of independence, "Boyer finally gained Haiti diplomatic recognition from France. Though the deal he made ended his country's political isolation, the president, in fact, offered Haiti a defeat disguised as a victory" (Dubois 2012, 99). In 1825, the French King Charles X declared that France would recognize Haitian independence for the price of 150 million francs. This amount was roughly 3 billion U.S. dollars in current currency or "around 10 times the amount the United States had paid for the Louisiana territory. The sum was meant to compensate the French colonists for the lost revenues from slavery" (Daut 2021, n.p.). To pay the indemnity, Boyer borrowed money from French banks, "which added interest to the crushing debt load. Though the indemnity was later reduced to 60 million francs by France, the cycle of debt only worsened. By 1898, fully half of Haiti's government budget went to paying France and the French banks. By 1914 [a year before the U.S. Occupation], that proportion had climbed to 80 percent" (Dubois 2012, 8). The indemnity and subsequent debt would thus instate neocolonial relations between Haiti and France.[11]

Soon after the indemnity, Boyer implemented the infamous Code Rural in 1826, which sought to establish state control over agricultural production to generate revenue for the state. The Code restricted the autonomy of Haiti's rural population or *peyizan* (peasants), outlawing agricultural cooperatives and farm stands, thus foreclosing the rural populations' subsistence and economic prospects. The Code also "limited the movement of rural residents, denied them the right to travel to towns or cities without authorization from a local official, and created a rural police to enforce these regulations. In addition, Boyer's new laws provided for so-called corvée labor, which allowed officials and police to temporarily force rural residents to work on road repair projects without pay" (Dubois 2012, 106; see also Castor 1987). In effect, the Code Rural constituted a new form of forced labor, wherein the government siphoned off the peasantry to benefit local and foreign powers (see Bastien 1961; Castor 1987).

Under President Boyer, elite men were some of the country's only people with access to higher education. Though some of these men continued to travel to France for higher education, others attended Haiti's exclusive Francophone Colleges of Medicine and Law. The intellectual elite would thus foster and advocate a Haitian national essence that was French in form and content (Bernard 1989;

Lahens 1990; Magloire 1997). Scholar Gérarde Magloire (1997, 14–15) writes that in postindependence Haiti,

> French civilization and later—more specifically—French language and culture continued to be ones of domination by which a small group of former *affranchis*, or freedmen, differentiated themselves from the masses of ex-slaves. The colonial socioeconomic system and sociocultural structures were perpetuated and education—largely inaccessible to the masses—remained not only a weapon of social control, but became an important locus for forging and preserving national identity for the elite. It was especially elite control of history writing that contributed to imposing the French civilization and French cultural models for over a century.

In other words, the intellectual elite valorized the French language and culture, rejecting Haiti's African heritage (namely, Kreyòl and Vodou) and advancing an exclusionary nationalism that conceived Haitians as so-called colored Frenchmen (Price-Mars 1919). This nationalism was not only French-oriented and elitist but also subscribed to masculinist understandings of citizenship: it marginalized women while using them to embody concerns about the nation's fate (Eller 2021).

In summation, the first decades after Haiti's independence saw the proliferation of overlapping fractures—between north and south, milat and Black, *moun lavil* (city dwellers or urban citizens) and *moun andeyo* (literally, "outsiders" or Haiti's rural citizens), French-speaking intellectual elite and so-called uneducated Kreyòl-speaking masses (see Barthélémy 1989; Casimir, Colon, and Koerner 2011; Castor 1987). Members of the intellectual elite furthered these fissures through French linguistic hegemony and French-style education. Women and girls experienced these fractures differently. Despite their vital contributions to Haitian society, women and girls were primarily excluded from national development plans and the educational opportunities open to some of their male counterparts (see Clément 1979a; Price-Mars 1919; N'Zengou-Tayo 1998).

COLLECTIVE BLACK RESISTANCE: HAITI AND THE BLACK RADICAL TRADITION

The secondary and higher education reforms of the mid- to late-nineteenth century paved the way for the early twentieth-century formation of Haiti's radical Black intelligentsia, men and women who called for mending societal fractures by engaging the "Black Radical Tradition." As Cedric J. Robinson (1983, 5) coined it, the Black Radical Tradition is "collective Black resistance inspired by an enduring cultural complex of historical apprehension" of Western modernity, which Black intellectuals did not so much create as articulate against colonialist regimes of thought. By the mid-twentieth century, Black radicalism dovetailed

THE DISPLACEMENT OF HAITIAN INTELLECTUALS 35

with and helped spur the global anticolonial movement, even as Haiti entered the repressive Duvalier years (1957–1986).

Secondary and Higher Education Reforms, 1860–1915

The formation of a radical Black intelligentsia in Haiti was due, in large part, to nineteenth-century education reforms that began under President Faustin Soulouque. When he became president in 1847, Soulouque was a sixty-year-old military officer and "black ex-slave, in contrast to most of the members of the Senate, who were light-skinned and often the descendants of free people of color" (Dubois 2012, 145). Though the milat political elite saw President Soulouque as a political puppet, he ousted the milat senators who elevated him to his position and ordered the execution of the milat political elite he suspected of conspiracy (Dayan 1995). On August 25, 1849, "Soulouque, following Dessalines's and Napoleon Bonaparte's imperial example, declared himself Emperor Faustin I" (Dayan 1995, 10). He thus established authoritarian rule over Haiti until his 1859 overthrow by General Fabre Nicholas Geffrard. Yet, in 1848, Soulouque would pass "one of the most important laws in the history of Haitian education. It was the law for the creation of rural schools. This law resulted from a growing need for rural schools and the repeated requests of some members of the House of Representatives. . . . This law had a significant effect on Haitian education during the second half of the 19th century. It opened up instruction to the masses of Haitians who never had the opportunity before" (Clément 1979a, 166). Under the milat president Nicolas Geffrard (Soulouque's successor who governed from 1859 to 1867), Haiti witnessed a promising period of educational reform.[12] In 1860, Geffrard's minister of public instruction, François Elie Dubois, "revived the law of 1848, which had not been enforced completely, and wisely applied it as much as his authority permitted. He established several urban and rural primary schools and two lycées. He introduced vocational instruction, reorganized the College of Medicine and the College of Law, and made attendance at school compulsory according to law, at least from six to sixteen years of age. During his administration, Dubois increased the number of schools from 118 to 229" (Clément 1979a, 167). From 1862 to 1915, other educational developments included the formation of more schools, the "establishment of secondary school for young women, introduction of a grading system, creation of several private law schools," and other minor improvements (167). These reforms would help pave the way for non-elite Blacks to access secondary and higher education for the first time (Bastien 1960/2006; Smith 2009).

Joseph Anténor Firmin (1850–1911) and Louis-Joseph Janvier (1855–1911) attended Haiti's colleges of law and medicine, respectively. Born in Port-au-Prince to a middle-class family, Janvier began his medical training in Haiti before moving to Paris in 1872 to complete his medical training. The Haitian government provided the scholarship that funded Javier's medical studies in Paris

(Acacia 2016). In his 1884 treatise, *Haïti aux Haïtiens* (Haiti for Haitians), Janvier provides a damning critique of French neocolonialism in Haiti, seeing the country's colonial past as a view into a non-sovereign future should Haiti not reassert its independence as the first Black Republic. Janvier writes:

> We can foresee the future through the past. They sought to humiliate us. They despoil and pillage us. They have held and every day they hold a knife to our throat. They have threatened us and they continue to threaten our very independence because we have a debt of forty million [this sum is in reference to the French indemnity]. Everywhere, they have spread the news that we are savages in order to better intimidate us and to better fleece us; those who licked our hand at home called us monkeys in Europe. Remember to be defiant from now on, Haitian people. Do not forget the September ultimatum and be careful. . . . Haiti for the Haitians. That is what our ancestors intended. It is also what the black race wants. (Janvier 1884, 55)

Yet, Janvier did not propose global isolation for Haiti. Instead, his scholarship and diplomacy sought to affirm Haiti's global importance and its role in challenging trans-Atlantic anti-Blackness. In her article, "Caribbean 'Race Men': Louis Joseph Janvier, Demesvar Delorme, and the Haitian Atlantic," Marlene Daut (2016, 12) observes the following concerning Delorme and Janvier:[13]

> [They] urged Haiti to the center rather than to the margins of not only a Caribbean world system that included the entire archipelago of the Caribbean and the broader continent of South America, but an Atlantic one that included Western Europe and the United States. Indeed, both writers envisioned Haiti as a central part of an interconnected global intellectual tradition of what we might call Haitian Atlantic humanism: a long-standing way of thinking about eradicating the problems of racism and slavery *through* and *from* the nation state of Haiti, but also *in collaboration* with European and American world powers.

In other words, Haitian Atlantic humanism countered a (white) humanism premised on Black abjection by challenging Haitian marginalization within the Caribbean, greater Americas, and the world.

Janvier's contemporary, Anténor Firmin, was born in Cap-Haïtien to a Black working-class family. Firmin was educated chiefly in Haiti, having completed "his secondary schooling in 1867 at the Cap-Haïtien Lycée National, where he was taught by one of the prominent educators of the day, Jules Neff, a graduate of the École Normale Supérieure of Paris" (Charles 2016, 27). After studying law in his hometown and working as a public servant, Firmin began a formal political career in 1878. In 1883, Firmin represented Haiti at the Simón Bolívar centennial celebrations in Caracas, Venezuela, at the request of President Lysius Félicité Salomon (1879–1888). Following this mission, he declined an offer to join the

THE DISPLACEMENT OF HAITIAN INTELLECTUALS 37

president's cabinet and instead traveled to St. Thomas (then in the Danish West Indies, today the United States Virgin Islands) and then to Paris. In 1884, he joined the Societé d'Anthropologie de Paris under the sponsorship of Louis-Joseph Janvier and French physical anthropologist Ernest Aubertin (Charles 2016, 28).

In 1885, Firmin published his pathbreaking study, *De l'égalité des races humaines (Anthropologie positive)*, which went largely ignored outside of Haiti until well after Firmin's death (Fluehr-Lobban 2000; 2005b). A response to Arthur de Gobineau's *Essai sur l'inégalité des races humaines*,[14] Firmin's text contested scientific racism through an "anti-biological argument for the equality of humans . . ." (Fluehr-Lobban 2005b, 98). In the preface of his book, Firmin reveals how the racist ideology he encountered in Western pseudo-scientific texts motivated his treaties. "Je n'ai pas à le dissimuler. Mon esprit a toujours été choqué, en lisant divers ouvrages, de voir affirmer dogmatiquement l'inégalité des races humaines et l'infériorité native de la noire. Devenu membre de la Société d'anthropologie de Paris, la chose ne devait-elle pas me paraître encore plus incompréhensibleet illogique" (1885, ix)? (I do not have to conceal it. I am always shocked whenever I come across dogmatic assertions of the inequality of the races and the inferiority of Blacks in various books. Now that I have become a Société d'Anthropologie de Paris member, do not such claims seem even more incomprehensible and illogical?) Employing Comtean positivism, Firmin's text provides unequivocal scientific proof of the illogic of anti-Black racism (see also Fluehr-Lobban 2005b).

In the book, Firmin argues that "Blacks are capable of 'perfectibility' through a continuous educational process and through civilization. To underscore this argument, he made reference to the glorious history of the ancient Egyptians, the Ethiopians, and the foundation of Haiti in the Americas as achievements of human intelligence, before they can be considered as accomplishments of the Black race" (Denis 2006, 330). This notion of Black "perfectibility" and reclamation of African cultural heritages would undergird a burgeoning Pan-African movement (Denis 2006, see also Fluehr-Lobban 2000; 2002; 2005b). In 1900, Trinidadian lawyer Henry S. Williams—in conversation with Firmin and Haitian journalist Bènito Sylvain—organized the first Pan-African Congress in London. The Congress included delegates, participants, and observers from Haiti, the colonial West Indies, Africa, North America, and Europe (Williams 2021). Firmin and Sylvain were the only two Haitian delegates at the Congress (Fluehr-Lobban 2000). The papers presented there by Bènito Sylvain, Henry Williams, W.E.B. Du Bois, and Anna Julia Cooper,[15] among others, centered Haiti, Liberia, and Ethiopia—as free Black countries—in discussions about colonialism, racialism, and Black independence (see Sherwood 2010).

Within a decade of Anténor Firmin's and Louis-Joseph Janvier's deaths in 1911, Haitian secondary and tertiary education reforms that continued under President

Salomon had produced a "new generation of writers, scholars and poets who exploited the educational opportunities and achieved prominent places among the intellectual elite" (Smith 2009, 8; see also Verna 2017). Many of these same intellectuals would follow in Firmin's and Janvier's footsteps to leverage anti-racist critiques and affirm Haitian and Black sovereignty. Firmin and Janvier can thus be seen as forebearers of the Black Radical Tradition in Haiti and across the Black diaspora. But, as I explain in the next section, Black radicalism in Haiti would take more precise shape in the interwar period with the work of Jean Price-Mars, Firmin's intellectual heir.

While Haiti made significant strides in expanding access to secondary and higher education for non-elite Blacks between 1860 and 1915, for the rest of the Caribbean, where colonial rule still prevailed, secondary and higher education in the colonies and metropole were gradually opening to select Black students. It is also worth mentioning that Caribbean students had the opportunity to travel within the region for education, a testament to how the colonial political economy connected conquered communities within a conquered region.[16] The increased educational access reflected shifting attitudes toward secondary and higher education in the metropole and changes in colonial administration. For instance, through the Island Scholarships, Imperial Britain created limited opportunities for gifted Caribbean students of color to pursue university education in Britain.[17] As British historian Anne Spry Rush (2011, 28–29) observes:

> Imperial authorities in the Caribbean began, as early as the late nineteenth century, to develop a system of state scholarships for gifted pupils who could not otherwise afford to continue their education. At first, they concentrated on helping only the very elite—those already able to attend secondary school. They established the Island Scholarships, administered by the local colonial governors, which enabled the top secondary student from each Caribbean colony (or for the smaller islands, only one from each region) to attend university in Britain. The first pupils to win these, in the 1860s, were white, but from the 1870s Island Scholars were almost always persons of color.

A similar process occurred across the Francophone Caribbean as the French Empire implemented its *Mission Civilisatrice* (1890–1945), which sought to bring so-called civilization to its colonies through assimilationist education. Forming an elite class through French university education was central to this task (see Harrison 2019; Segalla 2009). Thus, despite increased access, "higher education remained an elite process, based on European models rather than local conditions and designed to turn out gentlemen and administrators" (Lowenthal 1972, 67). Ironically, Black colonial subjects' exposure to and recognition of the contradictions inherent in Western modernity through colonial higher education would contribute to the formation of Black radicalism in the first half of the twentieth century.

Haiti and Global Black Radicalism, 1915–1957

The interwar period (1918–1939) was critical for inciting Black radicalism in the Caribbean and throughout the Black diaspora. The First World War (1914–1918) brought Black colonial subjects, conscripted into battle for the British and French Empires, into contact with Marxist political thought and blatant racial discrimination and segregation. In the interwar period, these factors, along with colonialism in the Caribbean and Africa and Jim Crow segregation in the United States, would propel collective Black resistance (Gilroy 1993; Robinson 1983). According to Cedric Robinson's *Black Marxism*, "When confronted with the limits of democracy under racial capitalism and colonialism and with the uprising of the Black masses whose access to bourgeois European culture was limited, the Black petit bourgeoise [read: intellectuals] was forced to choose sides. Abandoning the West was never an option . . . but critiquing and challenging it was" (Kelley 2000, xix). This critique and challenge took the form of global Black radicalism, which placed racialism at the center of criticisms of capitalism and Western modernity (Robinson 1983; see also Gilroy 1993; Kelley 2002). Haiti, too, was implicated in this global movement; however, one of the primary impetuses for Haiti's involvement was United States imperialism in the country.

By the early twentieth century in Haiti, "the demands of the French were [being] surpassed by the pressures of a new and powerful force"—the United States (Dubois 2012, 8). As Stephen Solarz (1995, x) notes in the forward to Hans Schmidt's *The United States Occupation of Haiti, 1915–1934*, "the United States was engaged in a kind of imperial competition with Europe [and] determined to keep the Americas for itself." Haiti was of great interest to the United States: U.S. military officials "considered Haiti strategically important, while entrepreneurs were eager to build new plantations in Haiti as they had elsewhere in the region" (Dubois 2012, 8). In 1915, with the prompting of the First National City Bank of New York (now Citibank), U.S. President Woodrow Wilson ordered a marine occupation of Haiti to purportedly restore order after a coup and the assassination of President Jean Vilburn Guillaume Sam (Renda 2001). "As with the occupations of Cuba, the Philippines, Puerto Rico, and the Dominican Republic, the United States installed a military government in Haiti. American military officials had virtually complete control over the operations of a parallel, client Haitian government" (Angulo 2011, 1). Thus, control of Haiti was part and parcel of the goals of U.S. imperialism and expansionism in the Caribbean and Latin American region.

During the nineteen-year occupation (1915–1934), the United States adopted a racist and paternalistic stance toward Haiti, claiming to develop the "child nation" by building roads and schools and providing medical care (Renda 2001, 74; see also Castor 1988). Within the higher education sector, the primary investments the United States made were the construction of the Schools of

Agriculture and Military (Bernard 1989)—reflecting the aims of the United States to direct Haiti's armed forces and agricultural sector by educating future generations of Haitians in U.S. methods and logics (see Angulo 2011; Pamphile 1985). Historian Laurent Dubois (2012, 9) observes that:

> The United States, like other colonial powers, touted its building of schools and roads, and it is still recognized and appreciated for having brought significant medical assistance. But while the United States justified the occupation as a project to improve and democratize Haiti's political institutions, it ultimately exacerbated the rifts within the society. As more and more U.S. agricultural companies entered Haiti, they deprived peasants of their land. The result was that, for the first time in its history, a larger number of Haitians left the country, looking for work in nearby Caribbean islands and beyond. Others moved to the capital of Port-au-Prince, which the United States had made into Haiti's center of trade at the expense of regional ports.

Although the U.S. Occupation deepened societal fractures and created new ones, it also inspired an anti-imperial nationalist movement, which encompassed both intellectual/literary and activist elements that often intertwined.

Jean Price-Mars (1876–1969) would significantly shape radical intellectual thought during the Occupation. Born in Grande-Rivière-du-Nord, Price-Mars began secondary school at Lycée Grégoire in Cap-Haïtien and later transferred to Lycée Pétion in Port-au-Prince. He began medical school in Haiti in 1895 and received a scholarship in 1896 that "allowed him to pursue medicine in Paris, where he also discovered the nascent social sciences at the Sorbonne and the Collège de France" (Magloire-Danton 2016, 213). Price-Mars served as *chargé d'affaires* in Washington, DC (1908–1911), Haiti's inspector of public education (1912–1915), and as minister to France (1915–1916) (Britannica, T. Editors of Encyclopaedia 2022). More than a physician and public servant, Price-Mars was also an adroit intellectual and social critic. In a series of public lectures—compiled in 1919 as *La vocation de l'élite*—Price-Mars condemned Haiti's French-oriented elites for betraying the Haitian people by allowing the country to fall under United States control, and he chastised the elite for conceiving themselves as colored Frenchmen and for rejecting their indigenous Haitian culture, namely Vodou and Kreyòl (see also Shannon 1996). "In attempting to ignore the existence of Haitian [Vodou] as beneath their intellectual dignity, he told them they were like ostriches hiding their heads in the sand. He applied the term 'collective bovaryism' because they were envisioning their society other than it was. He appealed to them instead to act 'as Haitians' who should appraise the values of their historical traditions and societal heritage realistically and who as elites should instruct all of their countrymen to be proud of their indigenous culture" (Shannon 1983, x–xi). *La vocation* outlined "a reworking of Haiti's educational system to better accommodate the country's black majority; a diatribe on the worthiness of blacks esthetically; and advocacy of the popular Creole language that 'holds an enormous place in our linguistic baggage and in our mental formation'" (W. Alexander 2018, 127). Price-Mars, therefore, led a vision for a decolonial future wherein Haitian identity and culture could exist on its terms outside of Western modernity and white supremacy.

The year 1927 saw the creation of Price-Mars's *indigéniste*—a radical literary movement predicated on Haitian indigénisme or the culture of the Haitian peasantry (see Byron 2010; Joseph et al. 2018; Magloire and Yelvington 2005). The movement's creation coincided with the formation of *La Revue Indigène*, a monthly journal that published six issues from the summer of 1927 to the beginning of 1928. Despite its brief tenure, the journal "proved extraordinarily influential among the Haitian intelligentsia. Its collaborators, who included Max Hudicourt, Jacques Roumain, Normil Sylvain, J. C. Dorsainvil, Emile Roumer, Étienne Charlier, Arthur Holly, and Jean Price-Mars, called for a new national program that explicitly rejected French [and by extension, United States] cultural values and promoted the acceptance of Haitian ones. They stressed the significance of Haiti's African heritage and promoted its inclusion in the development of a uniquely Haitian literature" (Smith 2009, 8). The same year as the review's final issue, Price-Mars published his seminal work *Ainsi parla l'oncle: Essais d'ethnographie*, which encapsulated the spirit of the indigéniste movement. *Ainsi parla l'oncle* draws on folklore and ethnology to investigate the national character of Haitian people. In the book, Price-Mars highlights the cultural influences of African civilizations and ethnic groups within Haitian society and maintains that the Dahomey (or the Fon people who reside in present-day Benin) left the most indelible mark on Haitian culture, especially in religion. Crucially, *Ainsi parla l'oncle* affirms the centrality of peasant culture by proclaiming Kreyòl and Vodou as the embodiments of Haitian national essence.

Ainsi parla l'oncle influenced Francophone Black identity formation, becoming "extremely popular with black students in Paris and elsewhere and established Price-Mars as an international scholar" (W. Alexander 2018, 127). Moreover, the indigéniste movement prefigured and influenced *négritude*, an anticolonial cultural and political movement founded in the 1930s by Francophone Black Caribbean and African students studying in Paris, namely, Léopold Sédar Senghor (elected the first president of Senegal in 1960), Léon Dumas of French Guiana, and Aimé Césaire, the great Martinican poet and public intellectual (W. Alexander 2018). In his homage to Price-Mars, Léopold Senghor indicates the influence of indigéniste on négritude. In Senghor's words: "For, as he [Price-Mars] showed me the wealth of Négritude he had discovered on and in Haitian soil, he taught me how to discover the same value, but virgin and stronger, on and in African soil" (cited in W. Alexander 2018, 128). Yet, as Jamaican historian Matthew Smith notes in his pathbreaking book, *Red and Black in Haiti: Radicalism, Conflict, and Political Change, 1934–1957*:

The indigénistes found their most important progeny among a small group of non-elite intellectuals in Port-au-Prince. As early as 1929 three young men who referred to themselves as Les Trois D met regularly in a rented house on Rue Fronts-Forts in downtown Port-au-Prince to discuss the significance of Price-Mars's work and the ethnological movement for the emerging black middle class. The group included Lorimer Denis, a lawyer from Cap Haïtien, Louis Diaquoi, Roumain's associate and a journalist from Gonaïves, and François Duvalier, from the capital who was then studying medicine at the Medical School in Port-au-Prince. All three first met at the Lycée Pétion, where they had been students in the mid-twenties under Price-Mars. (Smith 2009, 23–24)

Despite its popularity among Francophone Black intellectuals, the Haitian political elite who benefited from the U.S. Occupation never adopted indigéniste ideas: "Haitians in power chased many [indigéniste] writers for their proposals against the government and the U.S. Occupation. For example, on December 15, 1922, Louis Borno [the milat president who served under the U.S. Occupation from 1922 to 1930] passed a law that regulated the freedom of the press. During his government, U.S. military authorities controlled all forms of press" (Rodriguez Miranda 2018, 17). Various Haitian journalists were imprisoned for violating Borno's press law (Rodriguez Miranda 2018).

The anti-imperial nationalist movement also included actions of collective resistance. For instance, the *cacos*, a guerrilla peasant movement headed by Charlemagne Péralte, used a combination of intellectual, tactical, and physical means to lead collective resistance against the U.S. Marines. However, the cacos were brutally defeated in 1919 when the Marines executed Péralte and desecrated his body as a warning to other rebels (Alexis 2021). Despite this crushing blow, resistance to the U.S. Occupation continued in various forms, with another crucial moment of collective resistance, the Damien revolt, occurring a decade after the cacos' defeat.

In the fall of 1929, widespread anti-Occupation protests, known as the Damien revolt, erupted throughout Haiti. The insurrection began as a small student strike at the École Centrale de l'Agriculture (the School of Agriculture), which, as noted earlier, the United States had constructed to serve its financial interests in Haiti (Angulo 2011). John H. Russell, U.S. Marine major general and head of the U.S. Occupation, desired to increase U.S. capital and investments in Haiti and planned to use vocational and agricultural education toward that end:

In 1922, Russell began one of the greatest educational reform efforts in Haitian history.... He radically increased funding for the Department of Agriculture with the intent of starting an entirely new system of education.... He established the "Bureau of Technical Service of Agriculture and Vocational Education" as a division within the Agriculture Department. The division was to

THE DISPLACEMENT OF HAITIAN INTELLECTUALS   43

supervise the development of new institutions for technical education. His goal was for the program to rival and eventually overtake the entire educational infrastructure under the Ministry of Education. (Angulo 2011, 5)

George Freeman, who had received a doctorate in science from Harvard University and was a "former chief of the Division of Cotton Breeding at Texas Agricultural Experiment Station, was brought to Haiti to direct the [Bureau]" (Pamphile 1985, 102).[18] In October 1929, students at École Centrale went on strike to protest scholarship cuts Freeman proposed (Angulo 2011). The École Centrale strike quickly gained momentum, spreading among other Haitian university students, high school students, workers, and peasants, leading to demands to end U.S. control of Haiti (Angulo 2011; Castor 1988; Padmore 1931).

The anti-imperialist nationalist movement failed, however, to adequately acknowledge and address the experiences of Haitian women and girls under the Occupation. In her book *Framing Silence*, Haitian Canadian literary scholar Myriam Chancy (1997, 39) observes, "Nationalist agendas, focusing as they do on the generic 'people,' have, by and large, been gendered as male even as they espouse gender-neutral politics." As with the Haitian Revolution, women played a pivotal role in organizing against the U.S. Occupation and suffered abuse and violence at the hands of U.S. troops (Chancy 1997; Sanders Johnson 2023). To wit, "a report made in 1927 by the U.N. Women's International League for Peace and Freedom revealed . . . that U.S. troops had been responsible for innumerable 'war crimes' against women, including execution by machine gun, beatings, torture and burning at the pyre" (Chancy 1997, 39). Given these abuses, a defined feminist movement only formed after the Occupation (Chancy 1997).

Haiti entered a phase of leftist radicalism between the thirties and the forties (Smith 2009). In the early 1930s, Jacques Roumain led efforts to establish a communist party in Haiti. Roumain and his comrade Christian Beaulieu—a former member of the indigéniste movement—went to the United States in 1932 to secure financial support from the Communist Party of the United States (CPUSA). This support was contingent on forming an underground party—which Roumain and Beaulieu attempted in the context of depression-era apprehension (Smith 2009). Soon after his ascension in 1930, U.S.-backed milat president Sténio Joseph Vincent joined U.S. interwar efforts to quell communism in the Caribbean and Latin America. Vincent repeatedly instituted martial law and put anticommunist Élie Lescot, his interior minister from 1930–1934, in charge of "expelling various foreign nationals suspected of being linked to regional movements. The rationale for such drastic measures may be explained by the political nature of the battle between communism and nationalism in Latin America in the thirties. Across the region, communists were perceived as anarchists, the antithesis of what nationalism stood for" (Smith 2009, 17). Vincent's government intercepted

Roumain and Beaulieu's correspondence with CPUSA and charged the men with planning a strike to overthrow Vincent's regime and hasten the withdrawal of the United States (Smith 2009; see also Verna 2017).

Concurrently, the Haitian government moved to curtail the efforts of leftist Max Hudicourt, another former member of the indigéniste movement. Hudicourt, who had Marxist leanings but did not consider himself a communist, formed the radical organization La Réaction Démocratique in 1932 with J. D. Sam, Georges Rigaud, and Jean Brierre, some of the leaders of the Damien revolt (Smith 2009, 17). Vincent's administration arrested, tried, and imprisoned Roumain and Hudicourt for three months at the beginning of 1933. And U.S. Marines, "anxious to rid the country of Marxist influences before leaving, launched a widespread campaign for the 'Suppression of Bolshevist Activities' in Haiti, which they argued were 'being organized and spread among the working class.' The sentencing of these high-profile leftists [Roumain and Hudicourt] attracted much coverage in the local and international press and provoked criticism from labor organizations in New York, which lobbied for their release" (Smith 2009, 18). In 1934, the U.S. Marines officially withdrew from Haiti in correspondence with Franklin D. Roosevelt's Good Neighbor Policy. This policy stipulated that U.S. relations with Latin America and the Caribbean would rest on cooperation and trade (read: neoimperialism), not military force.

Within an atmosphere of newly won liberation, Haitian communists formed the Parti Communiste Haïtien (PCH) in the summer of 1934. The formation of the PCH revived the Haitian government's antagonism toward the left, leading to the sentencing of Roumain and other radicals to three years imprisonment for conspiracy and treason (Smith 2009). "The harsh verdict handed down to Roumain sparked a repeat outcry against the Haitian government, particularly among U.S. black intellectuals with whom he enjoyed close friendships. Langston Hughes, who visited Roumain in Haiti in 1931, participated in a 'Committee for the Release of Jacques Roumain,' and in the international black press appeals were made for readers to lobby against the Haitian government and push for his release" (Smith 2009, 21). After securing another presidential tenure and under international pressure, Vincent pardoned and released Roumain and other imprisoned leftists in the summer of 1936. But Roumain had caught malaria while imprisoned. "With weakened health and under constant police surveillance, Roumain left Haiti on 15 August, embarking on a five-year exile in Europe. From abroad Roumain worked to bring the repression in Haiti to the attention of the international left" (Smith 2009, 22). The PCH would begin to languish during Roumain's exile. By the early forties, a split in the communist movement would further weaken its mobilizing force (Dash 1981; Smith 2009).

The year 1934 also saw the formation of the Ligue féminine d'action sociale (Feminine League for Social Action). Cofounded by lawyer, sociologist, and educator Madeleine Sylvain, the Ligue was an activist organization that fought for

THE DISPLACEMENT OF HAITIAN INTELLECTUALS 45

"access to higher education, children's rights, social assistance, and women's citizenship rights, successfully obtaining suffrage for women in 1957" (Glover 2013, 10; see also Verna and Oriol 2011). The Ligue also published a literary-political journal, *La Voix des Femmes* (The Voice of Women), which connected women's emancipation to national liberation and "was celebrated for its scholarly rigor and style" (Sanders Johnson 2023, 103). Moreover, as literary scholar Kaiama Glover (2013, 10) notes: "Very much of a kind with the bourgeois, intellectual leftist groups active during the period, the Ligue was made up of primarily upper-class women who, entirely conscious of their own privilege, sought to create a site of community unconstrained by color or class." Unlike the communist movement, which would begin to splinter by the early forties, The Ligue was a formidable, albeit elite, force until its "deradicalization"—that is, its transformation into a charitable association under François Duvalier's *noiriste* (Black nationalist) dictatorship (Glover 2013).

Whereas Haitian feminists advocated for gender equality and women's suffrage and communists stressed the need to end socioeconomic class struggle, noiriste thinkers saw color as the significant dividing force in Haitian society. *Noirisme* grew out of the Griots movement, which François Duvalier, Lorimer Denis, Clément Magloire, and Carl Brouard had cofounded. "Coming of age in the late occupation years, the Griot intellectuals formed an important core of the mid-thirties' generation who identified themselves as 'nouveaux Haitians,' whose thought and approach regarding history, politics, and culture pointed the way forward for Haiti. The failings of the 'anciens Haitians' of the preoccupation years had, by contrast, created the circumstances for the occupation" (Smith 2009, 24; see also Sylvain 2013). Griot intellectuals, like the indigénistes before them, "perceived . . . the intellectuals and the artists as the conduit through which folk history and culture is transmitted" (Smith 2009, 24). Griots also followed nineteenth-century thinkers, like Louis-Joseph Janvier, in their stance that the "country's most basic problem [had] existed since independence," that is, "the constant exploitation of the majority of the Black inhabitants by a small privileged milat elite" (25). Though nascent in the early years of the Griots movement, noirisme would gain a more explicit expression in the 1940s.

By the forties, noirisme found its formulation as a radical form of indigénisme based on biological and historical arguments of Black Haitian nationalism (Smith 2009). Noirisme gained legitimacy through its recognition from négritude thinkers and Black U.S. and Caribbean Anglophone intellectuals. Even though "*négritude* never explicitly acknowledged the biological argument, nor the strong anti-*milat* tendencies of *noirisme*, the similarities were indeed significant. Most important was the fact that the early négritude writers, like many of the writers from the Harlem Renaissance a generation earlier, found in Haitian history the roots of an independent black culture. Aimé Césaire, following a visit to the island in 1945, noted that Haiti was where *négritude* began. For the *noiriste* writers

46 FRACTURES

of the period, *négritude* provided the international solidarity they long sought" (Smith 2009, 57). Black Haitian nationalism also spoke to Black intellectuals in the United States and Anglophone Caribbean. For instance, Black U.S. intellectuals—such as Harlem Renaissance leader Langston Hughes and Howard University professor Rayford Logan[19]—maintained ties with Haitian intellectuals and supported Black Haitian nationalism. Smith (2009, 57–58) writes that

> faced with their own civil rights struggles in the United States and the global crisis of World War II, many U.S. black intellectuals found in Haiti a strong example of racial pride and revolutionary change. . . . There was a simultaneous development among Anglophone Caribbean black intellectuals such as Trinidadians C. L. R. James and George Padmore. The former's monumental work on the Haitian Revolution, *The Black Jacobins*, presented a racialized perspective of the revolution within a traditional Marxist framework as a model for Third World nationalism, and was an important part of a general reappraisal of Haitian history in the African Diaspora. Black discourse on Haiti in the United States and the Caribbean, though less specific on the question of color, had parallels with the Griots interpretation of history.

In addition to gaining international support, noirisme expanded its political influence during and especially after the repressive regime of Vincent's successor—Élie Lescot, a milat politician who governed the country from 1941 to 1946. Lescot used ties to the United States and took advantage of the World War II political climate to maintain power (Bernard 1989). Lescot also sanctioned the violent persecution of folklore and Vodou and strengthened milat political control, "a move that made the social division more apparent to an increasingly politicized urban population" (Smith 2009, 69). For many Haitians, noirisme provided a helpful frame for critiquing Lescot and milat political rule.

As with the Damien revolt, students—specifically young Marxists studying at the newly established University of Haiti—helped lead the revolution that ultimately toppled Lescot's regime. Until the mid-forties, higher education in Haiti consisted of loosely related faculties or schools, each with its history and structure (Bernard 1989). Among the extant faculties—agriculture, applied science, engineering, ethnology, law, and medicine—the school of medicine was the most vocal in calls for restructuring (Smith 2009, 72–73). On March 31, 1943, President Élie Lescot

> issued one of a series of decrees [that would lead] to the standardization of higher learning under one head—the University of Haiti—under the control of the government (Le Moniteur 1943, Art. 2). During the period from 1943 to December 1944, a University Council was created by a presidential decree in an attempt to centralize and unite the facultés of higher education. The council was authorized to regulate examinations and raise the general standards

THE DISPLACEMENT OF HAITIAN INTELLECTUALS 47

of higher education in the country (Bunn and Gut, 1946, 80). "After 1944, the administration of the University was in the hands of the University Council. This council was composed of the Rector as presider, the deans of different faculties and the directors of the affiliated schools or institutes." (Bunn and Gut 1946, 80) (cited in Bernard 1989, 50–51)

However, the student body opposed the government's substantial influence over the University of Haiti. Frustrations over the government's aims to control the university dovetailed with a fervor of discontent among students who were becoming radicalized amid the global spread of Marxism. In 1945, a group of young intellectuals—poets, writers, and artists—founded *La Ruche*, a Marxist *revue* or journal. "The writers often went into the popular areas of Port-au-Prince and read the articles in Kreyòl for their largely illiterate audience. The *La Ruche* writings were often bold, defiant, and idealistic, driven by a revolutionary zeal and naïve optimism in Marxism. Unlike the noiristes, their resistance to Lescot did not derive from color politics but from the repressive nature of the state, which they equated with fascist Italy" (Smith 2009, 75). The 1946 New Year's edition of *La Ruche* called for a revolution and an end to the dictatorship. When Lescot forced the press to be closed, members of *La Ruche* and student supporters from the schools of medicine and law took to the streets in protest. Over the next couple of days, the protesters grew by the thousands. They included various political factions and organizations, including noiristes, populists, and the Comité Démocratique Féminin, a women's movement led by Nicole Roumain, Jacques Roumain's spouse. As it became clear that he could not quell the revolution, Lescot resigned and fled into exile on January 11, 1946. In August 1946, Dumarsais Estimé, a Black politician born in Artibonite, defeated his more radical opponents and became president of Haiti (Greenburg 2016; Smith 2009; Verna 2017).

La Révolution 1946 successfully toppled the Lescot government and ushered in a new era of Haitian politics where control shifted from milat to Black political rule. The revolution and "subsequent elections animated the popular classes and gave them a stake in political participation. With the slogan '*les noirs au pouvoir*' ['Blacks in power'], Black political elites could claim victory over the traditional *milat* elite and present Black rule as a necessity rather than a privilege" (Smith 2009, 101; see also Voltaire 1988). Pivotally, François Duvalier—cofounder of the Griots movement and noirisme, an alum of the University of Haiti's College of Medicine, and a former postgraduate medical student at the University of Michigan, was elected president of Haiti in September 1957 after defeating Louis Déjoie, a wealthy milat landowner from the north (Trouillot 1990a). Putting into play a warped version of *pouvoir Noirs* (Black power), Duvalier would establish Haiti's longest and most brutal dictatorship.

Returning Home to Continue the Task of Suturing

President François "Papa-Doc" Duvalier[20]—understanding first-hand that the intelligentsia could pose a serious political threat—swiftly moved to eliminate intellectual opponents and restrain academic freedom of expression by controlling the University of Haiti (see Remy 1974; Trouillot 1990a). In 1959, Duvalier established the Tontons Macoutes (Tonton Makout in Kreyòl, or literally, "Uncle Gunnysack," or simply "bogeymen"), a paramilitary force he used to persecute, imprison, and kill intellectual and political opponents, causing many to flee the country into exile. In 1960, Duvalier issued a decree stipulating that the "choice of the rector, deans, and directors of the [University of Haiti] be made by the president of the Republic upon the recommendation of the Minister of National Education (1960 Decree, Art. 4–5)" (Bernard 1989, 54). Students at the University of Haiti went on strike to protest the decree. Duvalier's response to the student strike was total suppression. He declared martial law on November 22, 1960, dissolved student associations, and prohibited the assembly of students and intellectuals (Special to New York Times 1960). Duvalier then ordered the closure of the University of Haiti and orchestrated its complete restructuring. On December 16, 1960, a presidential decree reopened the University of Haiti as the State University of Haiti. The order also forbade all communist doctrine— communist here "defined as any person who disagreed with or opposed Duvalier" (Bernard 1989, 56). Furthermore, Duvalier appointed all university personnel under the new decree, from the minister of education to deans and rectors to university professors (Bernard 1989). That year, eighty-something-year-old Jean Price-Mars—who had seen Haiti through the U.S. Occupation and helped shape the Black radical tradition in Haiti and globally—retired from his post as dean of the University of Haiti. In 1964, Duvalier declared himself "President-for-Life" as even more intellectuals fled into exile.

In addition to violent repression tactics and authoritarianism, the Duvalier regime used divisive political propaganda to set "inside" intellectuals against those living "outside" (Trouillot 1990a). "Inside" scholars became suspicious of those who had left, alleging that they had abandoned the country, while "outside" intellectuals accused those who remained of being Duvalier sympathizers (Trouillot 1990a). In the 1970s, when there was a slight opening in the regime after nineteen-year-old Jean-Claude "Baby Doc" Duvalier became president following his father's death, Haitian diasporic editorials "condemned any trip to Haiti as an implicit endorsement of Jean-Claude Duvalier's government and summoned 'outside' intellectuals (those living abroad) to take a stand not only vis-à-vis the regime but also vis-à-vis any 'inside' intellectuals thought to be Duvalier supporters because they were able to survive in Haiti" (Trouillot 1990a, 180). Then, in the late seventies, "President Carter ... put considerable pressure on Haiti to liberalise [sic] its political system and opposition groups began to organise [*sic*], openly voicing cautious criticisms of the administration. Although a number of independent journals appeared, influencing opinion among students and intellectuals in the larger cities, the major role was played by various radio commentators [e.g., Jean Dominique of Radio Haïti-Inter or Radyo Ayiti], whose caustic observations on government corruption and inefficiency were listened to by . . . peasants throughout the countryside. With the election of Ronald Reagan, Jean-Claude felt he could safely repress these opposition movements" (Nicholls 1986, 1242). For instance, in 1981, Jean-Claude closed the influential Radyo Ayiti and forced its founder, Jean Dominique, his professional partner and spouse, Michèle Montas, and other Radyo Ayiti journalists into exile (Wagner and Legros 2022).

By restricting intellectuals' freedom of expression and assembly and putting a geographic cleavage between scholars in Haiti and those abroad, the Duvalier dictatorship sought to quell the possibility of resistance. But more than this, the departure of countless Haitian intellectuals between the 1960s and 1980s adversely "affected all sectors of Haitian society, particularly the schools and universities" (Prou 2009, 37; see also Fass 1988), undercutting the hard-won advances in Haitian higher education that contributed to François Duvalier's intellectual formation. François Duvalier betrayed the principles he espoused as a young revolutionary thinker—choosing to hold onto power at all costs, even if that meant bleeding the country of its intellectual capital (Drumhiller and Skvorc 2018; Trouillot 1990a). And his son followed suit.

The conditions for the father-son Duvalier dictatorship existed long before François Duvalier came to power (Trouillot 1990a). The Duvaliers perfected previous mechanisms of state control, such as the exacerbation of color and class divisions; the elimination of political dissidents; and the acceptance of foreign capital, investment, and aid in exchange for international political recognition, support, or noninterference. As I will discuss in the next chapter, this latter move would create the grounds for neoliberalism in Haiti and contribute to ending the Duvalier dictatorship.

As seen in this chapter, Haitian intellectuals have historically vacillated between fostering social divisions or cohesion in Haiti. From 1791 to 1803, the gens de couleur and free Blacks joined the enslaved to upend slavery and French colonial rule. In the first decades of the twentieth century, Haitian radical intellectuals worked beyond class and color divisions to join the larger population in overthrowing U.S. imperialism. However, despite a moment of collective uprising in 1946, the promise of the postoccupation years waned in the face of still extant societal divisions, political factions, and U.S. neoimperialism. In 1960, as François Duvalier drove countless scholars into exile, Haitian anthropologist Rémy Bastien (1960, 849) called upon Haiti's intellectuals to again participate in mending the country's fractures; he asks: "Will the intellectual, once more, take up the task and teach union instead of class hatred, tolerance instead of persecution, some measure of freedom against dictatorship, and the priority of the masses' needs over personal ambitions?" This book is about the scholars who returned to Haiti to resume this task of suturing. As inheritors of the Black radical tradition in Haiti, these scholars held "open the prospect of living with the tension between our inheritance and our autonomy, of thinking with the visible sutures that render intelligible the histories of irreparable rupture and the aspirations for and against belonging"—to borrow a phrasing from David Scott (2013, 6). In the pages that follow, I draw on multivocal and multi-sited ethnographic research to discuss how returnees' aspirations for social transformation and belonging were shot through with hope as well as ambivalence and contradiction.

CHAPTER 2

Internal Displacements

TRACING THE GENERATIONAL ASPECTS OF EXILE AND DIASPORIC HOMECOMINGS

Future making is about communicability ... about giving from one generation to the next a sense of the future they are to inherit. That's how futures are made—not necessarily through deliberation but through infection.
—Matthew J. Wolf-Meyer, Theory for the World to Come

On a brilliant and dusty afternoon in April 2018, I arrived at a cultural foundation in Pòtoprens. Inaugurated in 2003 and envisaged by Haitian architect Gaylord Esper, the building was a sharp-edged, modern mélange of saffron orange, Haitian metal art, concrete, and glass. It towered over the simple structures surrounding it and, at a certain vantage point, seemed to match the height of the mountains in its far distance. I had visited the foundation a couple of times before, once to tour the community library and the other for a night of literary readings in the small yet state-of-the-art auditorium. That day, I was there to converse with Carole, a returned intellectual exile, former professor at ENARTS (École Nationale des Arts), and then-director of the foundation. Carole was a sixty-something white-appearing Haitian with cropped hair and a kind and open demeanor.[1] As we sat in her bright earth-tone-colored office, I felt entranced and transported by her story of return. Recalling the intergenerational tensions that she experienced on returning to Haiti in 1986, she told me with a certain sadness and resignation in her voice: "There is a real generational problem in this country—chronic! ... I think that in a country that doesn't have a culture of retirement—there aren't pensions or anything—people can't imagine leaving a job for someone younger. There's no financial security." Later in the conversation she noted,

Pa gen plas pou jenn nan peyi sa a [there is no place for youth in this country]. It's a young country.[2] But there is no place for young people. ... Elders ... are

51

afraid for youth to take their place. . . . There are practical consequences of this in terms of knowledge transmission. Take the [State] University for example. There are no structures in place to allow [junior professors] to learn from [senior professors so that they can eventually become senior professors themselves.] So, all youth felt, all they experienced was that there was no place for them.

This "generational problem" emerged as a salient theme in my interviews with returned scholars on their trajectories of return and reintegration. Drawing on these interviews or uneven dialogues (Scott 2014), I trace the generational aspects of return or how "location" and "temporality" informed the specific and separate homecomings of jenerasyon 86 and the jenn doktè. I use "location" to refer to the social positioning of the different cohorts (see Mannheim 1952) and "temporality" to mean the sociohistorical contexts of return that shaped returnees' relation to past, present, and future (see Scott 2014).[3] In developing my argument, I do not thoroughly attend to the various heterogeneities and conflicts within the generational cohorts but emphasize the divergences and overlaps between them.

Specifically, I argue here that generational differences between jenerasyon 86 and the jenn doktè converged in an environment of "neoliberal scarcity"[4] to create divergent and convergent experiences of internal displacement for each set of returnees, with the former constituting the "background of experience" (Kecskemeti 1972, 23) for the latter. When jenerasyon 86 returned post-Duvalier to join the fight for democratic transition, they found themselves displaced in a context of political uprooting (dechoukaj), intergenerational distrust, and rising anti-intellectual populism. Members of jenerasyon 86 would gradually move from the formal political arena to the more circumspect space of the university; they would also play a significant role in shaping the post-Duvalier State University of Haiti (UEH) and civil society institutions. Conversely, when the jenn doktè—who generally came from working- or lower-class backgrounds and had been undergraduate students at UEH—returned postearthquake to partake in reforming public higher education in the era of the neoliberal university and global knowledge economy, they found the top ranks of UEH still being occupied by members of jenerasyon 86. Given what Carole saw as an environment with "no culture of retirement"[5] and a generational chasm between their respective intellectual cultures, there was no apparent continuum between jenerasyon 86 and the jenn doktè.

The returns of jenerasyon 86 and the jenn dokté were motivated by the hopeful potential of revolutionary change toward realizing their visions of their homeland's futures. However, as Matthew Wolf-Meyer (2019, 16) maintains, "Future making is about communicability . . . about giving from one generation to the next a sense of the future they are to inherit." This communicability requires "intellectual friendship"—that is, an ability to work through shared problem-

INTERNAL DISPLACEMENTS 53

spaces regardless of divergence or the "dimension of friendship that offers a dialogical context for thinking" (Scott 2017, 12).[6] My conversations with members of each cohort presented an opportunity to bridge the generational chasm between them. I was a contemporary who did not share interlocutors' pasts and was only momentarily part of their presents. This positionality allowed me to listen to the perspectives of both groups to potentially facilitate a cross-generational exchange (see Scott 2017). It is to that end that I interweave the voices of both generations in a sort of artificial dialogue gesturing toward future-oriented communicability.

Post-Duvalier Intellectual Exile Returns

Carole, born a year before François "Papa Doc" Duvalier came to power, recollected the early years of the twenty-nine-year father-son Duvalier dictatorship that propelled the exile of numerous Haitians. The first to leave were primarily upper-class, biracial, or light-skinned intellectuals and political dissidents (see Laguerre 1984; Trouillot 1990a).

> I was born in '56. Duvalier came to power in '57. . . . The first thing I remember was the political environment [surrounding the rise of Duvalier]. Everything changed as we began to enter an absolute dictatorship. All the memories from my childhood were otherwise pleasant. There weren't problems within the family, but at the immediate exterior was a dramatic situation that would affect the family more and more.
>
> I am unsure if you're aware of the different movements opposing Duvalier. *Jenn Ayiti* [Haitian Youth], a group of thirteen, arrived in Grand Marie in 1964. Well, one of my cousins was married to one of the guys that were part of this group, and their child—they had a son, my little cousin—lived with us. We lived in an old gingerbread house with my grandmother, my parents, and my little cousin—he was young, about a year old.[7] With the rise of the Jenn Ayiti came government-led massacres in *Jeremi* [Jérémie]. The army did not kill [all the militants] and captured two. My cousin's husband died in battle. After that, they arrived in Port-au-Prince with the two captives: Marcel Numa. I don't remember the name of the other. Drouin. Drouin and Numa. Duvalier had them executed in front of the cemetery wall on November 12, 1964, and had the schools come to watch. All the schoolchildren came to witness the execution.[8] At that time, my parents removed me from school. I was very young. I was five years old and had just started school. They took me out of school. My sister left with [my little cousin], and my grandmother and I crossed over to the Dominican Republic, [then] soon after, New York.
>
> It was an exile that they did not explain. I was five years old. You know that in Haiti, they don't speak to children about serious matters. It is a harsh

memory for me—this *boulvèsman* [upheaval] that I didn't quite understand. But there were a lot of people crying, panicking, and afraid. My grandmother and I went from the Dominican Republic to New York and found ourselves in a housing project in Harlem with other people in exile.

Carole's childhood exile in 1964 overlapped with the expulsions of many others who huddled in New York City housing projects and flats in Paris and Montreal, awaiting Duvalier's departure. The boulvèsman of which Carol speaks describes a rupture in time, a period of indeterminacy that threw all that was certain up in the air. Salman Rushdie's *Satanic Verses* (1988) captures well this feeling of indeterminacy: "Exile is a dream of glorious return. Exile is a vision of revolution.... It is an endless paradox: looking forward by always looking back. The exile is a ball hurled high into the air. He hangs there, frozen in time, translated into a photograph; denied motion, suspended impossibly above his native earth, he awaits the inevitable moment at which the photograph must begin to move, and the earth reclaim its own" (Rushdie 1988, 212). As the Duvalier dictatorship deepened, those who stayed behind also experienced the uncertainty of the crisis of authoritarian rule (Trouillot 1990a).

When Carole returned home a year later in 1965, she lived the internal immobility that shaped life in Haiti at the time. She spent her childhood with her parents, whom she described as bohemian artist-intellectuals who "loved Haiti." Carole and her parents lived in a shuttered home in the countryside, unable to move freely about the country. By 1980, as the political situation in Haiti continued to deteriorate, Carole moved to Europe and later the United States to pursue higher education in the arts. This type of academic emigration became the trend among better-off voluntary exiles who could afford to attend university abroad. In addition to traveling to northern countries for education, various academic exiles also went to universities in the south, particularly in Mexico and Brazil.

In the mid-1960s, when Carole returned for the first time as a young child, François Duvalier was already permitting venues for the rise of neoliberalism in Haiti, allowing foreign businesses to operate in the country so long as they did not interfere in its politics. After a period of tensions with the United States and the suspension of aid, U.S. aid resumed under the Johnson and Nixon administrations (Dupuy 2012; Nicholls 1986; Trouillot 1990a). When François Duvalier died in 1971, the United States played a significant role in transferring power to Jean-Claude Duvalier and facilitating the continuation of liberal economic shifts in the country. In his short essay, *The Neoliberal Legacy in Haiti*, sociologist Alex Dupuy (2012, 23) notes how:

> In return for military and economic aid from the United States and other core countries (notably Canada and France), the regime of Jean Claude "Baby Doc" Duvalier (1971–1986) . . . turned over the formulation of economic policy for Haiti to the IFIs [international financial institutions]. These institutions

INTERNAL DISPLACEMENTS

pursued a twofold strategy that succeeded, on the one hand, in turning Haiti into a supplier of the cheapest labor in the Western Hemisphere for the export-assembly industries established by foreign and domestic investors, and, on the other hand, one of the largest importers of U.S. food in the Caribbean Basin. These outcomes were achieved through a series of "structural adjustment" policies that kept wages low, dismantled all obstacles to free trade, removed tariffs and quantitative restrictions on imports, offered tax incentives to the manufacturing industries on their profits and exports, privatized public enterprises, reduced public sector employment, and curbed social spending to reduce fiscal deficits.

Political scientist François Pierre-Louis (2011, 196) likewise analyzes how these neoliberal measures negatively impacted Haiti's rural population:

As part of the international community's strategy to decrease Haiti's dependence on subsistence agriculture and cash crops, the government of Jean Claude Duvalier in agreement with NGOs began to encourage Haitian peasants to migrate to Port-au-Prince to seek employment in the assembly industries that were being built. The Food for Work program was a means of paying peasants for building roads and installing drinkable water systems in rural communities and then paid them through surplus food that was donated by the United States, Canada, and other countries.[9] The impact of this program in the northwest of Haiti was a massive exodus of peasants from the countryside to urban areas. Peasants began to abandon their land since the surplus food that was dumped in the market was cheaper than the food locally produced. Since they were also attracted by the factory jobs in Port-au-Prince, they preferred to settle there instead of eking out a living off the land.

These burgeoning neoliberal procedures would eventually lead to massive food shortages as agricultural production drastically declined. Added to this, United States Agency for International Development (USAID) led the slaughter of creole pigs to purportedly stave off the African Swine Flu (ASF), which had been transferred to Haiti in 1978 from the neighboring Dominican Republic (Oliver-Smith 2012). The creole pig—a hardy animal that required little maintenance and could eat almost anything—was crucial to the livelihoods of the Haitian peasantry and afforded households the means to educate and clothe their children and make other financial investments.[10] After the killing of the creole pigs, "new pink pigs were officially distributed only to those who could guarantee imported pig food [from the United States] and sties with concrete floors" (Nicholls 1986, 1244). Few households could afford to maintain the imported pink pigs. As the food shortage deepened, peasants protested throughout provincial towns like Gonaives, Petit Goave, and Jeremie. High school and university students soon joined the peasantry in their protests. These protests led to mass demonstrations

56   FRACTURES

from May 23, 1984, to February 7, 1986, contributing to the fall of the Duvalier regime (Bellegarde-Smith 2013; Dupuy 2013; Nicholls 1986).

When Duvalier fell, Carole and numerous other exiles decided to return to Haiti to join the fight for social change.

DARLÈNE: What ran through your mind when you decided to return home?

CAROLE: When Duvalier fell, there was a wave of hope that things would change. I had to be there! I had to participate in the change. It is difficult to describe because we hardly live stuff like this anymore, these sentiments. But it was something extraordinary. It was like something was carrying you. "Things are going to change. We must collaborate with the change. We have to go fight!" So, Jean-Claude left on February 7, and by April, I was here.

DARLÈNE: What struck you the most when you returned? Because I assume you remained connected to Haiti through news and visits, but what struck you as the difference at the time?

CAROLE: Well, it was the departure of Duvalier. There was an extraordinary atmosphere in the country. There was indeed a loosening of restraints under Jean-Claude, but they still arrested people. There were a lot of political prisoners under Jean-Claude, many people I knew very well. [When Duvalier fell], it was like there was a gust of liberty, of hope. You could go anywhere in the country. Under Duvalier, you were stopped at military checkpoints when you traveled within the country. That was all over now, as Haitians had the right to circulate within the country. It was something extraordinary.

Duvalier destroyed the radio stations in the 1980s. Those who had run the radio stations fled into exile and closed Radyo Ayiti, et cetera. [Slaps table for emphasis.] Imagine that! In 1986 there was a fundraiser right away, eh?! Jean-Claude left, and right away, there was a fundraiser to permit the return of Jean Dominique and reopen Radyo Ayiti. It was an event in the country. . . . The first movement I participated in was the Women's March on April 3, 1986.[11] So, the first movement that emerged after Duvalier was the feminist movement. It was a massive march. Thirty thousand people were in the streets of Port-au-Prince of all social classes. It was exciting! Many people left the rally to attend the benefit of reopening Radyo Ayiti. They needed sixty thousand dollars to open Radyo Ayiti, and they raised the money! And eighty percent of the money came from the Haitian people. Eighty percent of the money came from five gourdes here and ten gourdes there.[12] Some people traveled from afar with goats to sell for cash to give to Radyo Ayiti. It was something extraordinary.

Jean-Claude Bajeux—a former exile whose entire family the Duvalier regime killed—was one of the first exiles to return. There was a mobilization of people who went to the airport to receive the former political refugees who returned. There was Gerard Pierre-Charles and Suzy Castor. And then, Jean Dominique and Michèle Montas returned to the country. The people invaded the airport. They brought a small car, perhaps a tiny Honda or Volkswagen, to get Jean and Michèle. The people carried the vehicle! They [Jean and Michèle] got into the car, and the people carried it! [Laughs joyfully.][13]

Carole explains in this exchange that the Women's March and Radyo Ayiti (Radio Haiti-Inter) fundraiser were hopeful indications that the collective will of the Haitian people would triumph over that of a self-interested political elite and that Haitians would finally mend social class and color conflicts to establish a liberal, populist democracy (see Castor 1994; Castor, Brisson, and McLeod 1998; Gilles 1990). In the words of Haitian activist Marx Aristide and U.S. scholar Laurie Richardson (1995, 183): "With the bit of the brutal Duvalier dictatorship out of the people's mouth, everything seemed possible. This newfound taste of liberty whetted an appetite for justice and a desire to organize collectively for fundamental change. For the first time in nearly three decades, the voices of Haiti's poor majority found expression in a myriad of grassroots organizations, some newly formed and others emerging from clandestinity. These groups began to articulate a range of concrete demands—from land reform to Creole-language literacy programs." The atmosphere of hope Carole and Aristide and Richardson (1995) describe can be seen as a collective momentum toward change. As Rebecca Bryant and David Knight (2019, 142) write:

Hope as teleoaffect emerges collectively in its various forms (optimistic, pessimistic, filled with certainty, filled with yearning) when people mobilize to push potential into the future actual. Hope, alongside such associated orientations as faith and love, operates to produce change, bringing fragments of potential otherwises toward indeterminate ends. This is never more so the case than during election campaigns or soccer matches [we can add to this: activist marches and fundraisers] where there is collective investment in virtual futures, a dimension of potentiality where there is an "energy" that can be collectively sensed. Hope harnesses this hidden but profoundly felt energy—the "incorporeal materiality," the unseen capacities of other people and objects—shaping the course of collective action.

Although I did not witness it myself, Carole's vivid recollection of the collective efforts following the regime's fall transferred some of the "energy" that filled the country then.[14] As Carole spoke, her eyes were wide with wonder and possibility and her voice sparkled with anticipation. But we both knew (her experientially, I intellectually) what would happen next.

Within months of the Women's March and Radyo Ayiti fundraiser, the optimism that swept post-Duvalier Haiti met the stark realization that although

Duvalier was gone, Duvalierism remained (see Trouillot 1994). Before fleeing the country, Jean-Claude had turned power over to the Duvalierist Conseil National de Gouvernement (CNG, National Council of Government), a U.S.-backed six-member military junta led by General Henri Namphy (Dupuy 2007; Trouillot 1990a). "Brutal section chiefs still ruled the countryside with impunity,[15] the public administration remained bloated with corrupt civil servants, and the Tontons Macoutes still held powerful government posts" (Aristide and Richardson 1995, 183). The fact of Duvalierism fueled the campaign of dechoukaj: an attempt at uprooting the remnants of the dictatorship. Dechoukaj took the form of "summary judgments and executions of Duvalierists openly carried out by a civilian mob, . . . the removal from office, by force or by popular demand, of known Duvalierists" (Trouillot 1990a, 222), widespread street protests, peasant mobilization against the repressive section-chief structure, and student struggles to eliminate state control of UEH (Aristide and Richardson 1995).

Dechoukaj also led to the increased distrust between intellectuals who stayed and those who left, as well as among returned intellectuals themselves. First, dechoukaj fueled political distrust between returned exiles and those who stayed, a distrust that had been mounting since the Duvalier years (see Trouillot 1990a). Whereas those who stayed would accuse former exiles of being out-of-touch bourgeoisie, returnees would denounce those who stayed as closeted Duvalierists (see Maingot 1987). For returned exiles, the length of time they spent abroad added weight to the suspicions against them, leaving them at a political disadvantage. As Trinidad-born sociologist Anthony Maingot (1987, 92) notes: "A lengthy exile tends to break contacts which are difficult to rebuild. . . . It also creates personal and family commitments abroad which are not easily abandoned for the uncertainties of a Haitian campaign. The temptation to run their campaigns from abroad, and/or through subordinates, can be fatal in a system which is at once so personal and so communal." Second, by Carole's account, ideological divisions soon emerged between returned intellectual exiles:

> I began working in popular education [at] *On pèp* [One people]. There, I encountered many former political exiles. But I remember [that], being a young person, I began to have a conflict with them. . . . All the signs of lack of cohesion and capacity to organize were there—the factions. But at the same time, the most leftist were the ones who had issues with the others. And then, when the military regime [CNG] started to depose people like Deroche, the Minister of National Education . . . I told the [older returned exiles] at *On pèp*, "We need to protest, even if Deroche isn't necessarily one of us. The government cannot continue doing what they did under Duvalier." They explained that, "Well, . . . [trails off].
>
> That is where the problems began. That is to say, we had difficulty—and it's the most significant issue we have in this country—coming together to fight

INTERNAL DISPLACEMENTS
59

for principle. We don't need to be part of the same political party, we don't need to be part of the same political groups, we don't even need to agree on everything, but we need to fight collectively. . . . It started then. I don't want to name names because these people are my friends, but they were highly sectarian. That's what happened. We were divided. We had our own ideologies. We were part of our own small groups. So, we couldn't find common ground to say "No!" immediately.

Here, Carole describes how her youthful enthusiasm began to diminish amid the ideological tensions that arose after post-Duvalier euphoria. Returnees fought among themselves about who was the most leftist, most radical, and most authentic—while remaining relatively silent on the CNG's blatant abuses of power. Backed by substantial U.S. financial aid,[16] the CNG and its allies were able to use their resources and control of major media outlets to launch "a propaganda offensive highlighting the street-justice aspect of dechoukaj and calling for national reconciliation" (Aristide and Richardson 1992, 184). More than this, the CNG perpetuated pervasive and open violence against Haitian citizens. In his book, *Haiti: State against Nation*, Michel-Rolph Trouillot (1990a, 222) observes that: "By the end of its first year in office, the CNG, generously helped by U.S. taxpayers' money, had openly gunned down more civilians than Jean-Claude Duvalier's government had done in fifteen years." The CNG thus brought dechoukaj to a halt by late-1986. And, as Carole indicates, the factionalism among intellectuals impeded collaborative resistance to the CNG and played its part in the failures of dechoukaj.

In 1987, major political shifts suggested a changing tide in Haiti. Returned exile Jean-Claude Bajeux performed a significant role in facilitating these shifts. In January of 1987, Bajeux helped found the Komite Nasyonal Kongres Oganizasyons Demokratik (National Committee of the Congress of Democratic Organizations, or KONAKOM), which aimed to "create a popular, progressive, and democratic government as an alternative to the discredited dictatorial system that benefited a privileged few" (Dupuy 2007, 59). KONAKOM, emerging as CNG's fiercest opponent, had a large part in ratifying Haiti's most progressive Constitution in March 1987 (Dupuy 2007). In his book, *The Prophet and the Power: Jean-Bertrand Aristide, the International Community, and Haiti*, Alex Dupuy analyzes the radical potentiality of the 1987 constitution. He writes: "Going beyond the traditional liberal provisions, the constitution embodied several social democratic principles and articles that conformed to the concept of social and economic justice. . . . It called for a thorough agrarian reform and declared that health care, housing, education, food, and social security were fundamental human rights, in addition to those of personal liberty and freedom of thought, religion, and political association. . . . The constitution [also] declared Creole an official language along with French, the language of the educated and properties classes" (Dupuy 2007, 60). Markedly, Article 208 of the 1987 constitution declared UEH "autonomous" from state control, called for the "creation of a parliamentary democracy," and barred "former close collaborators of the Duvalier regime from running for or holding public office for a period of ten years" (Dupuy 2007, 60). As such, the 1987 Constitution seemed to address not only Duvalierism but also the colonial-rooted social cleavages that had long plagued Haiti (see also Deshommes 2011).

The 1987 Constitution also helped pave the way for Haiti's first democratically elected president, Jean-Bertrand Aristide, who was elected in 1990.[17] However, since Haiti had not entirely uprooted Duvalierism, Aristide would suffer a coup d'état on September 29, 1991, months after taking office. The coup, led by Duvalierists Raoul Cèdras, Phillipe Biamby, and Michael François, precipitated mass arrests, killings, and the exodus of many from the capital. These events compelled various returned intellectual exiles to flee the country again to rejoin the ever-growing Haitian dyaspora (see Trouillot 1994). Yet, many returned exiles stayed even in the face of rising anti-intellectualism and the concomitant dislocation of public intellectuals in Haiti.

DE-EXILE AND THE SOCIAL DISLOCATION OF HAITIAN PUBLIC INTELLECTUALS

Throughout the late 1980s and early 1990s, intellectuals were losing their social role as intermediaries between the Haitian people and the state. With freedom of speech, the growing valorization of Kreyòl, and the proliferation of Kreyòl-language radio programs, the public no longer wanted (if ever they did) French-speaking experts to speak on their behalf. In local parlance, "*Baboukèt la tonbe!*" (The muzzle has fallen!). In my conversation with Yanick Lahens, a Haitian Francophone writer, she recalled:

> The greatest thing that happened in the eighties was that the majority who had been silent now wanted their voices heard. They were saying, "We exist! We exist!" And that made a big difference. . . . I think intellectuals have less symbolic capital worldwide, particularly in Haiti now, because those who want to make their voices heard can. And [the people] don't know what you're saying [in French]. The government knows this, so you don't suffer censorship or anything.

Similarly, other interlocutors emphasized the political impotence of and popular ambivalence toward intellectuals in Haiti. For instance, Michel, a public intellectual and journalist, exclaimed, "You hear them say about intellectuals, 'Oh, he is an intellectual, *yon en-te-lekt-yèl*'"—he said this in singsong—"as if to say, those who speak French, those who do nothing, et cetera." Similar sentiments to what Michel shared are captured in popular Haitian sayings such as "*Pale*

INTERNAL DISPLACEMENTS

franse pa di lespri pou sa" (Speaking French doesn't mean you're smart) and "*Li pale franse*" (They speak French [so is likely to be deceiving you]). For his part, Richard, a sixty-something-year-old psychology professor, emphasized the political dismissal of scholars: "Politicians don't want to know what scholars think. More than this, politicians often make fun of intellectuals. If former Haitian President René Préval called you an 'intellectual,' it was an insult. President Martelly thinks the same way. He was like—he doesn't mess with people with all those diplomas. Because it's like collecting degrees is a bad habit." Most striking for me was what Alex, an Ivy League–educated sociology professor, described as the simultaneous use and disregard of academics: "You [as a scholar] don't have an audience! So, the Haitian intellectual is a bit of a problem. I wrote an article a few years ago in which I argued that intellectuals don't have a place in this country. So, you speak, and they [the public] don't listen; you write, and they don't read you! So, it's like that!" He continued that, while the state and INGOs consult academics, they never implement their recommendations. "That is the kind of rapport the intellectual has with state and private institutions. But it is not a rapport where they respect your expertise, where they respect your knowledge," he lamented. This ambivalent anti-intellectualism had salient social class undertones, where diplomas and French literacy became markers of a privileged class who were seen as not truly understanding the realities of life in Haiti.

In my interview with her, Suzy Castor—a feminist historian and activist—used "de-exile" to describe a never-ending process of reintegration rooted in Haiti's ambivalent anti-intellectualism:

> I still remember this writing by this Latin American, Mario Benedetti—he was a Uruguayan. Benedetti spoke of exile, and he came up with another concept, "de-exile." He said that de-exile is just as hard as exile. Because with de-exile, you're reintegrating into an unfamiliar milieu. There are a series of codes you lose and people who you no longer recognize. Naturally, Benedetti ended the work this way, "Exile, I did not choose exile, but de-exile I chose." But reintegration is always tricky.

For Suzy, de-exile represented a tension between the desire for and actualization of national belonging. Despite the returned exile's willingness to do so, they cannot actualize national belonging if those who stayed refuse it to them. Although it had been decades since her return, Suzy described her continued efforts at "reintegrating." Here, reintegrating is not restoring unity or retrieving a former self who once belonged to their community. As Suzy admitted, such a retrieval was impossible. She had changed while she was away, as had her country. Instead, reintegration as de-exile was a choice of ongoing relearning and iterative readaptation. Suzy needed to relearn and continuously readapt to the country—and had chosen to do so. But this process was especially tricky for her given her positionality as a radical intellectual.

I first met Suzy, a distinguished and vibrant woman in her seventies, at the Center for Economic and Social Development (Le Centre de recherche et de formation économique et sociale pour le développement or CRESFED). She had cofounded CRESFED in 1986 with her late husband, Gérard Pierre-Charles, who had been an economist and leader of the Unified Party of Haitian Communists. As we sat talking in Suzy's sunny and lightly furnished CRESFED office, I noticed the iconic black and red image of Che Guevara that hung on her wall, indicating her leftist leanings. After completing her undergraduate studies at UEH École Normale Supérieure (ENS), Suzy traveled to Mexico City in 1959 for graduate education at the National Autonomous University of Mexico (UNAM). There, she met Gérard, who had been forced into exile by François Duvalier (see Beauvoir-Dominique 2016). Upon earning her doctorate in history at UNAM, Suzy stayed on as a professor, supported anti-Duvalier resistance from Mexico, and published works on Caribbean and Latin American history, including a book based on her dissertation on the U.S. Occupation of Haiti.[18] In 1986, Suzy and her husband returned to Haiti ready to participate in democratic transition through political action, "research, and education." In addition to running CRESFED, Suzy was a politically active scholar who taught at UEH, where she "introduced many students to the basic tenets of Marxist economic theory" (Beauvoir-Dominique 2016, 87).

As with other intellectual exile returnees, Suzy had supported Aristide's first campaign for president in 1990. By the mid-1990s, "the political party Organisation du Peuple en Lutte (Organization of People in Struggle, or OPL) broke away from the Lavalas movement, largely due to disillusionment with its former leader Aristide. Castor ran unsuccessfully for a Senate seat as a member of this new party" (Beauvoir-Dominique 2016, 87). On December 17, 2001, under Aristide's second presidential tenure (2001–2004), Aristide's Lavalas party supporters set Suzy's home on fire and destroyed the CRESFED offices (Organization of American Societies 2002). "Castor resolutely decided not to leave the country despite this act of intimidation. Instead of exile, she returned to live at the ruins of her home, and she rebuilt CRESFED with the help of supporters" (Beauvoir-Dominique 2016, 87). In the previous year, Jean Dominique (returned public intellectual, journalist, and Radyo Ayiti cofounder) was assassinated outside of the radio station. In 2014, a judge charged nine, including members of the Lavalas party, in the assassination (Baron 2014). These violent acts signaled a fundamental shift in the relationship between the popular party and radical intellectuals (see Dupuy 2001). As Suzy told me in her characteristically kind yet assertive manner, the state and larger population were "very ambivalent" toward intellectuals, treating them with a level of admiration and a degree of disdain.

De-exile thus functioned as "internal exile" for intellectual exile returnees, particularly those whose social class created a barrier between them and the

INTERNAL DISPLACEMENTS

Haitian majority. In my interview with her, Yanick Lahens defined internal exile as being physically within the nation but outside it linguistically, socially, and culturally. Yanick was a sixty-something-year-old woman with a regal quality to her movements. Her eyes seemed to hold a smile even as she discussed serious matters. At thirteen years old, Yanick left Haiti to go to Paris for secondary school. She would go on to earn a degree in comparative literature at la Sorbonne. When she returned to Haiti, Yanick began teaching at UEH École Normale Supérieure and stayed for seventeen years (Metz 2016). Yanick was now an acclaimed writer, novelist, and lecturer. As I conversed with Yanick in the expansive living room of her Pétionville home, she said that there were, in fact, "two Haitis: the one of the haves and the other of the have-nots." "To which Haiti do you belong?" I inquired. "Oh," she began, "those who have. I'm a have because I received an education. I live in a house, I went to university, and I've never known hunger. I'm from a middle-class background, but I still belong to those who have." Although she had been born and raised in Haiti until her teenage years, Yanick's class background had initially kept her from "encountering" the Haiti of the economically "poor majority." She told me that she would first learn about the dual reality of her home country while studying in Paris, where she met other Haitian students with a better grasp of Haiti's sociopolitical landscape. Yanick explained that she wrote to encounter and learn about her country. Yet, for her, the very act of writing lent itself to the internal exile of the intellectual. She told me as if repeating an oft-cited excerpt from one of her books, "The internal exile of the intellectual in Haiti is the exile of any creator. The exile of language, the exile of the fact that you're in an oral country, but you write, an exile that is not only social but also cultural."

In 1990, Yanick Lahens published *L'Exil: Entre l'ancrage et la fuite l'ecrivain Haïtien* (translated by Cheryl Thomas and Paulette Richards and reprinted in 1992 as "Exile: Between Writing and Place"). This short book attempts to rethink the inside/outside binary of intellectualism in post-Duvalier Haiti by exploring the relationship between exile, identity, and literary creation. Moreover, it is in this work that Lahens formulates her concept of internal exile. Concerning the returns of nineteenth-century intellectuals like Demesvar Delorme and Louis-Joseph Janvier, Lahens (1992, 740) writes:

> They all left . . . to finish their studies, as if the detour was necessary in order for them to return with the faith in having found, through elsewhere, the true country in which to take root. But upon returning, none really found the nodal point at which to replant himself. And, in light of the discovery of the impossibility of taking root, the pangs and torment were not long in resurfacing. Political exile therefore appears to a great extent as a redundant effect of the internal exile which it prolongs, perfects and flaunts at the very moment where it forces the writer to assume an external exile.

This internal exile or rootlessness is not so much a problem of geographic location as it is a problem of coloniality's ruptures. In this view, Lahens illustrates the linguistic non-belonging of Haitian Francophone writers:

> The writer outside the French language is also outside his native Creole community. His apprenticeship in the written word takes place elsewhere, in French. The new literature he writes in this language is not enriched by the Creole tradition of orality. There has been a discontinuity and a rupture. He gravitates in spite of himself toward the edge of an abyss. But he always avoids focusing on this void which he carries within himself, preferring to fill it in an imaginary fashion by looking beyond it. This writer therefore does not inhabit the Creole language either. (Lahens 1992, 737)

In other words, the Haitian creator writing in French cannot fully inhabit any language. This linguistic non-belonging is a vector of coloniality where one is educated away from themselves and their native language and, simultaneously, can never fully be at home in the colonizer's tongue (Lahens 1992; see also Thiong'o 2023). Lahens thus suggests that Haitian Francophone creators necessarily write from a space of rupture and emptiness they carry within themselves due to their linguistic (and cultural) non-belonging.

Connecting this non-belonging to returned intellectual exiles, she writes: "Now that neither external nor internal exile can be considered a political fatality, the differences between writers tend to crystallize in a divergent and antagonistic manner around paradigms of inside/outside referring once more to an essentialism, whether territorial or national. It seems possible and urgent on the eve of the twenty-first century to rethink the question of identity, of nationality, and of origin in order to get out of the inside/outside alternative" (1992, 745). Here, Lahens problematizes the inside/outside binary of Haitian intellectualism, which binds intellectual legitimacy and national authenticity. She concludes, therefore, that a way forward for Haitian intellectuals (returnees and those who stayed) is to embrace their shared and inherent exile: "Nos écrivains sauront-ils ouvrir le champ du territoire imaginaire, en intégrant ces mutations et en acceptant d'abord l'exilé, l'étranger, en eux?" (Lahens 1990, 72) ("What if we opened the sphere of imaginary territory by first accepting exile and thereby the alterity within ourselves?" [1992, 745]). It seemed to me that Yanick had accepted her own internal alterity, seeing it as a way of being and a point of creative departure.

Lyonel Trouillot, an acclaimed novelist and poet who came from a family of *"intellectuels traditionnels,"* shared a similar experience to that of Yanick. Lyonel was a relatively short man in his late fifties. He had a raspy voice from years of smoking, an infectious laugh, and a serious yet jovial demeanor. He spoke in an open but curt manner as if meaning could be derived from silences and well-placed expletives. I conversed with Lyonel at the cultural center he and his siblings had founded in memory of their mother, a long-time community organizer.

INTERNAL DISPLACEMENTS 65

Lyonel had moved with his mother to New York in 1971 after his parents' divorce, then returned to Haiti in 1976, under Jean-Claude Duvalier's reign. "So, at the time many people were trying to leave, I decided to come back," he exclaimed. Continuing, he added:

> At the time, I was very involved in what people would call now "leftist movements." There was a dictatorship in Haiti and a very young president. It seemed to us that the only way to get rid of the motherf-cker was to get involved in politics. I was born into a very well-off family, I would say. I didn't know Haiti when I left. I knew the best school in the country. I was a student at the school. I knew people in my circle, but I did not see the reality of the people, even the existence of poverty. And I—it's like I needed to discover or encounter my country. I believe mostly that that's what made me decide to come back here.

When I asked Lyonel what struck him most when he returned, he quickly replied: "The social differences—how they function as a barrier. I was born in a neighborhood called Saint-Antoine. When I left at fourteen, I left one neighborhood. When I returned at nineteen, I found another. There was another population that wasn't at all the same social origins." As indicated in the quote, by the mid-1970s, Port-au-Prince had already begun to witness what would become a significant influx of Haitian peasants, whose agricultural livelihoods had suffered under Duvalier-era political and economic policies. This massive rural-to-urban migration collapsed the "spatial barrier" between country and city and "threatened to collapse the social barriers of difference and distinction too" (Beckett 2019, 30). But as more and more peasants populated and transformed formerly middle- and upper-class neighborhoods like Saint-Antoine into so-called shantytowns (*bidonvil yo*), many well-off Haitians moved to maintain physical and social distance. Lyonel, however, remained in Saint-Antoine from his return in 1976 onward (except for a brief period of exile in the 1980s). He earned a law degree as a sort of "family tradition," but he never practiced law. He instead pursued his love of literature and poetry.

Lyonel Trouillot's first book, *Les fous de Saint-Antoine* (1989), is set in his childhood neighborhood. The book is a masterful mix of fact and fiction that tells the story of Saint-Antoine's transformation from an upper-middle-class residential area to a bidonvil. The story centers on Antoine—a middle-class intellectual named after the neighborhood and its patron saint. Antoine lived in both versions of the community. In an interview about the novel, Lyonel Trouillot (1992, 404) describes how Antoine's sense of unhomeliness in the Saint-Antoine of the past and of the present led him to die of suicide: "He suffocated, in the first Saint-Antoine, because of his mother who was very possessive and prevented him from being free; and when there was no relationship between him and his mother, he found himself entrapped in the second Saint-Antoine without a job or a future. Thus, from his birth to death, Antoine never found a way to live, and that's why he commits suicide." Antoine's suicide serves as the novel's book-end and its driving force. In view of the public intellectuals' decline in post-Duvalier Haiti, literary scholar Marie-José N'Zengou-Tayo (2004, 332) writes the following concerning *Les fous de Saint-Antoine*:

> With the suicide of Antoine, Trouillot marks in *Les fous de Saint-Antoine* the end of the leading role usually assigned to the politically committed intellectual in Haitian literature. . . . In his novel Trouillot captures the depressing and stifling atmosphere of the Duvalier era, the impact of mass exodus on the ones left behind, and the overwhelming presence of the rural migrants. The figure of the powerless intellectual must be associated with the 1986 events. In the movement that overthrew Jean-Claude Duvalier and the Macoutes, intellectuals were left on the sidelines. In spite of the efforts made by intellectual circles to take over the movement, various political events since 1986 showed that they had no control over the masses.

The parallels between Lyonel Trouillot and Antoine are so evident that one may read the novel as a semi-autobiographical text. As discussed earlier, Lyonel returned home in 1976 to encounter his country and change it through political activism. He would, however, witness the transformation of Saint-Antoine, the social dislocation of the public intellectual, and, perhaps, his own powerlessness as an activist-scholar (see N'Zengou-Tayo 2004). But unlike Antoine, Lyonel "found a way to live." He found inhabitability through his teaching and writing and by creating a space for emerging poets and writers from diverse social class backgrounds to share their work (chapter 4).

The post-Duvalier social dislocation of Haiti's politically engaged scholars should not be read as proof of Haiti's "uninhabitability" (Munro 2007) but as a specific manifestation of the decline of public intellectuals in the wake of postcolonial disenchantment.[19] For some members of jenerasyon 86, this dislocation meant disengaging from formal politics and achieving livelihoods as academics, for others, it meant having one foot in activism and the other in academe. Either way, various jenerasyon 86 members seized upon the post-Duvalier liberation of UEH and develop it into their domain—as space in which their thoughts and scholarship found relevance and audience. When the jenn doktè returned postearthquake, the quality of education at UEH had significantly declined since when they were students at UEH in the late 1990s and early 2000s. The jenn doktè tended to blame UEH's deterioration on jenerasyon 86. For the jenn dokté, jenerasyon 86 refused the administrative and structural changes requiring this older generation to hand over the reins of leadership to the younger generation. But, as we will see in the following section, the decline of UEH was more due to the rise and spread of neoliberalism and the global knowledge economy, which reshaped higher education in the Caribbean and globally.

Neoliberal Higher Education in the Caribbean and Postearthquake Academic Diaspora Returns

Outside of Haiti and the Spanish-speaking Caribbean, the establishment of public higher education in the Caribbean began in earnest between the late 1940s and 1980s as formal colonization was ending across the Anglophone and Francophone Caribbean. In the Francophone Caribbean, the Université des Antilles was founded in 1982, although its origins date back to 1850 with a School of Law. In the Anglophone Caribbean, the University College of the West Indies (UCWI), currently the University of West Indies (UWI), was established in Jamaica in 1948. UCWI was initially "established as a regional institution with a mission to meet the higher education needs of the Anglophone-Caribbean and to promote regional identity" (Coates 2012, 349). However, UCWI had difficulty attracting students within the first decades of its establishment. As Alan Cobley (2000, 15) observes: "During the late 1940s and 1950s, the UCWI had only limited success in establishing itself as the natural destination for West Indians in search of higher education. The initial enrolment in 1948 of 33 students (23 men and 10 women) had risen to 555 (354 men and 201 women) by 1957–58, an increase of more than sixteen times in ten years. But this was still only a fraction of the university college's potential." This was due in large part to a lack of scholarships and aid for qualified students, as well as the "continuing preference on the part of many potential students to go to universities and colleges overseas" (Cobley 2000, 15). Yet, between the 1960s and the 1980s, with formal decolonization, the Caribbean would witness a rise in public higher education enrollment as demands increased among non-elite populations (see Coates 2012; Howe 2000).

Between the 1970s and early 1980s, various newly independent Caribbean states aimed to improve access to and the quality of secondary and tertiary education (Hickling-Hudson 1989; Rose 2002). For instance, under Prime Minister Michael Manley's democratic socialism, "Jamaica focused on further access to secondary and post-secondary education to meet the demands for skilled labor as evidenced by the rapid growth in enrolment in higher education until the mid-1980s" (Welsh 2012, 119). In Grenada, the People's Revolutionary Government (PRB), under the leadership of Prime Minister Maurice Bishop, attempted to tackle the exclusionary colonial education system by forwarding a "revolutionary policy of integrating educational development, political mobilisation [sic] and economic growth" (Hickling-Hudson 1989, 95). Grenada allotted over 22 percent of its 1982–1983 national budget to education, "the highest amount anywhere in the region" (Rose 2002, 333). However, Caribbean states would borrow development loans from the International Monetary Fund (IMF), the World Bank, and other lenders to meet their educational and social goals. For example, "changes in the lending policy of the World Bank enabled Jamaica to obtain loans for the extension of educational facilities placing great emphasis and importance on the expansion of secondary and post-secondary education. Between 1966 and 1980, 50 new secondary schools were built and a Canadian loan scheme at the same time sponsored the building of 40 primary schools" (Welsh 2012, 119). Increasing under Jean-Claude Duvalier, Haiti saw continued international aid, witnessing an unprecedented influx of funds in the mid-1990s—1.8 billion between fiscal years 1995 through 1999 (Schuller 2007). The Haitian government channeled a portion of its national budget to the continued implementation of the 1979 Bernard Reform through the National Plan on Education and Training (NPET).[20] In 1997, the NPET sought to overhaul Haiti's French-style education system, which systematically disadvantaged Haiti's Kreyòl-speaking majority (Prou 2009). Yet, these development loans and financial assistance would contribute to economic crises throughout the Caribbean, paving the way for implementing neoliberal policies (see McAfee 1991).

Between the 1980s and 1990s, economic neoliberalism spread throughout the postcolonial Caribbean as multilateral financial organizations like the World Bank and the IMF directed Caribbean development through structural adjustment programs (SAPs)—loans and grants that came with neoliberal stipulations. Amid the 1980s global recession, the IMF and World Bank used SAPs to compel Caribbean governments to adopt neoliberal policies, such as the privatization of social services and the reduction of government spending on health and education, among other austerity measures (McAfee 1991). In the case of Jamaica, analysts trace the country's hefty external indebtedness and myriad economic inequalities to the IMF/World Bank–proposed structural adjustment policies (see Lundy 1999; Nelson and Clarke 2020). In Haiti, the foreign development funds received in the mid- to late-1990s "contributed to a severe imbalance of imports to exports, which led to the 1998 debt crisis and a $54 million bailout. Consequently, the . . . IMF imposed austerity measures in Haiti" (Dubuisson 2020, 65). Anthropologist Mark Schuller (2007, 73) notes that "when Haiti's government failed to deliver, the IMF triggered a freeze of all international funds to Haiti." Hence, the implementation of SAPs throughout the Caribbean ultimately led to increased external indebtedness and neocolonial dependency.

Neoliberal policies through structural adjustment programs also facilitated disinvestment in public higher education. In 1994, the World Bank released a report on higher education that "outlined the rationale on which the Bank had dramatically reduced lending for higher education to developing nations in favor of primary and secondary education: '. . . higher education investments have lower social rates of return than investments in primary and secondary education and investments in basic education can also have more direct impact on poverty reduction, because they tend to improve income equality' (World Bank, 1994; 12)" (cited in Stephenson and Zanotti 2019, 116). The Bank decreased its support for higher education from 17 percent of its lending portfolio between

INTERNAL DISPLACEMENTS

1985 and 1989 to about 7 percent in 1995–1999, supporting the 1994 report's findings "that developing nations could ill afford to treat higher education as a public good" (Stephenson and Zanotti 2017, 116). Higher education would gradually shift from a public good to a commodity—a transformation that merged with the needs of the emergent global knowledge economy.

With the rise of the global knowledge economy, higher education became increasingly incorporated into neoliberal logic. In 2000, "a World Bank-UNESCO Task Force on higher education encouraged the Bank to reconsider its lending policies based on the need to address the global knowledge economy. The group contended that lesser-developed nations might be lifted from poverty by cultivating citizen capacities to engage in the so-called 'knowledge economy' through improved access to strengthened higher education institutions" (Stephenson and Zanotti 2017, 116). This new development logic has contributed to the formation of the neoliberal university system. Within this system, "as educational institutions aspire to be more like each other, causing homogenization and hybridization, governments are also attempting to rationalise [sic] institutions through processes of differentiation, in their attempts to maximize their benefits for economic purposes. At the same time, local knowledges about particular societies and home-grown solutions for development—endogenous development— through education, are dispensed with in favour [sic] of solutions from external lending sources offering economic support to fledging economies" (Green 2016, 6). Moreover, in postcolonial Caribbean contexts, neoliberal higher education has resulted in the proliferation of private institutions, the migration of students and scholars to the Global North, and the transformation of local academic culture. In the case of changes to local academic culture, Megan Sylvester (2008, 280) notes how "the discursive construction of the UWI has shifted from that of a community of scholars producing knowledge as a public good for community uses, to that of a market-led business producing knowledge as a private good for individual consumption." In brief, neoliberal higher education has altered local and global intellectual landscapes—transforming and restructuring higher education institutions in the Caribbean and worldwide (see also Shahjahan 2014).

By the 1980s, the quality of education at the State University of Haiti (UEH) steadily eroded. As discussed in chapter 1, UEH "historically provided quality training for the socioeconomic elite, producing mainly lawyers and economists, as well as physicians, pharmacists, engineers, administrators and accountants, and writers who were the top echelon of the country" (INURED 2010, 5). Investments in Haitian public higher education began to decrease even as the demands for higher education grew among Haiti's popular classes (see Louis 2021). Between 1990 and 2014, Haiti's higher education sector averaged 0.33 percent of the country's GDP (Cela 2021; Jacob 2020). Yet, from 1981 to 2005, enrollment at UEH exponentially increased, outpacing the growth in instructors: "The number of instructors grew from 559 to 700," while the number of university students enrolled jumped from 4,099 to an estimated 15,000 (INURED 2010, 7; see also Cela 2021). As in various other postcolonial countries, public university in Haiti has been "all but abandoned, increasingly left to compete with better-resourced private distance education corporations and national private universities financed by international capital" (Louis 2021, 78). Indeed, from the mid-1980s onward, private universities mushroomed as an alternative for the thousands of Haitians who could not gain admittance into UEH. As INURED (2010, 8) reports:

> Of the 145 private institutions of higher education whose founding dates are known, only 3 predate 1980, and 10 predate 1986. This reveals the unchecked proliferation of private institutions of higher education (many of which are universities in name only), following the Constitution of 1987 [I return to this in chapter 3]. The National Strategy for Action on Education for All (SNAEPT), which guides government action on education in Haiti, concludes that, "regarding the sub-sector of the Haitian higher education, the most obvious conclusion is that it generally operates outside the law. Without any concern for basic standards of education, institutions of higher education are emerging and calling themselves universities." (MENFP 2007, 48)

People often referred to low-quality private universities as "*invèsite bolèt*" (literally, "lottery" universities)—meaning "students do not gain credits based on merit, but rather based on tuition payment" (INURED 2010, 10). The term also suggests that achieving academic success at such universities might be as unlikely as winning the lottery.

The 2010 earthquake nearly destroyed Haiti's already stressed higher education system. The quake demolished an estimated 90 percent of higher education institutions and took the lives of an estimated 120 to 200 professors and administrators and 2,599 to 6,000 students (INURED 2010, 2). Given a growing development logic where skills and knowledge, gained through higher education, were read as a path to sustainable development in an information-driven global knowledge economy (Guruz 2011), the Haitian state and international development apparatus vowed to rebuild and reform the Haitian higher education sector (see Cela 2021). Soon after the earthquake, then-president of Haiti René Préval "created a presidential task force on education, which was charged with drafting a five-year 'Operation Plan' for reforming Haiti's education system. It proposed expanding higher-education enrollments and raising more than a half-billion dollars to rebuild and revamp the system" (Downie 2012, A8). International actors like Inter-American Development Bank (IDB) and the Clinton Bush Haiti Fund promised millions to help rebuild UEH's Faculty of Sciences and other destroyed schools.[21] In 2011, UEH launched a ten-year strategic plan, *Horizon 2020*, that declared a seven-point strategy for reform the mirrored international standards:

1. Streamline university governance, organization, management, and communications.

INTERNAL DISPLACEMENTS 71

2. Provide the university with infrastructures enabling it to carry out its mission and create a welcoming and motivating environment.
3. Strengthen the commitment and qualification of the teaching staff, including professors and temporary workers.
4. Strengthen the adequacy between the training offered and the development needs of Haitian society.
5. Develop research.
6. Develop community services and partnerships in Haiti.
7. Develop international relations.[22]

It was not clear to me to what extent foreign funding requirements shaped these priorities. But I recall my conversation with a UEH dean who told me that international funds for rebuilding his campus were tied to requirements regarding implementation of Northern practices and procedures. "We were promised money to fix [the school], but couldn't meet their expectations," he said, pointing to the barely standing building in the center of the campus.

The catastrophe and potential for institutional transformation postearthquake also propelled the returns of numerous diaspora academics. According to a survey I administered to over one hundred returnees working at UEH, 55 percent of respondents had returned after the 2010 earthquake from places like France, Canada, the United States, Belgium, Spain, Mexico, and Brazil. Through conversations with UEH students, professors, and administrators, I learned that degrees from certain countries were considered more prestigious than others based on a perceived hierarchy of academic knowledge. For example, degrees from France and Belgium were often considered more valuable than those from the United States and Canada. Additionally, universities in Mexico and Brazil were viewed as superior to other Southern universities and were associated with certain stands of leftist radicalism. Irrespective of where a degree was obtained in the Global North, it was still considered better than one earned in the Global South. Therefore, the jenn doktè, who had generally earned doctorates from universities in the Global North, expected to have a competitive edge at home. But, as I will show in the next section, the jenn doktè's expectations—influenced by academic audit culture or Northern-oriented standards of accountability and productivity—would clash with local institutional realities, impeding their emplacement at UEH.

STRUGGLING FOR PLACE

One afternoon in 2018, I met with Pierre, a jenn doktè, in the upstairs lobby of the Marriott Hotel, a meeting place for Haitian, dyaspora, and expatriate professionals. Pierre was a thirty-something-year-old man who carried himself with a mixture of nervousness and confidence. As we conversed, I heard hints of a slight stutter in his otherwise quick and philosophical speech. Pierre was born and raised in the countryside. Although his parents only had primary school educations, they emphasized the importance of education for social mobility and invested what little they earned into their children's schooling. In 2001, Pierre enrolled at UEH just as Aristide was starting another presidential term. Pierre described this period as a political "drama or film with several acts" that would end in 2006 with the presidential reelection of René Préval. "The political context in Haiti is determinant," he explained. "When the state does not function, nothing functions." The political tumults under Aristide resulted in intermittent closures of UEH, which forcefully interrupted Pierre's undergraduate education. While several of Pierre's classmates left the country, he stayed and finish his undergraduate degree in 2007. After graduation, he received a scholarship to pursue a doctorate in Belgium. He completed his graduate studies there in 2012 and promptly returned to Haiti. When I asked him why he decided to return, he replied, "I always said that if I went abroad for a doctorate, it would not be predicated on departure but return." He continued, "[In Haiti,] I studied at a university and department plagued with problems and aspired to return in order to bring a contribution to the department, the University, [and] the country."

I heard similar versions of Pierre's story across my interviews with the jenn doktè: most said that they left to come back. Jacques, a lively and robust man in his late thirties or early forties, returned from Brazil in 2014 with a doctorate in political science. He was influenced by the late Haitian sociology professor and radical activist Jean Anil Louis-Juste, who also studied in Brazil, to choose Brazil over Europe for his studies. Jacques told me:

> When I was in Brazil, I never saw myself as an immigrant. I wasn't an immigrant. I emigrated specifically to study. When they speak of the Haitian dyaspora, I am not included since I was counting down the days until when I would return. . . . In UEH, we are used to the reality of returned academics. . . . But there are those who stay [abroad] . . . there are a lot of people who stay [abroad] when they get the chance.

Here, Jacques distinguishes himself from the average member of the Haitian dyaspora because he did not "take root" in Brazil and oriented his actions toward returning to Haiti. Like Pierre and other jenn doktè with whom I spoke, Jacques emphasized the voluntary nature of his return. "Brazil wanted me to stay, as opposed to returning to Haiti. They even asked me to stay to do a post-doctorate," Jacques explained. For him, returning was a choice—one he jokingly admitted was perhaps grounded in "sentimentality" or "insanity."

Several jenn doktè described an interesting paradox surrounding their return: even though they had prepared themselves mentally or psychologically for return, they nevertheless experienced disillusionment. I recall my conversation with Mehdi Chalmers at a pizza shop/hangout spot in Turgeau or Port-au-Prince's Gingerbread District. Medhi was a young man in his mid-twenties who displayed an easy cosmopolitanism. He had returned to Haiti in 2013 after

INTERNAL DISPLACEMENTS

living in Paris, where he earned two degrees: one in the history of philosophy at the University of Paris I and the other in library sciences at la Sorbonne. After returning, Mehdi began working at a bookstore called Librairie La Pléïade and teaching part-time at ENS. When I asked him why he returned, he gave the standard response among the jenn doktè: "It had never been my plan to stay abroad." Continuing, he added: "But I knew return would be brutal."

"What do you mean by 'brutal'?" I probed.

Drawing a menthol cigarette from the pack of Comme il Faut on the bistro table between us, he replied:

> Well, I knew it would be and I had prepared psychologically for [the brutality]. I remember that I argued with my girlfriend [when I was deciding to return]. She is French and agreed to follow me to Haiti. But she wanted us to take reprieve every few years—to stay for five years—to acclimate but not to stay. This upset me. I was like, "No, I cannot leave [after I return]. If I stay for a year or two and I then leave, I may never come back." In the minds of the people, in minds of the people here, I will always be a dyaspora.
>
> When you come back, people notice how you speak. They say, "You're a *ti grimo* (light-skin).[23] You speak French." They analyze everything. They say, "You don't know anything. You're not one of the guys. You don't drink the same. You don't move the same." [They even ask,] "Who are you sleeping with? Do you sleep with the same women as us?" In effect, "Are you part of the same world?" Well, aside from that I could find work and started teaching at the university without a problem. I am young and I returned with new knowledge that I didn't have before. I get along with the students.
>
> But there is animosity just the same. There's hostility against young professors who just arrived, who have cars. I don't know how many times people ask me if I am Haitian, understand? If you aren't completely unmoved by this, it will be difficult. If every time someone asks you if you're Haitian, it hurts your feelings, you're screwed! If you don't have some level of distance, if you don't have a sense of humor and the capacity to realize that you're in a situation where people are always testing you, you won't be able to acclimate. But it's not that it's impossible.

Unlike many others in his generational cohort, Mehdi came from a middle-class background, but still experienced rejection as an unwitting dyaspora. His counterparts who stayed questioned his national belonging due to his migration status, class, and color, but Mehdi approached these interrogations with a critical distance. He embraced the brutality of return—that is, the blunt experience of recurrent deracination—seeing reintegration as difficult but not insurmountable.

Conversely, academic diaspora returnees with tenuous middle-class status described feeling deceived and even betrayed by the lack of livable salaries they found as professors in Haiti. Jacques explained that his stipend as a student in

Brazil was more than his current salary. And had he taken the postdoctorate position in Brazil, his salary would have been three times the salary he earned in Haiti as a full-time professor. "So, return would seem like a suicidal mission. But I was conscious of this," he chuckled. Taking a more somber tone, Jacques went on that "the net salary for a UEH professor isn't more than 1,000 USD a month." According to Jacques, this salary was not enough for him to take care of his young family, especially considering postearthquake housing inflations:

> When I returned, the first thing I experienced was a massive deception. Renting a house was a mystery because, after the 2010 earthquake, the [INGOs] that invaded the country created a housing crisis. First, the earthquake destroyed many homes, and INGOs rented those that remained in US dollars! There were housing ads that were priced for INGOs workers [who could pay thousands a month]. I eventually found a place to rent but was evicted after three months [on the previous tenants' eviction notice].

In addition to being a full-time professor at UEH, Jacques held a part-time teaching position at a private religious university but still could not make ends meet. Pierre, for his part, summed the financial situation of the jenn doktè this way:

> [With reintegration], the question should be in terms of income. Is this going to allow you to live or not? If you cannot live on what you're doing, you are going to want to go abroad or do a series of jobs overseas, which causes the university [and] people who want to dedicate themselves to the university to suffer. Today—if you consider those who returned—there is a phenomenon where many had come back with a fire ignited within them. But [the living conditions] soon squelched that fire, causing many to re-emigrate. A person who enters UEH simply cannot live day-to-day.

For many jenn doktè, their ability to make a decent income was equivalent to staying and fulfilling their aspirations of contributing to their country through higher education. As Pierre illuminates above, if the jenn doktè could not afford to live, the hope that propelled their returns would soon diminish, forcing them to leave again.

In addition to being discouraged by the meager salaries they received as professors, several jenn doktè were dismayed by the disjuncture between the academic and professional standards they found abroad and those they returned to at home. For instance, Pierre found UEH's academic standards and reintegration of newly minted doctorates to be subpar:

> Therein lay the "shock of return." The university doesn't even have the resources to support research. And with a lack of resources comes a lack of time to undertake research. From 2012 to 2018, I worked hard to publish several articles, either here or in France. The researcher [in Haiti] is autonomous, which allows him to pursue his research interests. However, there is a problem with

valorization. You're a transnational researcher in a national context [where research is not valued].

Mickael, a professor and director at Institut d'etudes et de recherches Africaines (the Institute of African Studies and Research or IERAH), expressed indignation at what he saw as mediocre teaching and recruitment standards. Sitting behind the desk in his university office, Mickael decried:

> People here teach anyway and anyhow . . . there are no metrics for evaluation. And becoming a professor here is too easy, even to become a director. You don't even need to have a diploma . . . to become dean or even rector! . . . Back in Europe, there was a process to fill a vacant position. Here, it's: "Are you friends with the dean? Are you friends with the rector?" . . . "Are you competent?" is people's last resort. That is the difference . . . Politics are destroying the university . . . the games people are playing to hold on to power—manipulation to hold on to his job . . . no research. But it's "How can I hold on to my resources and keep those in power that helps me hold on to my power?" . . . There is no tenure . . . you enter, and they call you, "Professor"!

For various jenn doktè with whom I spoke, the "shock of return" lay in the fact that they could not secure well-paid positions based on the academic criteria that shaped the profession elsewhere. Diverse interlocutors told me that UEH had no definitive tenure track to climb, and promotion rested on length of employment and political alliances, as opposed to scholarly output and other standard (read: Northern) metrics of academic productivity.[24] In short, although many of the jenn doktè had been students at UEH and some part-time instructors before going abroad, they returned differently than they left. And upon returning, they found themselves struggling for a place in the very institution they sought to transform.

Intellectual Friendship

Intergenerational conflict soon emerged between the jenn dokté and members of jenerasyon 86. The former generally viewed the latter as beneficiaries of the status quo, who were neither qualified nor motivated to lead what they saw as the badly needed transformation of UEH. In 2013, Pierre, Mickael, and other jenn dokté led a movement to raise academic scholarly production, standardize professor evaluation, and make pay commensurate with qualifications. The movement generally viewed jenerasyon 86 as unqualified and publicly argued that UEH would not be a real university until it fostered scholarly production and transparent promotion processes. In Pierre's words,

> Today, we have [young] professors who are more qualified than those who are leading the University. . . . These leaders remain behind the scenes as pillars

of an ineffective academic system that they don't want to change. There is also the problem of the jenerasyon 86. Members of jenerasyon 86 are generally those who left after completing *premye sik* [the first academic year], or they started a premye sik that they never finished. They had already started working at the State University and soon fled into exile or forced exile because of Duvalier's persecution. They didn't study while abroad. When they returned in 1986, they took the University as a *chanm* [private space], or better, *an otaj* [hostage]. These people don't want [change]. When the movement began in 2013, people derisively called it, "*mouvman ti dòkte,*" "*les petits Médecins,*" "*mouvman jenn doktè.*" But those who said this didn't have diplomas but were still professors or administrators, or people who had fake degrees. They even say that even the Rector doesn't have a [graduate] degree.

Pierre's view of jenerasyon 86 was based on a generational apprehension that casts a long shadow of doubt on the older generation's ability to lead. Moreover, the idea that the jenerasyon 86 held UEH an otaj or hostage suggests that the older generation would rather see the university perish than give up their place to younger scholars. Interestingly, other UEH factions leveraged this same accusation against those they perceived as trying to control or dominate the university space (chapter 3).

Several members of jenerasyon 86 described the jenn doktè as self-interested agitators, seeking to rapidly transform UEH for their benefit. A UEH dean and jenerasyon 86 professor told me with frankness and self-amusement: "There are a lot of ti doktè [Laughs mockingly]. We have a phenomenon where more young people are returning, who earned doctorates in Europe. We [the older generation] are in a miserable situation that we are fighting to change. But they want to disrupt things rapidly, very rapidly." That members of jenerasyon 86 grasped onto more secure positions at UEH and tended to block the placemaking strategies of the most recent generation of returnees was largely a symptom of neoliberal higher education, which has altered and fragmented the global and local landscape of intellectual and academic labor. But going back to Carole's pronouncement at the start of this chapter: what the jenn doktè felt, what they "experienced was that there was no place for them."

The struggle that emerged between jenerasyon 86 and the jenn doktè for place at UEH had as much to do with power as with different worldviews. Summing up Karl Mannheim's work on the relationship between intellectual competition and social power, Paul Kecskemeti (1972, 25) writes: "Every group has its own interpretation of the world and seeks to make it the universally accepted one. Thus, theoretical discussions may be conceived of as an instance of the general struggle for power. When social power is monopolized by one group, then one world interpretation reigns supreme; no contrary position to the official prevailing one is allowed to be expressed. However, monopolies of power inevitably break down sometime; when they do, rival theories and interpretations of the world begin to compete among each other." While both generations expressed similar desires for a well-resourced university that privileged teaching, research, and service, they had divergent theories on how this might be achieved.

A way forward is what David Scott (2017, 14) terms "intellectual friendship"—a "rough harmony of interests"—that solicits "an attitude of attentive receptivity, a readiness to appreciatively hear where the other is coming from." Intellectual friendship, while not devoid of conflict, rests on mutual respect and rigorous dialogue—not as a means of arriving at convergence, but as a way of thinking and working through shared problem-spaces. Carole described longing for this sort of friendship with older exile returnees: "There was a lot of generational distrust. One-sided! The older generation, I think, was afraid of us who were in our twenties. This was excruciating because we loved them. We wanted to work with them, but they were very guarded. . . . It hurts your feelings." Mickael, who returned in 2011—twenty-five years after the returns of jenerasyon 86—likewise explained: "The first challenge I faced [when I returned] was from the person at IERAH with whom I had come to work. I should have been seen as a collaborator, not a threat." Conventional understanding reads the intergenerational transfer of knowledge as a one-way process, where the older generation deposits knowledge into the minds of the newer generation. Yet, as Carole and Mickael suggest, learning from one generation to the next should be based on friendship and collaboration:

> From this angle, we can see that an adequate education or instruction of the young (in the sense of the complete transmission of all experiential stimuli which underlie pragmatic knowledge) would encounter a formidable difficulty in the fact that the experiential problems of the young are defined by a different set of adversaries from those of their teachers. Thus (apart from the exact sciences), the teacher-pupil relationship is not as between one representative of "consciousness in general" and another, but as between one possible subjective center of vital orientation and another subsequent one. This tension appears incapable of solution except for one compensating factor: not only does the teacher educate his pupil, but the pupil educates his teacher too. Generations are in a state of constant interaction. (Mannheim 1952, 301)

Given their temporal and locational differences, jenerasyon 86 and jenn doktè had varying and complementary perspectives and competencies. But within the neoliberal illogic of scarcity and competition, the conditions for sustained and institutionalized dialogue and sharing between the cohorts tended to go unmet, fueling tensions and even a multi-year crisis at UEH.

CHAPTER 3

The "Crisis Factory"

IMPROVISING PLACE IN THE (STATE) UNIVERSITY OF HAITI

> *Crisis was . . . a salient imperial category, typically mobilized in relation to the security issues provoked by one or another colonial insurgency, or one or another capitalist contraction. But crisis, in recent Caribbeanist ethnography, has also been oriented toward understanding the extent to which people feel it is possible to imagine different futures.*
>
> —Deborah A. Thomas, What the Caribbean Teaches Us: The Afterlives and New Lives of Coloniality

I stand in Chan Mas in late October 2017, taking in the area surrounding UEH Faculté d'Ethnologie (Fakilte Etnoloji, Faculty of Ethnology, or FE). Chan Mas is a public square that houses the statues of Haiti's revolutionary heroes, including the iconic *Nèg Mawon*—a Maroon crouched on one knee, blowing the siren call of freedom into a conch shell. The square's proximity to the National Palace, which now lies in ruins, makes it a popular site of public protests. Today, Chan Mas is quiet, with *machann* (street vendors) dotting the sidewalks, selling candy, liquor, shoeshines, photocopies, and used and outdated textbooks. Despite being located across the street from FE, I do not see signs of university students. The quiet and relative emptiness of the square unsettles me. I cross the street toward FE, and then, standing at its shuttered gates, I notice the handwritten signs (figure 3.1).

"ABA Impunité" (Down with impunity)
"Viv Libète ak Byennèt" (Long live liberty and well-being)
"Nou vle etidye tankou moun" (We want to study like people)
"Viv yon Leta Fò / Ann Revisite Rèv Papa Nasyon a" (Long live a strong
    state / We must resurrect the dream of the Nation's Father)
"Blot Kriminèl" (Blot is a criminal)

THE "CRISIS FACTORY"

Figure 3.1. Protest posters at FE gates, October 2017. Photo by author.

"Fòk etnoloji relouvri / Fòk Goug jwenn jistis/ Fòk Blot al nan prizon" (Ethnology must reopen / Goug must get justice / Blot must be imprisoned).

As I would learn, these demands and proclamations signaled the then ongoing crisis at UEH.

Conventional discourse has often read Haiti through a lens of "perpetual crisis"—meaning, a pervasive state of chaos and precariousness (Polyné 2013b). For many Haitians, "crisis" informs how they understand and experience the seemingly intractable failure of the Haitian state and its institutions. For instance, one interlocutor explained how people often refer to the Université d'État d'Haïti (State University of Haiti, UEH) as a "crisis factory"—meaning a place that produces disorder. Yet, this lens of perpetual crisis occludes historical, geopolitical, and epistemological realities, creating a "space-time singularity ... that warps one's capacity to see, assess, proceed" (Polyné 2013b, xiii). To contextualize and disrupt this notion of Haitian perpetual crisis, I examine in this chapter the historical, structural, and embodied aspects of the specific 2016–2018 UEH crisis.

I divide the chapter's multiscale analysis into three interrelated segments. In the first part, I discuss various approaches to crises in Haiti. I also highlight Greg Beckett's (2013; 2019) conceptualization of *kriz* (embodied crisis), and, taking it further, I use "articulation" and "embodied space" to forward a place-based understanding of kriz. In the second section, I analyze the national and international processes that, I argue, articulated UEH as a crisis factory by constituting it as a state-nonstate entity located in a United-Nations defined "yellow zone," a site of insecurity. I posit that the embodied space thus created was one of "affective uncertainty." Affect, here, means "the generalized concept for all those embodied processes that, when they reach the conscious mind, can be understood on the one hand as feelings, or on the other as physiologically charged emotions" (Brown and Phu 2014, 6). Thus, I use affective uncertainty to describe how ambiguities become embodied feelings that inform place-making. In the final section, I use a composite narrative to retell the story of the 2016–2018 UEH crisis. I also draw on observant participation at three UEH faculties (schools) to trace kriz through the affective experiences and embodied practices of UEH students, professors, and administrators. My central argument, here, is that the 2016–2018 UEH crisis was a manifestation of the so-called crisis factory articulation that geographically situated individuals incorporated and reified through a "habitus of improvisation."

I use habitus of improvisation to mean that differently situated groups used competing modes of improvisation to navigate uncertainty and demand change. Habitus—that is, "a subjective but not individual system of internalized structures, schemes of perception, conception, and action common to all members of the same group or class" (Bourdieu 1997, 86)—is a helpful way to appreciate how similarly situated groups perceive, feel, and act within a given space. Improvisation, for its part, connotes spontaneity, immediacy, and even reactivity. "[But] in its most fully realized forms, improvisation is the creation and development of new, unexpected, and productive co-creative relations among people. . . . Improvisers work with the tools they have in the arenas that are open to them, in order to imbue the world with the possibility of making right things happen" (Fischlin, Heble, and Lipsitz 2013, xii). Improvisation, therefore, may provide a way out of crises, at least to the extent that improvisers can coalesce around a shared vision of the future that can drive systemic change.

Haitian "Perpetual Crisis": Toward a Place-Based Understanding of *Kriz*

The ongoing crises in Haiti have been approached primarily as either a problem of culture or of the state. The former, dating back to the early responses to the Haitian Revolution, treats crisis as a historical problem rooted in Haitian "culture" (Beckett 2013; Polyné 2013b). The intensely punitive global marginalization that was the dominant response to the Haitian Revolution thwarted early nation-building efforts in the country and exacerbated preindependence social divisions (chapter 1). Rather than acknowledge the role of dominant countries, nineteenth-century and twentieth-century Western powers claimed that Haiti's problems were caused by its culture of so-called barbarity and savagery (Dash 1988). Indeed, during the U.S. military Occupation of Haiti (1915–1934), U.S. journalists "wrote popular accounts that portrayed Haiti as a dismal, backward place, full of lazy (if at times charming) peasants in the thrall of Vodou" (Dubois 2012, 2). The idea that culture is to blame for Haiti's problems continues to inform Haitian abjection in U.S. popular and news media (Pierre 2013; Ulysse 2015a).

Nineteenth-century Haitian intellectuals forwarded an alternative understanding of the country's problems: as a political problem of a state mired in deeply rooted class and color divisions. International observers located the country's troubles in the dysfunction of the Haitian state (Beckett 2013; Fatton 2014). U.S. officials used the language of political instability to justify recurrent political and economic interventions in the country. The idea has endured that "perpetual crisis" is a problem of the dysfunctional Haitian state. Today, international relations typologies define Haiti as a "weak" or "failing" state, albeit an atypical one: its frailty is positioned not so much as a problem of conflict as a consequence of persistent poverty (Nesbitt 2013b, 36). Yet, the "weak state" and "poorest country in the Western Hemisphere" monikers that have been attached to Haiti occlude and justify systemic imperial processes and interventions that have ensured that Haiti's survival depends on "nongovernmental organizations and U.N. life support" (Nesbitt 2013b, 5; see also James 2010). Thus, both political and economic unrest as well as natural disasters are problematically read as symptoms of a frail state that needs ongoing foreign and humanitarian intervention and control.

Some scholars have examined how fragmented globality creates the conditions for insecurity in the country. Nancy Glick Schiller and Georges Fouron (2001, 213–214) define Haiti as an "apparent state," arguing that postcolonial countries like Haiti sustains "only the formal apparatus of a state without any possibility of setting an economic direction that can begin to meet the needs of the populations [it claims] to represent." Conversely, in his book, *Haiti: Trapped in the Outer Periphery*, Robert Fatton (2014, 1) locates Haiti within the neoliberal "outer periphery"—meaning "a zone of generalized inequities and ultracheap wages whose politics offers a simulacrum of electoral 'democracy' under the tutelage of a self-appointed international community. This zone is often besieged by wars, natural disasters, regime change, and foreign occupation." Within the outer periphery, crises are used to justify state control, in which "the state" also pertains to the processes and practices of international and nongovernmental institutions (Fatton 2014; Trouillot 2001). While conceptually useful, neither the apparent nor outer periphery state types offer means for examining how state and state-like processes and practices converge and are experienced as crises on the ground.

By forwarding a person-centered and phenomenological understanding of crisis, Greg Beckett (2019) examines crisis as lived. Beckett's 2019 ethnography,

There Is No More Haiti, focuses on what Raymond Williams (1977, 173) called the "'structure of feeling'"—that is, the "affective elements of consciousness and relationships: not feeling against thought but thought as felt and feeling as thought." Beckett (2013, 41) employs the Kreyòl term *kriz*, which is a translation of the French *crise*: the "French and Kreyòl terms render crisis an embodied condition that is rooted in the social and psychological experience of an individual." Although Haitians use kriz to describe "a political crisis or the aftermath of a disaster," they also use it to convey a "sense of an unmediated bodily response to trauma" that leaves one open to a "sense of sudden rupture and vulnerability" (41) or illness or even death. Beckett (2019) examines kriz through the personal narratives and experiences of various interlocutors, pointing to the ways that local and global political, socioeconomic, and ecological factors converge to create a thin line between death and life in Haiti. Beckett's vividly and beautifully written ethnography centers around a "forest" turned botanical garden and illuminates how death in Vodou cosmology may also signal rebirth.[1] Notwithstanding its path-breaking gestures, the book tends to reify notions of Haiti's "uninhabitability" by treating "crisis" as an enduring reality from which interlocutors theorize, while Haiti remains a relatively undifferentiated crisis zone. Like any country, Haiti is not monolithic but is a composite of specific sites that each have their own distinct "feel" even while located within the same national territory.

Building from Beckett's (2019) work, I employ the concepts of "articulation" and "embodied space" to further a place-based understanding of kriz. Articulation describes how ideological, cultural, and material elements combine to create reality or construct place (see Deluca 1999). While "space" is abstract and open, "place" is how individuals inscribe space with meaning (Low and Lawrence-Zúñiga 2003). Embodied space, therefore, is the "existential and phenomenological reality of place: its smell, feel, color, and other sensory dimensions" (Low 2003, 13). The concept of embodied space also recognizes that, while individuals are receptacles of meanings and behaviors derived from trans-spatial articulations, they are also "grounded at any one moment in a specific geographical location" (Low 2009, 22–25). Vanessa Agard-Jones similarly illuminates the interconnection and interbeing of bodies and places. Through her ethnographic research, she shows how the body can be "an important site of (inter- and intra-) action, a site 'on the ground' that encourages us to look *in* the ground—a position from which we might ask new, and more finely calibrated questions about how individual bodies and individual people come to be, in dynamic relationship to the worlds around them" (Agard-Jones 2013, 192). I suggest, therefore, that to properly understand kriz as embodied crisis, one must first examine the articulations that construct a site of crisis and then look at how individuals incorporate these articulations in their inhabitation of the site. I thus next examine the transnational articulations that constructed UEH into a "crisis factory."

The "Crisis Factory": The (State) University of Haiti

The UEH construction as a so-called crisis factory was due, in part, to its articulation as a state-nonstate institution; that is, it was both struggling against and dependent on the state. The Université d'Haïti (the [State] University of Haiti) was historically a locus of political resistance.[2] As discussed in chapter 1, when Duvalier took over the university in 1960–1961, he renamed it Université d'État d'Haïti, or the State University of Haiti. Under Duvalier, "faculty and students at the State University of Haiti were ... tamed, and all independent student organizations were banned. Faculty and students at the university were henceforth chosen on the basis of their loyalty to the president" (Dupuy 2007, 34). After the fall of Duvalier's dictatorship, the university sought to safeguard itself against future state control. The country's 1987 Constitution officially declared UEH's autonomy from the state (Chap. 5, Article 208). Crucially, although the Haitian state theoretically could not impede the intellectual freedom of the university, it remained responsible for setting the university's budget, supplementing students' tuition, and paying professors' salaries (see INURED 2010). The university had no real means to hold the state accountable, let alone defend against state political interference. Thus, UEH became situated in a liminal space as a state-nonstate entity.

As I previously discussed in chapter 2, the rise of neoliberalism in Haiti led to the debilitation of UEH. After the 1991 coup that deposed Jean-Bertrand Aristide, overlapping political and economic turmoil further contributed to a lack of resources for the university, which was growing exponentially in the number of enrolled students (see INURED 2010; Prou 2009). After Aristide was restored to power in 1994, he promised to reform the education sector and announced the government's plans to purchase school supplies, refurbish schools, and provide scholarships for the poor (Prou 2009, 44). His successor, President René Préval, oversaw the continuation of these reforms with the 1997 National Plan on Education and Training (NPET) (Prou 2009).

In 1997, the school's liminal existence as a state-nonstate entity solidified when the university's Provisional Council and the state's Ministry of Education adopted the *Dispositions Transitoires* (Transitional Arrangements).[3] This policy proclaimed that the university is responsible for appointing its leaders and managing its organization, but it stopped short of amending its dependent legal status. Under the Dispositions Transitoires, each of the nineteen UEH schools have their own internal regulations, while the Conseil de l'Université (University Council, CU) maintains control of the overall structure and arbitration for UEH. The CU is made up of thirty-six members, including the three members of the Conseil Exécutif (executive board)—the rector and two vice rectors—elected every four years. One of the vice rectors is responsible for academic affairs, administrative

84 FRACTURES

training, and research. The remaining thirty-three members of the CU are appointed delegates of the different schools—deans, professors, and students. During my fieldwork in 2017 to 2018, UEH was still operating under the Dispositions Transitoires.

From 2002 to 2004, during Aristide's second presidential tenure, open and sometimes violent conflicts occurred between the university and the state. As Haitian sociologist and professor at UEH Faculté d'Ethnologie, Ilionor Louis (2021, 78–79), writes in "Repression and Resistance in the Neoliberal University": "This moment was primarily characterized by President Jean-Bertrand Aristide's inclinations to control UEH and by the organized struggle to overthrow his regime. This period was also a time of uprising and politicization of the student struggle." For example, on December 5, 2003, "Aristide gangs, such as the *chimères* (ghosts), and police attacked the State University, where students were holding anti-government protests. They ransacked buildings, gutted two departments, and injured dozens of students and administrators" (Luzincourt and Gulbrandson 2010, 7). In 2004, UEH students joined anti-Aristide protests, which dovetailed with a paramilitary coup that eventually contributed to the overthrow of Aristide on February 28, 2004 (Dupuy 2007).

Soon after Aristide's ouster, the United Nations declared a political crisis in the country, which was argued resulted from "a prevailing culture of violence, widespread corruption and the criminalization of armed groups" as well from "neglect by the international community" (Faubert 2004, 4). In June 2004, the United Nations Stabilization Mission in Haiti (MINUSTAH) took on the task of restoring "the rule of law," which included police reform, the disarmament and demobilization of street gangs, and the organization and monitoring of elections (Lemay-Hébert 2018). Scholar-activist Jemima Pierre illuminates the (neo)colonial underpinnings of the U.N. Occupation of Haiti. She writes:

> What most solidified this occupation was the creation and operationalization of the Core Group. An international coalition of self-proclaimed and non-Black "friends" of Haiti, the Core Group was established as part of the 2004 U.N. resolution that brought foreign soldiers and technocrats to the country. While the group's membership has fluctuated since its initial formation, it currently has nine members: Brazil, Canada, France, Germany, Spain, the United States, European Union, OAS, and United Nations Organization. Significantly, the group has never had a Haitian representative. The Core Group's stated goal is to oversee Haiti's governance through the coordination of the various branches and elements of the United Nations mission in Haiti. But in practice, the Core Group represents an insidious example of (neo)colonialism driven by white supremacy. (Pierre 2023, 247)

Like the U.S. Occupation of Haiti nearly a century earlier, foreign definitions of crisis in Haiti were employed to justify processes of (neo)colonialism through

THE "CRISIS FACTORY" 85

international policing and control. As the first part of the opening epigraph suggests, crisis as imperial category has long been used to further coloniality.

In 2006, with the second-term election of René Préval, the university began implementing modest reforms, but this was not enough to forestall crisis or even violence. During the 2006–2007 academic year, the CU adopted an election charter that effectively replaced the appointment process for leaders in the schools in the metropolitan Port-au-Prince area. The Commission Électorale Centrale (Central Electoral Commission) was established to work with the local electoral commissions that organized elections at the schools, including of the executive board. However, as noted earlier, even though UEH managed its own governing structure and electoral process, the state retained control of the university's budget, thereby curtailing UEH's ability to implement desired institutional and structural changes. In 2009, tensions boiled over when the administration of the School of Medicine announced that it was forced to eliminate over ten courses from the curriculum and cited state budget constraints that prevented the hiring of qualified teachers. This led to a university-wide student strike and then widescale public protests to demand reinstatement of the courses plus a national minimum wage increase and MINUSTAH's removal (Losier 2013). The demonstrations, which began in April 2009, peaked on June 3, 2009, when over seven hundred UEH students protested. "[They were] strategically blocking Port-au-Prince streets near the National Palace as well as the offices of an educational NGO previously run by Préval's prime minister. Despite repression by police and MINUSTAH soldiers, the students continued to take to the streets for the next two days throwing stones, erecting barricades, and setting government vehicles on fire. Over the next several weeks, students drew hundreds of people to the streets. Their signs and slogans increasingly targeted not only Préval, but also the U.N. MINUSTAH troops, describing the soldiers as an occupying force" (Losier 2013, 216). Despite a turbulent spring and summer, classes at UEH commenced with the fall 2009 session. Then, on January 12, 2010, a new crisis struck with the 7.0-magnitude earthquake. The earthquake killed approximately 300,000 people (roughly the entire population of some mid-size U.S. cities like Pittsburgh) and displaced millions. Far from withdrawing, the U.N. ramped up its presence significantly in the wake of the earthquake (Schuller 2016).

In 2011, Haiti witnessed the installation of the Tèt Kale Party (PHTK)—an extreme-right, neo-Duvalierist regime led by U.S.-backed president Michel Martelly (Lamour 2021). Sometime after the establishment of PHTK, a troubling alliance arose between the regime and certain UEH leaders: "Paradoxically, leaders of the UEH, who in the past had defined themselves as democrats or progressives, formed an alliance with this regime to suppress student protest and to nip in the bud an attempt to unionize administrative staff" (Louis 2021, 78). As I will show next, this unprecedented alliance would also contribute to the 2016–2018 UEH crisis.

86

In addition to its construction as a state-nonstate entity, UEH was also articulated by its geographic location within a U.N.-identified yellow zone, or site of insecurity. Nicolas Lemay-Hébert (2018, 66) notes: "Interventions in a (post-)conflict or (post)disaster context are increasingly seen through a risk-assessment lens, where security zones are spatialized depending on perceived security or insecurity for international staff. In Haiti, security mapping has taken shape through color-coding—with green zones deemed 'safe,' yellow zones 'risky,' and red zones 'to avoid.'" In Haiti, color-coded security mapping—created in coordination with the United States, the United Nations, and the country's upper classes—did not reflect "any actual crime or violence assessment" but was drawn along socioeconomic divisions. The mapping legitimized "political control over certain residents, perhaps particularly those who may demonstrate a greater propensity to challenge the political status quo" (Dirksen 2019, 330–331). Deployed first in Haiti in 2004, MINUSTAH continued to use color-coded security maps as a means of "justifying their presence and use of force to meet [purported] local threats, stigmatizing local actors deemed 'problematic' and reading local politics through their own security lens" (Lemay-Hébert 2018, 90). MINUSTAH placed UEH schools in Port-au-Prince within the yellow zone, which meant the geographic space around the schools received stricter security measures and greater presence of military and police (see Lemay-Hébert 2018). This geographic designation allowed MINUSTAH greater means to surveil and restrict student activism. For instance, in 2010: "Brazilian soldiers of the MINUSTAH entered the campus—a violation of constitutional guarantees of the inviolability of university space—and arrested Frantz Junior Mathieu as students occupied the Faculty of Ethnology in May 2010 to denounce the presence of foreign troops in the country and demand the immediate departure of MINUSTAH" (Louis 2021, 80). This led to another wave of student protests against the U.N. occupying force (Louis 2021).

MINUSTAH's placement of UEH within the yellow zone reinforced (or influenced) how people perceived UEH. Even after MINUSTAH's departure in 2017, I witnessed that whenever political or economic tensions heightened in Port-au-Prince, news outlets and word of mouth warned the public to avoid UEH. This geographic imaginary also marked UEH students as embodiments of *dezòd* (disorder). When I asked students how the public perceives UEH students, many said that they were often considered *vakabon* (troublemakers) or *militan* (radical activists). Indeed, whenever protests or civil unrest occurred in the capital, the public generally believed that student protestors would be involved, burning tires in the street, throwing rocks at cars, and impeding foot traffic. Samuel, a UEH alum and former part-time professor, described the public's perception of UEH students this way:

> The society sees UEH students as violent, as people who are defending causes that don't concern them. [People say], "What's up with these students?! They

THE "CRISIS FACTORY" 87

are against the society, not simply against the government or the leaders of the University." Student protests have created tensions, an impasse. Moreover, students are fighting for the university to remain *their* space. They don't see themselves as individuals who must one day graduate from the university. The university has become a living space and a community for them. It's extraordinary! Many students eat and bathe at the university *every day*. They leave their house in the morning and go to the university even when they don't have classes. They live at the university. . . . It is their house. So, they prefer to keep the university as it is.

In the above quotation, Samuel implicitly alleges that UEH students were indeed vakabon, who intended to keep UEH hostage—as *"their* space." Yet, it seemed apparent that widespread class biases informed this perception of UEH students, as many UEH students came from economically poor and working-class backgrounds and perhaps needed to find "living space" at the university. Placing the onus of disorder on UEH students (that is, those with the least power) not only criminalized them but also served to delegitimize their claims while absolving powerful actors of responsibility.

The UEH Crisis, 2016–2018

Because of the contested nature of this 2016–2018 UEH crisis, I use a composite narrative to retell the story of the crisis. I combine information from interviews with professors, administrators, individual students, and student activist groups, as well as published news reports and official university documents. From these diverse sources, I construct the following braided multivocal narrative.

The causes of this crisis are difficult to pinpoint. Many interlocutors blamed it on the *mouvman jenn doktè's* (movement of young doctorates) protests of the 2016 rectoral election. The mouvman jenn doktè, led by Pierre, Mickael, and others, advocated for changes to the administrative structure of the university (chapter 2). The movement also argued that professors with doctorates should be paid more than those without this higher education and be given leadership roles as well. This merged with ongoing student demands for better learning conditions and better qualified faculty. Professor Charles, my faculty sponsor, who had earned his doctorate in Europe and was a graduate program director, told me that if UEH had had a clear tenure process, then younger professors would not have fought with the directors and deans for promotions, creating "the problems we have now."

The mouvman jenn doktè saw the 2016 rectoral elections as an opportunity to replace the "aging" jenerasyon 86, whom they believed kept the university from meeting global academic standards. The movement specifically protested that the front-runner for the UEH rector position, Fritz Deshommes, was

88 FRACTURES

unqualified because he did not have a doctoral degree. "Nowhere else would you see someone with [only] a master's as the head of a university!" Pierre told me. Yet, Deshommes did meet the criteria for office according to the Dispositions Transitoires, which specified only a master's degree.

The opposition against Deshommes escalated when nineteen students occupied the office of the rectorate on February 5, 2016; they would remain there for over five months. On May 17, 2016, the election for UEH's new leadership was held in a secret location and without the full complement of CU members. On July 29, 2016, the newly elected rector Deshommes had the national police remove the students from the office of the rectorate. But many were surprised when the CU voted a few months later to expel the students. Local newspapers ran the full names of the expelled students, echoing university accusations against them of "theft and breakdown of public and private property, the destruction of archives and academic, administrative, and financial documents, acts of aggression and violence of all kinds against professors, students, administrative staff, and applicants" (HaïtiLibre 2016, n.p.). The newspapers also stated that the students' accomplices would be identified and charged. Although the students' coconspirators were never discovered, a jenerasyon 86 professor told me that the jenn doktè had manipulated the students into occupying the rectorate.

Regardless of whether the students had accomplices or even instigators among the faculty, many students and professors considered their expulsion as unjust. Dr. Christophe, a longtime UEH professor, explained that Deshommes had prosecuted the students without due process. Christophe added that it was extremely difficult to be accepted into the university, and that being expelled would irrevocably alter the course of these students' lives. During the 2016–2017 academic year, UEH students, mainly from Faculté des Sciences Humaines (School of Human Sciences, FASCH), Faculté d'Ethnologie (School of Ethnology, FE), and École Normale Supérieure (Teachers' College, ENS), disrupted university operations in protest against the expulsions. Peter, a maintenance worker at FASCH, told me that student protestors created a menacing environment by intimidating people and preventing them from entering the campus, and some even threw excrement over campus walls.

The situation took a more drastic turn at FE during a general assembly on June 12, 2017. Members of the mouvman etidyan (student movement), a moderate group of student activists, told me that the feeling at the assembly was already tense. There are differing accounts of how it happened, but a professor seriously injured a protestor.

Professor Jean Yves Blot, an FE dean and anthropology professor who was still working toward a doctorate, explained that he did not see the protestor before he ran him over, and he believes the protestor deliberately jumped in front his vehicle. Others claimed that Blot intentionally ran over the protestor, asserting that there was no way Blot had not seen him. Opinions notwithstanding,

THE "CRISIS FACTORY" 89

what is certain is that Blot ran over a protestor. Students subsequently physically retaliated against professors, burned cars, and vandalized buildings. Marc, a student movement activist, maintained that it was the more radical students who had set the fires and that moderates, like himself, tried to convince them that burning down FE and FASCH would not result in change. A cell phone picture of the injured protestor, bloodied and leg unnaturally contorted, later circulated on social media and in the news, fueling the public's perception of UEH as a "crisis factory." The state did not bring charges against Blot, and UEH sided with his version of events in multiple official statements.

In December 2017, the Communication Unit of UEH held a session to discuss the crisis. In an unprecedented move, the unit adopted a resolution asking the executive board to take "all necessary measures," including the use of police force, to take back control of FE and FASCH. The resolution cited both the Dispositions Transitoires and the 1987 Constitution as the basis for authorizing the National Police of Haiti (PNH) to "reestablish order" at FE and FASCH. On January 25, 2018, two different forces, the Brigade d'Opération et d'Intervention Départementale (Brigade for Operation and Department Intervention, BOID) and Corps d'Intervention et de Maintien d'Ordre (Intervention and Law Enforcement Corps, CIMO), took over FE and FASCH, respectively. CIMO was modeled after U.S. Special Weapons and Tactics (SWAT) teams, and CIMO members received SWAT training and equipment. BOID was a new division of PNH, trained by MINUSTAH and the United Nations Police (HaïtiLibre 2015; United States Bureau of Citizenship and Immigration Services 1999). A few days later, on January 31, 2018, a constituency of UEH professors wrote an open letter that denounced the presence of PNH at FE and FASCH and reaffirmed UEH's autonomy. The letter read in part:

> We condemn the decision taken by the university authorities to invite specialized bodies of the national police—who, moreover, have a proven and often denounced repressive tradition—to invade the premises of the FASCH and the Faculty of Ethnology. This decision, which betrays the spirit of the 1987 Constitution and which risks fueling the authoritarian temptations of the ruling power, is not likely to contribute to the resolution of the crisis. This occupation can only create new conflicts, unnecessary tensions, and fuel acts of violence while further polarizing the protagonists of the crisis.

The fact that those arguing for and against the police occupation both used the 1987 Constitution in their arguments highlights the ambiguity surrounding the parameters of UEH's autonomy. Moreover, UEH leaders requesting interference indicated an unsettling alliance between UEH leaders and the extreme far-right regime (see Louis 2021). In February 2018, FASCH reopened but with CIMO stationed outside the campus. BOID remained stationed inside FE's gates, and the school remained closed because of the physical damage that had occurred in the wake of violence after Blot ran over the protestor. Still, the presence of BOID and CIMO at FE and FASCH signaled a (tenuous) end to the 2016–2018 UEH crisis.

AFFECTIVE UNCERTAINTY

When it comes to studies of crises and disasters, it is not enough to ask: What went wrong? As Roberto Barrios (2017, 153) cautions: "[This query] steers the observer's evaluation away from the quotidian and normative practices that engender such occurrences as economic recessions and the flooding of cities . . . and presents catastrophic outcomes as the effect of errors or accidents that are aberrations of the normal operation of things." Instead, we must ask: What conditions prepared the ground for the crisis? What was the fertile soil from which this crisis grew? I draw on observant participation at ENS and FASCH and as an instructor in the FE Masters of Anthropology program to examine the affective experiences and embodied practices of individuals at UEH in the context of the ambiguous state-nonstate status of the university and the siting of the university in a yellow zone.

Faculté des Sciences Humaines

When I began observations at FASCH in late February 2018, it had just begun normal operations but under CIMO's watch, after having been closed for several months. Although FASCH's dean, Josué Vaval, approved of my conducting research there, Dr. Charles warned me against going to FASCH because he could not guarantee my safety, and he felt that violence might erupt again at any moment. The day I arrived at FASCH for my first observation, I saw a small group of CIMO officers, dressed in green and tan army fatigues, standing outside the faculty's gates. Carrying rifles across their chests, the officers appeared ready to defend the school against any enemy who might emerge at any moment. CIMO's presence made me aware that I had indeed entered a yellow zone. According to Vaval, it took weeks of negotiations after CIMO's arrival to get professors to return to FASCH, because many had suffered trauma from the events that transpired during the recent crisis.

After passing through security and entering FASCH, I was unsettled by a scarred landscape: a four-story white and green building, fractured and falling apart; makeshift classrooms and administrative offices; graffiti painted on buildings, walls, and on the surface of a burned-out white van (figures 3.2 and 3.3). There was also a large mural dedicated to Jean Anil Louis-Juste—a sociology professor who had been gunned down blocks from the campus by two unidentified political assassins—which served as a reminder that violence between the state and the university had been long-standing (figure 3.4).[4] In 2007, Louis-Juste, other professors, and students created the Association of Dessalines University Students

Figure 3.2. A van with graffiti, February 2018. Photo by author.

(ASID) to fight for a national minimum wage increase the from 75 HTG/day (US$1.75) to 200 HTG/day (US$5.00). In 2009, a march for minimum salary increases, which included ASID members and workers, met a violent confrontation with police and MINUSTAH soldiers (Losier 2013; see also Deshommes 2010). Then Louis-Juste was murdered in 2010, several hours before the earthquake.

Additionally, the presence of CIMO proved unnerving for those who had experienced persecution under Duvalier and Aristide. Dr. Christophe specifically vowed not return to FASCH as long as CIMO remained stationed outside. He told me that Aristide's police had once dragged him out of his classroom, beaten him in front of his students, and imprisoned him for his stance against the government. "They ruptured my ear drum. No matter what I've tried, I still can't fully hear out of this ear," he explained in a vulnerable and cracking voice. In effect, FASCH was now a living monument to the history of crises at UEH, a commemoration of multiple traumatic events that shaped how individuals felt and related to one another in the space.

The 2016–2018 crisis shifted how FASCH professors related to students. Professor Jean, who had returned to Haiti from Canada in the 1990s, explained:

> The crisis affected all of us professors because we observed a shift in how students treated us. I always said that a lot occurred during the crisis to which university administrators contributed. Students protested against certain professors . . . but I don't want to go into details because I too am a product of FASCH [or, a FASCH alum]. So, I—we knew what obstacles we would encounter

Figure 3.3. A school wall with graffiti, February 2018. Photo by author.

as professors. But I think student protestors crossed a line . . . during the crisis that left a lasting impression on all the professors at FASCH. . . .

We, professors, started questioning ourselves. If we had the choice, would we do something else? Finally, we said that we're here because we like what we're doing. But there were a lot of professors who said that they would not maintain the same level of engagement with students. . . . But then, it was only a small

Figure 3.4. A mural of Jean Anil Louis-Juste, February 2018. Photo by author.

minority of students—the majority didn't do it. For me personally, I find that students respect me and show their affection toward me. I can't say students aggressed me, understand? But with what just happened here [the recent crisis], there is nothing to say that they won't.

Although students had not been aggressive toward Jean, she still felt unease because she could not be sure that students would not eventually turn on her. The unpredictability of professor-student interactions created feelings of doubt

94 FRACTURES

among professors about the very profession to which they dedicated their lives.

Faculté d'Ethnologie and École Normale Supérieure

My own uncertainty took the form of indeterminant waiting. I expected that I would begin teaching in the FE graduate program at the start of the fall 2017 semester. In October 2017, I met with Dr. Charles at the UEH Rectorate to discuss the course I intended to teach. The atmosphere was unwelcoming. Security guards insisted that I wait in the reception area and retained my passport and backpack. I waited until Dr. Charles appeared at the door leading to the administrative offices and ushered me in. When I asked him where the course would be held, he explained that given the destruction of FE, he did not yet know, but he assured me that he would find a place and planned to meet with Deshommes and others to decide a way forward. Between October 2017 and January 2018, I waited with fraught anticipation and growing doubt. In late January, I finally got the news that the program would begin in February at the ENS campus downtown. My anxiety began to ease, but I had, to an extent, experienced the affective uncertainty that held sway at that time and place.

During the months that the anthropology master's program was suspended, a few students found jobs, others moved back home to the countryside, and some left the country altogether. Ronald, a third-year master's student enrolled in my class, explained that students could not wait for the school to reopen—they had to *chèche lavi* (look for life; that is, make a living). Ronald himself had started working for an NGO as a part-time consultant and missed a few of our classes due to work obligations. Of the students enrolled in the course, a handful never attended while several arrived midway through the semester. For example, Richard arrived six sessions into what was only an eleven-session course. He explained that he lived in a dangerous area, so it was difficult to commute to the university. With the help of fellow classmates, he was able to catch up. Other students who joined partway through the seminar stopped showing up again after a class or two. This was the general pattern across UEH: frequent interruptions to students' education, which caused many to drop out.

For my students, the pursuit of a graduate degree in Haiti was an unclear journey with no predictable end. They blamed this on two factors: frequent crises at the university and the lack of programmatic consistency and support. In the case of UEH's crises, students blamed undergraduates, whom they believed held the university "hostage." (Remember, this was the same offense the jenn doktè had alleged against members of jenerasyon 86.) Ronald complained that many undergraduates would insert themselves into UEH politics instead of focusing on finishing their degrees. As for programmatic failures, students lamented that they could not fulfill the degree requirements because core courses were not always

THE "CRISIS FACTORY"

offered, they received inadequate methodological training, and they lacked supervision to complete their theses. Responding to these two latter concerns, I had students write research proposals that used methods found in activist anthropology. At the end of the semester, students asked if I would return to teach a methods course, and some requested that I become their thesis adviser. Because I was there only temporarily, I could not commit to seeing them through the program. I, as a transient researcher-instructor, was part of the problem. Despite having a few core instructors, the master's program relied on foreign or dyaspora instructors who would teach an accelerated seminar and then leave— just as I would at the end of my ethnographic fieldwork.

Still, some of my students tried to persevere despite the indeterminate nature of their graduate education. In December 2019, about a year after I had left UEH, I received an email from Dani that she was in New York visiting family and wanted to meet to discuss research for her master's thesis. Dani was a fifty-something-year-old doula, studying the traditional birthing practices and knowledges of the *fanmsaj* (midwives) with whom she worked. After a couple of failed attempts, Dani found her way to my Brooklyn apartment. She arrived at my door, wearing a large winter coat and holding the proposal she had written for my class. We sat around my small kitchen table and discussed revisions to her proposal and her intentions to continue research once the general strikes over fuel prices (*peyi lòk*) had passed. As of this writing, Dani has yet to complete her master's degree.

École Normale Supérieure, the teachers' college, was not only implicated in the UEH crisis but also experienced additional layers of turmoil with student-teacher placements, because to meet their degree requirement, ENS students had to work as student-teachers. ENS students had difficulty finding placements, and those who did found administrative barriers that impeded their graduation. According to an article in 2017 in *Le Nouvelliste*, "an administrative personnel strike, demand for student appointment letters, student expulsions, and student hunger strikes were among the key events that have severely affected the operation of the institution in recent months" (Worlgenson 2017, my translation). Although ENS had been open for a few months when I began observations there, the residual effects of overlapping crises were clear. Take, for instance, my fieldnotes on the interactions among undergraduate students and administrators.

A student comes in the secretary general's office to discuss his repriz [regrade] with Paul, the program administrator. Two male students approach David, a young professor, about a grade discrepancy. David tells the students that if they don't like their grades, they need to discuss this with the professor. Another student interjects that each student should sit with the professor, who will explain why the student received the grade they did.

Eight more students enter the administrative office looking for their repriz on an exam. News/music plays in the background. The students speak loudly about the repriz. Paul tells them to go as they aren't supposed to be congregating in the office (said half-jokingly). David tells them that there are procedures/rules for dealing with a repriz. A student with a long, knit bag hanging across his right shoulder says that this hadn't always been the case. David replies that before was a special case (situation under crisis). The student replies that the administration should let all the students know about current procedure/processes. David tells the students that they are making too much noise (said half-jokingly). The student continues, "If you want us to return to order, we'll return to order." Sensing that the students would continue to press the issue, David removes the onus from the administrators and places it on the professors, reiterating that it would be up [to] the professors to submit the re-examination. Facing a dead-end with the administrators, the students leave the office. (Fieldnotes, February 9, 2018)

While seemingly mundane exchanges between students and administrators, this excerpt reveals tensions around normal procedures, and even suggests residual trauma from the crisis. The student's comment about "return to order" hinted at students' reputation as agents of disorder, and perhaps the potential for renewed violence. Meanwhile, David's comments imitated (albeit half-jokingly) the words of police, reflecting administrators' reliance on armed guards to protect them from student violence. The crisis had left chaos and uncertainty in its wake: rules were unclear, leaving room for students to make demands on a case-by-case basis. The students put the onus on administrators to set clear standards, but the administrators were hesitant to do so. Were they afraid? The administrators were clearly unsettled by the students' clamors, yet they were also reluctant to tell them to leave. It seemed to me that Paul and David used humor to mask their discomfort, but by shifting the onus onto professors, they left the matter unresolved, which contributed to, rather than alleviated, the students' frustration and the prevailing atmosphere of uncertainty about their grades.

Thus, as with the graduate students, undergraduates also carried uncertainty about their academic futures. The majority of UEH undergraduate students, who came from Haiti's lower classes or rural backgrounds, viewed higher education as the only way out of poverty. In my interviews with students, many expressed doubts about their futures in Haiti; some said that if they had the opportunity, they would study abroad. Similarly, the *Nouvelliste* article found that ENS students were tired of crises and increasingly feared that their educational aspirations would remain unfulfilled. Citing ENS students, the article includes:

"For some time now, it's been bothering me to say that I study at École Normale Supérieure," admits a student who, outside these times of crisis, would have completed her studies in contemporary literature at ENS in one year. Kirsthie, a native of a provincial town, admits to growing tired, like many of his comrades, by the endless crisis that ravages the institution. "I feel like my dream is escaping. I had a goal to reach at a certain point in time, but the study conditions are not yet met," says the student, expressing his frustration. (Worlgenson 2017, my translation)

Faced with ongoing and pervasive precarity and anxiety, students took a variety of actions to try to create pathways forward for themselves and prohibit their dreams from escaping.

HABITUS OF IMPROVISATION

Individuals at UEH were embedded within a habitus of improvisation as a means of navigating uncertainty and demanding change. For example, during fieldwork, I witnessed everyday acts that employed improvisation to navigate uncertainty: undergraduates compensated for the lack of electricity at home by studying under streetlamps; faculty used connections from abroad to gain access to academic texts; my graduate students who handwrote their papers because they had no access to computers; and other quotidian acts of future-making. While similar to the Kreyòl term *degaje*—meaning, "to make do with what one has to keep going"—these everyday acts of improvisation were more about creatively inventing possibilities for realizing better futures. In my interviews with students, professors, and administrators, I heard numerous accounts of how differently situated groups used competing modes of improvisation to affect change: students created alliances with professors as a means to pressure the administration to improve learning conditions; university leaders formed agreements with the state to quell protests; high-level administrators leveraged government ties to secure their positions; students vandalized the university and inscribed their demands on the walls of classrooms and administrative buildings.

Dean Vaval provided this analysis of UEH's habitus of improvisation as it related to the crisis from 2016 to 2018:

> The UEH crisis can be understood in two dimensions. The first dimension is rooted in the fact that we are in a country that is in perpetual crisis . . . meaning, political crises. . . . This perpetual crisis has an impact on all institutions, including the university. . . . The second dimension is the internal crises, problems across the university itself and within each faculty. Don't forget that each faculty functions like a *kasi ka*—a separate entity. Because the University doesn't have cohesion—synergy—that allows us to pursue the same objectives, crises emerge that manifest as movements. For example, the [2016–2018] crisis was a matter of the election of Deshommes. . . . Inevitably, there will be another crisis that will take another form.

Haiti's location on the neoliberal outer periphery contributed to overlapping crises that exacerbated the fractures throughout Haitian academia and UEH specifically. In the above quotation, Vaval suggests that these fractures, mirrored in UEH's structural ambiguities and lack of unified vision, leave individuals with no choice but to align themselves with particular causes. When a new cause emerges, so do new alliances or movements. "Improvisation is a strategy for re-novating what was already there ... for showing the passage from 'there' to a re-novated 'there'" (Lussier 2009, 3; see also Peters 2009). At UEH, improvisation was enacted to renovate UEH from a "crisis factory" (from "there") to visions of what UEH ought to be (to "there"). Thus, UEH became a "contested space," a site "where conflicts in the form of opposition, confrontation, subversion, and/or resistance engaged actors whose social positions were defined by differential control of resources and access to power" (Low and Lawrence-Zúñiga 2003, 18). Interlocutors' claims that one faction or another held the UEH an otaj (hostage) encapsulated UEH as a contested space. Thus, we may read the 2016–2018 UEH crisis in light of competing modes of improvisation, in which UEH leaders, faculty, administrators, and students butted up against each other, creating a cacophony that reified UEH as a "crisis factory." A unified vision, Vaval implied, could have led to the renovation of UEH, but in the absence of such vision, affective uncertainty led to improvisation that only reinforced the uncertainty.

Improvisation may reinforce uncertainty but is also a longstanding feature of activism and successful grassroots transformation. In their 2013 book, *The Fierce Urgency of Now*, interdisciplinary scholars Daniel Fischlin, Ajay Heble, and George Lipsitz effectively connect improvisation to rights activism. They argue that "improvisation is at its heart a democratic, humane, and emancipatory practice, and that securing rights of all sorts requires people to hone their capacities to act in the world, capacities that flow from improvisation" (Fischlin et al. 2013, xi). They add that improvisation as a strategy for social change must be grounded in an "ethics of cocreation"—an understanding that "the permutations of interconnection that bind people together enable a multitude of potential practices that can give rise to new lived, embodied, material realities" (xi). As such, improvisation may be used to transform the unequal power relations that undergird crises—to the extent that improvisers coalesce their efforts around a shared and dynamic vision, achieved through "dialogical relations that respect heterophony and difference" (55). Such dialogical relations did occur, particularly outside UEH, in meeting places beyond coloniality's fractures. I turn to these meeting places or spaces of decolonial suturing in part II of this book.

PART II

Sutures

Since colonization has produced fragmentation and dismemberment at both the material and psychic levels, the work of decolonization has to make room for the deep yearning for wholeness, often expressed as a yearning to belong that is both material and existential, both psychic and physical, and which when satisfied can subvert and ultimately displace the pain of dismemberment.
—*M. Jacqui Alexander,* Pedagogies of Crossing

It is the gift, the concept, the inhabitation of and living into otherwise possibilities. Otherwise, as word—otherwise possibilities, as phrase—announces the fact of infinite alternatives to what is.
—*Ashon Crawley,* Blackpentecostal Breath: The Aesthetics of Possibility

CHAPTER 4

Rasanblaj

ASSEMBLY BEYOND COLONIALITY'S FRACTURES

Rasanblaj (n.)
Resist the impulse to translate; pronounce it first. Think consciously of the sound. Let the arch of the r *roll over the* ah *that automatically depresses the tongue; allow the hiss in the* s *that will culminate at the front of the teeth to entice the jaw to drop for the* an *sound while unsmacking the lips will propel the* bl *surrounding the depressed* ah *again ending with* j. *Play with its contours. Know what this word feels like in your mouth.*

In Haitian Kreyòl 3 syllables. Ra-San-Blaj.

Defined as assembly, compilation, enlisting, regrouping (of ideas, things, people, spirits. For example, fè yon rasanblaj: do a gathering, a ceremony, a protest), rasanblaj's very linguistic formation subverted and resisted colonial oppression.
—Gina Athena Ulysse, Why Rasanblaj, Why Now?

Throughout Caribbean history, people have gathered in the spirit of rasanblaj—"defined as assembly, compilation, enlisting, regrouping (of ideas, things, people, spirits) (Ulysse 2017, 58)—to bring desired futures into the present. Take the case of Haiti. It was a Vodou ceremony that propelled emancipation, collective protests that helped end the U.S. Occupation and dictatorships, and "long traditions, practices of cultural conscientization and sensibilities toward self-making and determination" that allowed Haitian people to "continue to make life, to ingeniously survive and in fewer instances thrive, to 'create dangerously'" (Ulysse 2017, 71). Given the transformative potential of rasanblaj in Haiti, those in power instituted laws to prohibit its occurrence. The 1685 French Code Noir "forbade slaves of different masters to gather at any time under any circumstances" (Ulysse 2017, 69). From 1939 to 1942, the Catholic Church, with the support of presidents Sténio Vincent and Élie Lescot, led an "anti-superstition" campaign—a crusade

101

that prohibited Vodou ceremonies and popular ritual practices and included "raids, arrests, the destruction of temples, and the widespread confiscation and burning of drums and other sacred objects across the country" (Ramsey 2011, 108). And let us not forget how, in 1960, François Duvalier issued a decree that forbade the assembly of intellectuals and student organizations (chapter 1). As a decolonial praxis, rasanblaj still threatens to unsettle, dismantle, and reassemble extant colonial arrangements toward the creation of worlds otherwise (see Ulysse 2015b).

In 2015, Haitian American feminist interdisciplinary artist, professor, and theorist Gina Athena Ulysse introduced the concept of rasanblaj in her role as invited guest editor of *e-misférica*—a publication that Ulysse (2015b, 3) praises as having "been on the cutting edge as a multimedia platform/space that has consistently and boldly explored the complex intersections of performance and politics in the hemisphere." As guest editor, Ulysse curated *Caribbean Rasanblaj*, a multidisciplinary and multimodal volume that assembled visual arts, performance, conversations, and scholarly works that engage rasanblaj "as a way to express and think through the Caribbean" (Ulysse 2015b, 3). Drawing on the insights of this work, Ulysse's 2017 keynote address at the twenty-ninth annual Haitian Studies Association (HSA) meeting discussed the pressing need for a Haitian rasanblaj. As the afterlives of colonialism and slavery choked off lives through racist violence and toxicity, as sea levels continued to rise, threatening the margins first, as those on the margins witnessed aggressive waves of displacement, rasanblaj took on an urgency that required moving beyond disciplinary boundaries and academe. Taking the Caribbean "as the ultimate site of decoloniality" (Ulysse 2015b, 3), Ulysse urged those gathered at the HSA conference to embrace both performance and politics in projects of rasanblaj:

> [Rasanblaj] calls upon us to think through Caribbean performance and politics. . . . [W]ith unequivocal evidence that the past and the future exist in the present, rasanblaj not only presupposes intent (an awareness of self/position/agenda) and method but also offers possibilities for other modalities and narratives. Thus, it allows us to contemplate the performative—in subjectivity, agency, communities, and citizenship—that constitutes Caribbean futures imagined as possible realities. An explicitly decolonial project, rasanblaj demands that we consider and confront the limited scope of segregated frameworks to explore what remains excluded in this landscape that is scorched yet full of life, riddled with inequities and dangerous and haunting memories. (Ulysse 2017, 70)

Since Ulysse introduced the concept of rasanblaj, it has flourished, fueling various projects of decoloniality.

More specifically, rasanblaj is inspiring a burgeoning body of decolonial scholarly and creative works, primarily among Caribbean, Black, feminist, and/or queer scholars, creators, and activists (e.g., Beasley 2017; Decena 2023; Douglas 2022; Felima 2022; Gill and Ulysse 2023; Jean-Charles 2022; Sargsyan 2021; Smalls 2021; Wagner and Legros 2022). For instance, queer Dominican scholar Carlos Ulises Decena's provocative book, *Circuits of the Sacred*, "fè yon rasanblaj" by performing "a gathering of every thing for black Caribbean study, arguing that black queer paths to the divine swerve from the transparent 'I' of the academic and drift toward the intuitive, the sensorial, and the disreputable" (Decena 2023, 5). Decena employs creative writing, ethnography, memoir, and theoretical analysis to model what he terms "faggotology"—the erotic in the divine found in excesses of "sensation, pain, struggle, joy, and pleasure" (4)—which shapes "Black Latinx Caribbean immigrant queer life and spirit" (n.p.). Through this work, Decena radically affirms queer Black life and futures. Conversely, in her 2022 book *Looking for Other Worlds*, Black feminist literary scholar of Haitian descent Régine Jean-Charles brings together the works of Haitian feminists, Caribbean feminists, and Black feminists in a "Spirit of reassembly" (5), analyzing how the works of these feminist thinkers and creators suggest "alternative possibilities that . . . imagine the world otherwise" (8). I read Black and Caribbean futurity at the core of these and other engagements with rasanblaj. Thus, my insistence on engaging with rasanblaj is what I see as the concept's prefiguration of "otherwise possibilities." In the words of scholar-artist Ashon Crawley (2016, 2): "It is the gift, the concept, the inhabitation of and living into otherwise possibilities. Otherwise, as word—otherwise possibilities, as phrase—announces the fact of infinite alternatives to what is."

I posit that as with "creolization" and "bricolage," rasanblaj describes practices of Caribbean worldmaking. Creolization, a term borrowed from linguistics, defines the historical process whereby the forced contact between African, Indigenous, and European peoples resulted in new (read: modern) sociocultural formations (Glissant 1989; Hall 2015). Sidney Mintz and Sally Price (1985, 6) have posited creolization as "a particularly apt illustration" of how we may see the Caribbean region as a unit despite "the tremendous diversity of experiences represented by its various political, social, and cultural entities." Concurrently, bricolage describes combining available resources in improvised creation (Altglas 2014; Bastide 1970). "The etymological foundation of bricolage comes from a traditional French expression which denotes crafts-people who creatively use materials left over from other projects to construct new artifacts. To fashion their bricolage projects, bricoleurs use only the tools and materials 'at-hand' (Lévi-Strauss 1966)" (Rogers 2012, 5). Various scholars of the Caribbean have used bricolage—much like creolization—to analyze Caribbean creativity. For instance, "Raphaël Confiant sees creolization itself as dependent on the intermixture of fragments through bricolage . . ." (Knepper 2006, 70). For its part, rasanblaj creatively prefigures multiple belongings beyond coloniality's material and immaterial fissures.

Although creolization, bricolage, and rasanblaj may thus appear as slipping signifiers describing how Caribbean peoples create worlds out of physical and psychic fragments (meaning "remains," not "breaks"), I suggest important temporal distinctions between the three terms. Whereas creolization signifies "the past" as in a historical process of sociocultural formation under colonization and enslavement and bricolage connotes "the present" as in the creation of artifacts with materials "at hand," rasanblaj designates "the future" as in assemblages that anticipate potential realities. I see rasanblaj as the prefiguration of decolonial Black and Caribbean futures through everyday gatherings that resist coloniality's physical and psychic fractures—fissures that are at once generational (ways of relating in/to time and location), social (ways of relating to others), epistemological (ways of knowing), and ontological-spiritual (ways of being in and with spirit). Moreover, as a Kreyòl term, rasanblaj is as unapologetically Haitian as it is Caribbean: it brings Haiti to the center of imagined Caribbean futures and the Caribbean to the center of imagined planetary futures.

In this chapter, I contemplate how the Haitian scholars I worked with created places of gathering beyond coloniality's fractures. I show how these places of gathering performed assembly beyond generational, social, epistemological, and ontological-spiritual divides to instantiate multiple belongings in the present and, thus, forward a decolonial praxis that prefigures the possibility of "re-memberment" (see Ulysse 2015b). Similar to Decena (2023, 5), I seek here to perform "a gathering of every thing." Operating in the vein of Black and intersectional feminisms wherein poetics and politics convene (see Jean-Charles 2022), I specifically gather drama, poetry, and ethnographic prose to discuss instances of rasanblaj as they occurred at four spaces of gathering: a weekly *salon* (Soup nan Kay Sonson), a poetry night (Vandredi literè), a televised debate (Café Philo), and a bookstore (Librairie La Pléiade). If hope is a futural orientation that "bridges the gap between potentiality and actuality" (Bryant and Knight 2019, 136), then rasanblaj is a glimpse of the actual realized. It is proof that "other worlds" beyond coloniality are possible because "some of these 'other worlds' [have already been] alive" (M. Jacqui Alexander with Ulysse 2015, n.p.).

Soup nan Kay Sonson

Soup nan Kay Sonson is an example of "ethnographic drama" in that it places an ethnographic moment on an imagined stage. Ethnographic drama offers a "powerful way for ethnography to recover yet interrogate the meanings of lived experience. Constructed as dramatised [*sic*] field notes, audio-recordings, video-recordings, digital messages, and interviews, ethnographic drama employs theatre techniques to present live performance of research participants' experiences and researchers' interpretations. Ethnographic drama has the potential to refocus the gaze of the ethnographer, and open the audience to new ways of seeing research participants when they are presented as characters on stage" (Blackledge and Creese 2022, 590–591; see also Denzin 1997). Through *Soup nan Kay Sonson*, I want to convey fieldwork's dialogical and alive nature in a decolonial centering of interlocutors' voices, theorizations, and presences (see Harrison 1991; Madison 1999). Thus, I resist retheorizing interlocutors' theories; instead, I invite the reader to imaginatively sit with those gathered at the weekly salon and engage with these thinkers as thinkers.

TITLE *SOUP NAN KAY SONSON*

Setting A weekly salon at kay Rodolphe Mathurin (Sonson*)*, a small, bright yellow gingerbread house *anba zanman an* [under a walnut tree]. The house is in a neighborhood in metropolitan Port-au-Prince, Haiti. An intergenerational group of men and two women sit outside around a long rectangular table. People are smoking and sipping cups of coffee. A canister of coffee and a pot of *soup joumou*, or "Haitian freedom soup," sit at the center of the table. There are empty-or-near-empty bowls on the table. Sonson is not present.

CHARACTERS DARLÈNE/NARRATOR: A thirty-two-year-old Haitian dyaspora member born and raised in the United States.

MEHDI: A man in his late twenties who was raised in Haiti but attended university in France.

PAUL: A thirty-something-year-old man raised and educated in Haiti.

SAMUEL: A twenty-something-year-old man raised and educated in Haiti.

JEAN: A sixty-something-year-old man who returned to Haiti from New York in 1986.

RALPH: A man in his late thirties to early forties, raised and educated in Haiti.

RAOUL: A sixty-something-year-old man who lived abroad for twenty years.

ALEX: A thirty-something-year-old man.

CLAUDE: A sixty-something-year-old man.

FRITZ: A sixty-something-year-old, balding man.

MARIE: A twenty-something-year-old woman with short-cropped hair.

Translation// *The conversation occurs in mixed Kreyòl and French and is here translated into English with some words and phrases left untranslated.*

DARK STAGE.
(*Unseen female narrator.*)

NARRATOR: I pull myself up into Mehdi's dark green truck. "Kijan w yè?" I ask as I tug the seatbelt across my chest with my right hand and feel for the buckle. "Mwen tris," Mehdi replies with heaviness in his voice. His response catches me off guard. He explains that Manno Charlemagne, a Haitian folk singer, artist, and political activist, passed away that morning. I offer my condolences and notice Manno playing on the radio.

"AYITI PA FORÈ" [Haiti Isn't a Forest] PLAYS OVER HOUSE SPEAKERS.

Ou voye papa w al achte twa bonm
Pou vin bonbade lajenès an ayiti
Ki deklare ke dechoukay la poko fini
Konsèy gouvenman
Gen Régala ladann
Dechoukay la poko fini
Konsèy gouvenman
Gen twòp vòlè landann[1]
MUSIC FADES.

NARRATOR: Manno's plaintive and sonorous voice accompanies us on our short drive to *Anba Zanmann Kay Sonson Mathurin,* a weekly salon.

HOUSE LIGHTS COME ON, REVEALING THE STAGE.
(*Medias res.*)

PAUL: There is inevitable misery and isolation with being an intellectual. The more knowledge one has, the more distress one experiences.
SAMUEL: Read Kafka, man!
PAUL: (*Continues to recount his story but softens the language because Darlène is there.*) A friend introduced me to this woman whom I slept with. I found out later that the woman "belonged" to another man and feared that her man would retaliate. I looked over my shoulders whenever I would go out, eventually staying inside for weeks. I cried a lot as I was genuinely fearful for my life. At the height of this misery, I asked myself: "Why doesn't God exist so that I could pray to him?" (*Laughs*). Even at the height of my misery, I couldn't concede God's existence. I do not doubt that there's no God. And even in a moment of terror, I couldn't pray!
JEAN: Why do you say this is the predicament of an *intellectual* and not simply a person or atheist?
PAUL: Unlike most Haitians, I don't believe in God. I am not a mystic. It is a burden when you live in a society and understand how things work in that society. You can't even have a romantic relationship.
MEHDI: I disagree—there is a lot of vocabulary for this. "Go read Kafka?!" Don't you have more avenues for comfort and consolation that aren't the church? The person in misery and suffering can find other outlets.
PAUL: You don't have peace of mind as an intellectual, a nihilist. I am living in solitude in the middle of a crowd. If someone saw my illness, my anxiety from afar (*trails off*).

RALPH: (*Arrives and shakes everyone's hand.*)

MEHDI: (*Goes to look for another cup for Darlène and returns with a plastic cup.*)

DARLÈNE. (*Pours coffee into the cup.*)

PAUL: The first philosophy book that I read, I had to borrow from Institut Français. They [people in society] think I'm crazy.

MEHDI: Yeah, man. They say, "Be careful. Books will make you crazy."

JEAN: Yes-yes, they do say this.

PAUL: I can't be comfortable in a group of my peers. While *they* save money to go out and impress women, *I* spend my extra money on books.

RALPH: There is also family pressure to be an intellectual. For instance, Gustave Flaubert came from a family of lawyers, and Proust from a family of doctors. There was a sensibility toward intellectualism on my father's side. He used to have gatherings at the house and would sit with his legs crossed, drink his "drug," and speak French. He'd sit with his hand on his face like his thoughts were a beast. (*Acts this out.*) We've all experienced this putting on of airs—all of us in the popular classes.

MEHDI: (*Addresses Darlène.*) Sonson created this space where we meet on Sundays. There are people of older and younger generations who come together in a spirit of sharing, solidarity, and intellectual debate. We discuss the social sciences, art, politics, literature, culture, etc. There are only a few women. They sometimes come with boyfriends but leave once their boyfriends leave.

(*All laugh, except for Darlène, who feigns amusement.*)

MEHDI: This is Darlène. She's researching intellectuals, notably returned dyaspora.

(*People nod, their interests peaked.*)

RAOUL: I lived outside the country. I spent 20 years outside. My eyes weren't the same when I returned. The country was different. *I'm going to have difficulty living here in Haiti,* I thought. When you leave—you aren't a part of the country. You're a stranger. You're not connected. But I stayed connected and interested in political developments in the country.

MEHDI: Some people want to leave but can't. There is the question of going abroad to study and then returning. There is also the question of the prestige of migration, of living abroad. But people don't speak about this. From 1986 to 1996, some people came back. They returned with distinction. They went into exile, but they didn't leave Haiti. Others needed to follow the development of the country. These people became established abroad and didn't think of returning. Others came back after retirement but didn't come back to establish themselves here or to *create*—people who come from the United States without any knowledge but can get positions. There are many trajectories of return. But people are intimated by the dyaspora.

RALPH: I think of Appadurai's *After Colonialism*, which provides an understanding of displacement. I am thinking of globalization, of technology, *eh, eh, (searching for the word)* the technoscape. Physical displacement doesn't mean anything with technology. Then there is transnationalism—the images and objects that circulate. The way I see it, every Haitian who leaves believes he'll return.

RAOUL: *(Turning to Ralph.)* I have to disagree with you about the dynamic of leaving. I did K-12 in Haiti. I went to university here and left after my first semester. My classmates were excellent students. These are the people who left, and 90% of them stayed abroad.

RALPH: I find it interesting that when someone leaves and comes to visit, people say, "*Li retounen*" ["s/he returned"]—even if it's just for a short visit.

MEHDI: What was their profession when they returned? Engineering, finance, etc., you'll be okay. But what about the critical thinkers, the writers, and the poets? How are they going to make a living here?

ALEX: A bunch of people don't think of coming back. They act as if they are in Haiti when abroad . . .

MARIE: *(Sits back in her chair, smoking. Silently listens.)*

PAUL: No one goes to the provinces and thinks they are in a foreign country—not anymore. The idea of "*andeyo*" is passé. They [those andeyò] have technology too.

(Overlapping, indistinct conversation.)

PAUL: I don't understand the concept of "brain drain." Does the country even produce intellects? They think the returnee is an "intellect," but he's not an "intellect." They give these returnees preference over those of us who are already here.

MEHDI: It's not black and white, *man*.

PAUL: They search for papers/degrees to be well-positioned in Haiti. How will these "intellects" who come back behave? And what is the social perception of the people who came back?

DARLÈNE: Is there tension between those who return and those who stay?

MEHDI: Well, we need to look at empirical cases. For example, people talk highly about the professors here who have studied abroad.

PAUL: There's a particular perception the society has of returnees.

MEHDI: This [those gathered at Kay Sonson] *is* the society.

RAOUL: It is about valorization. There is a practical aspect, too: The way knowledge is transmitted here versus abroad. Our educational system, the space of knowledge transmission, has degenerated over the past decades.

We are at the bottom when it comes to how knowledge is transmitted. We are far from international standards. *Mòd de transmisyon enferyè* [the mode of knowledge transfer is inferior], as with developing countries with less infrastructure.

RALPH: The standards of knowledge transmission are Northern.

RAOUL: The mode of transmission influences the knowledge transmitted.

MEHDI: Yes, publication, "The Cannon," English as a language of instruction.

RALPH: Why don't *we* give a Nobel prize? As a society, we are seen as the "Orient," getting our educational standards from the "Occident"!

RAOUL: You must go to school to be a great writer (*said sarcastically*).

MEHDI: Publication as criteria of evaluation. Isn't there another way we could look at it? *Mòd de transmisyon* is good criteria.

RALPH: Look at the C.V.s! They say they did seminars in the North, not the South—Harvard, la Sorbonne. They are all bluffers. The professor who studies abroad constantly refers to his schooling abroad. Students laugh at this. These professors need a firm basis! When a parent sends their child to study overseas, they know they will be someone when they return. They are *idiots*, but they get their doctorates. It's sad. Take [the Vice-Rector of the State University]; he can't even organize his thoughts, let alone organize a syllabus so that students learn. Who has the better *bèt* [beast]?

JEAN: The way I see it, there isn't one Haitian dyaspora. There are divisions along the lines of place (U.S., Dominican Republic) and social class. There isn't one dyaspora. I was abroad for eighteen years and worked with Haitian immigrants in Miami.

Leaving is like an elevation of social class, even for the lower classes, because the places they go are more advanced than where they came from. They had another life experience. So, for them, they've had a better experience. The general attitude of the dyaspora is that they think they know more than people in Haiti.

I am a former dyaspora and had to relearn Haiti.

You can't put it in your head that you know more than those in Haiti or are more developed than those here. Their attitude is irritating! "Why aren't they doing this? Why are they doing that?"—I am speaking in a general manner. They value themselves; others love them. Going abroad gives them authority, which poses a problem. Someone who studies abroad—because of where and the type of education they received—thinks we should respect them. But they're missing something that people have *here*. Take law. People who study abroad think they know more than those who studied in the School of Law here, but they don't remember the Haitian context. They need to have a humbler attitude.

MEHDI: It's about *reclassement*. But the country has a way of conforming you. It will reshape you. There is a point where they [the dyaspora] will hit a wall, where others will put them in their place. But I'm an optimist. The arrogance of those who return makes them into a caricature.

FRITZ: Students think that so-and-so who teaches at *Syan Imen* is a caricature. The dyaspora cannot reintegrate.

(*Begins rambling on nostalgically about how Haitian education used to be.*) Haitian schools were a reference in the Caribbean.

RAOUL: The schools have degenerated.

ALEX: When I left and went to Peru (not the North), people saw me as someone with more knowledge. As Foucault said, we are measuring ourselves against European standards.

RALPH: A professor once asked me if I had studied in France, which bothered me because you must have a lot of determination to pass school here. I remember that when I was growing up, I used to see parents bringing their children to school. There was a lot of parental pressure to learn. I went to school if I wanted; if not, I didn't. From 9 to 10, I went to school at École Frère André. When you grow up in the popular class, you consider École Frère André a prestigious school. I even spoke French to valorize myself.

As a new professor at UEH, I wanted to do a good job. I would go to bed late, etc., but the administration didn't care. We [those who received their education in Haiti] are heroes. It takes *a lot* of determination to finish school here. You persevere through hard work. We are the *reskape* [survivors]. The state could make the State University a good school if it wanted.

JEAN: I returned when Duvalier fell. I left my children in New York because it was the middle of the school year. When I brought them here for school, I asked Pompilus [a mathematician who returned in the mid-70s after François Duvalier's death] to help me find a place to put my kids. We went to the school where Yvette teaches. And my son (9 or 10 years old at the time) said to me as we walked out of the school, "Dad, are you sure this is a school?" It looked like a little house. (*Laughs.*) He had gone to PS 180 and had specific standards.

CLAUDE: There's a psychological aspect as well. These were great schools, e.g., Lyceè Pétion. What happened? Long ago, schoolteachers were respected.

RALPH: Even if it *is* something colonial, you're learning; I did have the chance to go to a good school.

(*Indistinct, overlapping conversation. Someone brings up Manno Charlemagne.*)

JEAN: Let's toast to Manno Charlemagne.

(*Everyone raises their cups in a solemn toast.*) (*Silence.*)

RALPH: (*Trying to add some levity to the moment.*) It's a great thing that France isn't a world power anymore. We must look at other models, like those in Latin America, Africa, etc. There are two theories: theories that can develop Haiti and those that can't.

LIGHTS FADE OFF. END SCENE.

Soup nan Kay Sonson describes an instance of assembly across generational differences grounded in "intellectual friendship"—a relationship based on mutual respect and rigorous dialogue to work through shared problem-spaces (Scott 2017). In chapter 2, I discussed generation as both social location and temporality. I also highlighted a desire for intellectual friendship among members of jenerasyon 86 and the jenn doktè—a longing largely unmet within the neoliberal university system. Kay Sonson was where these two generations, and those in between, could meet and form intellectual bonds. Rodolphe Mathurin (Sonson)—educator, writer, poet, and radical activist—created the weekly salon, *Anba Zanmann Kay Sonson Mathurin* (Under the Walnut Tree at Sonson Mathurin's House), in 2012 as "un espace de rencontres et de discussions où la parole devient lieu de libération de soi et partage d'expériences dans le respect de l'autre" (a space for meetings and discussions where speech becomes a place of self-liberation and experiences are shared with respect for others) (Petit Frère 2021, n.p). Intellectual friendship, therefore, was a core principle meant to cement all gatherings.

The layered and meandering conversation that animates *Soup nan Kay Sonson* captures how people of different generations understand societal fractures amid capitalist globalization and neocolonialism. The discussion begins with a somewhat sexist story about romantic relationships and the isolation of the intellectual. The story's tone reflects Kay Sonson as a male dominated space, although women were welcome to attend. After Mehdi introduces me and my research, the conversation turns to questions of migration and the global marginalization of Haiti. Drawing on their experiences, interlocutors discuss how migration and return elevate one's standing in Haitian society. There is also a critique of the returned dyaspora who evaluate Haiti through Northern criteria and refuse to accept Haiti on its terms. Yet, Mehdi contends that Haitian society has a way of "conforming" and "reshaping" returnees. This sentiment echoes Mehdi's earlier assertion that reintegration for returned dyaspora is challenging but not impossible (chapter 2). Orienting the stream-of-consciousness discussion is a shared concern with Haiti's future. The older generation reminisces about the "good old days" while critiquing the degradation of Haitian education; the younger generation—sharing the older generation's concerns—see possibilities for change. Mehdi, for instance, describes himself as an "optimist." And Ralph believes that the Haitian state could still reform UEH into "good schools" and considers the decline of France's global dominance as an opening for Haiti to forge a new path forward. Overall, we get the sense that those gathered, although differently positioned along social location and temporality, are thinking through the shared problem-space of coloniality.

Vandredi Literè

Below is a "fieldpoem" (Zani 2019) that describes a scene from Vandredi literè (literary Fridays)—a weekly poetry night at a cultural center in Saint-Antoine. Anthropologists have long engaged poetry by studying "ethnopoetics" (e.g., Abu-Lughod 1986/2016; Rothenberg 1985), defined as the "aesthetic principles of indigenous oral poetry (and how these might differ from those of Western literary traditions), as well as the translation of oral poetics" (Maynard and Cahnmann-Taylor 2010, 4–5). Elsewhere, I have written about this scene from Vandredi literè within the vein of ethnopoetics, discussing how the spoken word performance was a "practice of tire kont (literally, 'to turn out a story' or call-and-response storytelling found throughout Africa and the diaspora)," which is grounded in Creole oral traditions of the Caribbean and Latin America (Dubuisson 2022a, 222). Unlike ethnopoetics, fieldpoetry is less a study of subaltern or non-Western poetry than "how poetry may help anthropologists write more insightfully about how we and other people live" (Maynard and Cahnmann-Taylor 2010, 4). In a recent meditation on fieldpoems, anthropologist and award-winning poet Leah Zani (2023, 83) writes: "Poetry and ethnography are twin forms of attention. Fieldpoems are fieldnotes written as poems, or poems written out of fieldwork material. . . . Fieldpoetry encourages researchers to work through their material with a poet's sensibility for experience and writing, including a greater awareness of the senses, syntax and line, word choice, mouthfeel, and sonics. Sensing and re-sensing the world, fieldpoetry is both a research method and a genre of writing." In the following, I draw on my former training in literature and early identity as a poet to say something that prose cannot, echoing Marvin Bell (1997, 45) that sometimes poetry "can say in words more than words can say." The poem attempts to capture a moment in time just as I experienced it, in colors and sounds, movements and whispers, arrivals and settlings, rhythms and repetitions. While I render the poem in English, I leave Kreyòl words and phrases untranslated to invite inhabitation in sound rather than in meaning.

> Nou Tout La, Ansanm
> We gather in the pavilion with burnt-orange, tiled floors
>   and thatched tin roof
> Together, we'll enter dreams and metaphors
> Ancient drums and ancestral rhythms
>
> Lyonel is home *here*
> Happy *here*
> Swaying and singing along to French bossa nova

He gets up abruptly
Motions for a youngster to battle him in *baton*
The young man picks up a stick from somewhere unseen

And   they   play

BAT
            BAT
BAT
            BAT

Lyonel's dexterity captures me
As he glides across the burnt-orange floor
Floating and light with a menthol sitting between a wide smile

The game ends as abruptly as it began
Now Dambala plays on repeat
Holding us in the embrace of Simone's transcendent voice

> *You slavers will know*
> *What it's like to be a slave*
> *Slave to your heart*
> *Slave to your soul*
> *Oh, Dambala come Dambala*
> *Oh, Dambala come Dambala . . .*

Sam leans over and says something in a practiced French
I reply in American-accented Kreyòl

Lyonel saunters over, "*Kilè wap fin ekri?*"
"*Jamè*," I say, scribbling into my turquoise notebook
I *must* capture this scene, this feeling of belonging *exactly*

As Dambala becomes *racine*
I sip my kola and wait for the night to begin
People start arriving . . . one by one

A tall, slender man wearing a fedora—the type that folk guitarists wear
Strums into the mic
Signaling us to start

We begin

Haitian folk music plays on two guitars
As raindrops hit the roof in rhythm to the strings
A drummer—with the flag of our nation wrapped around his head—joins in
Some sway, others sing

Nou tout la, ansanm
All immersed in versions of Haiti's glorious past

"Al danse lwa!"
Lyonel shouts, inviting a performance for the spirits

Travayyyyyy nap travayyyyy, oh . . .

Some sway, others sing
Nou tout la, ansanm

CAPTURED

The music fades and bodies become still
As the featured poet meets a raised platform
This Black young man in polka-dot white peasant shirt

Who had lived *andeyò*
Then on the streets of Pòtoprens

Now sits elevated and reads from his newly published book of poetic
    konts–*TiGri*
The spoken words pay homage to Haitian folktales with hidden morals
He is the *TiGri* of the *konts*

His life a moral tale of running
Running from beatings, bullies, and bullets.

He reads in a staccato-ed *Kreyòl.*
That matches the quick flow of the poems
With the refrain, *TiGri kouri*

    Li Kouri
Li Kouri
    Li Kouri
Li Kouri

Created by Lyonel Trouillot in 1994 around the reinstallation of Aristide to the Haitian presidency, Vandredi literè attracted artists from diverse socioeconomic backgrounds. Lyonel founded Vandredi literè to counter deep social class divisions. As Lyonel explained in our conversation in 2013, "People of all social origins come here to read their texts. This thing, which has been going on for 19 years, started in 1994 and works [long pause]. It does work. So, in the literary world in Haiti, there are fewer social frictions. Now, we have poets of very modest origins, and people recognize them as good writers. And they are good writers." The above scene from Vandredi literè was an instance of social assembly where individuals from different socioeconomic backgrounds created multiple belongings in the spirit of poetry—a shared medium of expression where those from popular or lower-class backgrounds could take centerstage as thinkers and creators.

Vandredi literè's focus on poetry was intentional. Lyonel once explained that since the late nineteenth century, poetry "has taken upon itself the task of saying 'we' to counteract [the] disunity, which, he believes, contributes to the nation's instability and to eventual political catastrophe" (Aquilanti 2011, n.p.; see also Kadish and Jenson 2015). Indeed, Haiti's independence "gave birth to poems celebrating Haiti's newly gained freedom and its founding principles of equality, justice, courage, and national pride. . . . The first republic of [formerly enslaved people] . . . viewed poetry as a powerfully persuasive influence [and] envisioned it in a positive light as the foundation of all culture, to be embraced in the founding identities and practices" (Kadish and Jenson 2015, xxi). Yet, these early postindependence poems were often written in French, the colonial language. The post-Duvalier era would, however, witness burgeoning Haitian Kreyòl poetry, which has been particularly unifying in its valorization of Creole oral traditions and the language of the Haitian majority (see Chalmers, Kenol, Lhérisson, and Trouillot 2015). As the late Haitian intellectual exile and poet-activist Paul Laraque (2001, xiii) writes, Kreyòl "is a beautiful language with the rhythm of a drum and the images of a dream, especially in its poetry, and a powerful weapon in the struggle of our people for national and social liberation."

In addition to Vandredi literè, Lyonel led *atelye jeudi soir* (Thursday night workshops), a writing seminar for seasoned, new, and aspiring authors. During the closed workshops, I encountered an intimate and diverse group of men and women—Haitians and expatriates, returnees and those who stayed, and members of the middle and popular classes—who worked through their texts together. Atelye jeudi soir thus directly contributed to the publication of fiction, nonfiction, and poetry, including Mehdi Chalmers's 2019 book of poems, *Mer libre et autres lieux imaginaires* (Open Seas and Other Imaginary Places). The atelye, much like Vandredi literè, anticipated a future of belonging through literary and poetic cocreation. Yet, despite the success of these initiatives in bridging socioeconomic differences, Lyonel confessed that they were "far from being sufficient" because the Haitian state had not taken up similar projects of inter-class solidarity and historically fueled color and class conflicts to its benefit (see also Michel-Rolph Trouillot 1990a). Lyonel added that at least the economically poor young poets who attended Vandredi literè (and I would add, atelye jeudi soir) "belonged to something larger than them—than the small and poor houses in which they lived."

Café Philo Haïti

The Café Philosophique (Café Philo) or Café Scientifique movement started in Paris on December 13, 1992, when French philosopher Marc Sautet gathered friends at Café des Phares to debate philosophical issues. Sautet would open these weekly debates to the public. The discussions gained popularity and drew over a hundred people, including university students, off-duty cab drivers, and many others (Courouve 1998, Diament 2003; Tozzi 2002). "British science journalist Duncan Dallas took this notion further to create the Science Cafés in 1998 in the U.K., followed by other initiatives in cities in the rest of Europe, Australia, the USA, South America, Southeast Asia," and Sub-Saharan Africa (Mutheu and Wanjala 2009, 245). The Café Philo and Science movement placed scholars in "a coffee shop, restaurant or bar, aiming to encourage them to communicate their work and enable the public to question their approaches, findings and discipline" (Mutheu and Wanjala 2009, 245). Philosophy and science cafés thus instantiated the collapse of the public and university divide.

In 2011, French philosopher and professor Héléna Hugot introduced the Café Philo movement to a group of her students at UEH École Normale Supérieure (ENS). Together, they laid the foundations of l'Association Café Philo Haïti. In 2012, Ralph Jean-Baptiste, a Haitian philosopher and public intellectual, helped lead the transformation of the association into a local institution, stating that "un café philo en Haïti ne peut être qu'haïtien" (a Café Philo in Haiti can only be Haitian) (*Le Nouvelliste* 2014, para 1). Under Ralph's leadership, Café Philo Haïti developed into a weekly filmed debate, where scholars and activists with different, and sometimes opposing, perspectives met at a local bar to discuss issues ranging from art and aesthetics, morality and religion, gender and sexuality, citizenship, and political crises. Ralph described Café Philo Haïti as "un espace qui pose les problèmes de l'Haïtien mais aussi de l'Homme car . . . 'être haïtien c'est s'inscrire dans l'universalisme de la philosophie, c'est se reconnaître du lieu de l'humanisme'" (a space that poses the problems of Haitians but also of humans because . . . 'to be Haitian is to be part of the universalism of philosophy, it is to recognize oneself from the place of humanism') (*Le Nouvelliste* 2014, para. 1). From this perspective, Café Philo Haïti can be seen as a site of epistemological assembly—a compilation of different views, beliefs, and ways of knowing that anticipate the possibility of moving beyond epistemological divides and disciplinary boundaries to claim what Marlene Daut (2016) termed Haitian Atlantic humanism, which may be summarized as an approach to humanism that centers Haiti as a site from which to theorize and work through the problems of coloniality, but in relation with other places. By recognizing Haiti as a site of philosophical production, Café Philo Haïti also worked "against commonly believed myths such as 'blacks don't do theory'"—to borrow an apt phrase from Faye Harrison (2008, 40).

On an evening in April 2018, I conversed with Ralph at his home, a two-room apartment filled with neatly stacked books and framed photographs of local intellectuals and artists hanging on yellow-tinted walls. I met Ralph in December of the previous year at Kay Sonson. That night, we sat on a small sofa as his friends busily prepared for a party they were throwing for Ralph's younger brother, an up-and-coming videographer. As Ralph and I conversed, the rhythmic sounds of someone grinding *epis* (spices) with a mortar and pestle and the alluring scent of the epis and *fritay* (fried food) floated into the room.

Ralph was raised under humble circumstances by parents who valued education despite not having completed fundamental schooling. He told me that in Haiti, "education is the only recourse low-income families have. . . . Many Haitians, therefore, fight to obtain an education." Ralph received his entire schooling in Haiti and earned degrees in philosophy and law from UEH. Before the 2010 earthquake, he taught at private universities and for a semester at ENS. Ralph explained that the students at ENS challenged his credentials because he had earned his degrees in Haiti instead of abroad. The dean at the time let Ralph go after one semester because the dean was facing reappointment and wanted to avoid trouble with the students. Ralph never got paid for that semester of teaching and ceased teaching altogether. Ralph now worked in the state's intellectual property division as a public relations specialist—a job he believed allowed him to make a broader impact.

During our conversation, Ralph identified three salient problems within the Haitian intellectual sphere. The first issue was that media (namely, radio, television, and, increasingly, social media) had contributed to a "perversion" of Haitian intellectualism. According to Ralph, many Haitian public intellectuals were more interested in gossip or verbosity than "profound reflection." Invoking Italian novelist and social critic Umberto Eco, Ralph continued: "In the past, the idiot used to philosophize after he got drunk at a bar. Nowadays, the idiot dominates the public space, creating 'alternative facts' and commenting on important social issues!" In short, with increased access to public media outlets, anyone with an opinion could assert claims to knowledge, whether or not that knowledge was verified.

Ralph also identified a need for better-resourced Haitian academic presses and distributors. While some Haitian academic presses, such as Éditions Cahiers Universitaires and Éditions de l'Université d'État d'Haïti,[2] have published over a hundred scientific and scholarly texts in Haiti, these publications did not receive adequate distribution in Haiti or internationally, highlighting the inequalities present in the global knowledge economy. As sociologist Fran Collyer (2018) notes, The English-language Global North dominates the academic publishing industry due to various neoliberal outcomes, such as market concentration. Collyer (2018, 61) writes:

> *Market concentration* is a fundamental and very recent development within the publishing industry. Indeed the industry has been transformed over the recent two decades, with the market becoming both more competitive and, contrary to orthodox economic theory, concentrated. A glance at the current

global market shows a highly skewed pattern, with a handful of very large publishing companies in the lead, followed by a "long tail" of medium and small publishers. In 2015, the top 10 world publishers combined accounted for 54% of all revenue generated by the 57 companies on the list, up from 53% in 2013 (*Publishers Weekly*, 2015). The headquarters of the major publishers, the major scholarly journals, and the major scientific societies and associations are largely found in the Global North.

The fact that the Global North dominates the academic publishing industry corresponds with an "academic culture oriented toward the [G]lobal North and having the authority to define the standards and models of 'good' science" (Collyer 2018, 66). This issue caused concern for the UEH professors and graduate students who attended the academic research seminar I led. They said they were often years behind current scholarly debates due to the delay in translating English research into French for accessibility in Haiti. They contended that this delay often prevented them from making relevant scholarly contributions and interventions. Given this reality, various scholars I worked with oriented their scholarly production toward the Global North, whether by consuming English-language texts or publishing with Northern academic presses.

Finally, Ralph expressed a need for productive academic critique in Haiti. According to him, when someone wrote a critical analysis of an author's book, the author often perceived it as a personal attack instead of constructive feedback. He further explained that the academic community in Haiti thus lacked healthy debates and was more focused on mutual admiration. "It's a community of mutual admiration as there isn't much debate. If you disagree with me, you're automatically a 'bad person.' It's like that. And we're all fanatics! We still agree with so-and-so because we like him, even if his thesis doesn't persuade us." Continuing, he added that scholars in Haiti often financed their research and self-published their books. This personal investment in their work contributed to the perception among such scholars that criticisms of their work were personal attacks rather than a necessary component of academic practice.

The three issues Ralph identified—the decline of reflective and critical thinking due to increased media access, the marginalization of Haitian academic presses and book distributors, and the need for dialogical critique among Haitian scholars—contributed to an environment of epistemological factionalism in Haiti. This environment created siloed ideological echo chambers that impeded the possibility of addressing collective problems and sometimes even fueled hate. Ralph provided this example of the adverse effects of epistemological factionalism:

> At Café Philo, we had two broadcasts with Charlot Jeudy. Charlot Jeudy was the leader of Kouraj (Courage), an organization that defended the rights of LGBT+ and low-income communities. We knew that we were taking a signifi-

cant risk. There were even divisions within the [Café Philo] committee: some committee members said they didn't want to have a *"masisi"*[3]—Jeudy was openly gay—come and speak at Café Philo. But many of us stood our ground and invited him anyway.

Exposing unpopular views might lead to ostracization or physical violence. Charlot Jeudy eventually lost his life for his public stance against homophobia and classism in Haiti. In 2019, the thirty-five-year-old LGBT+ activist and film-maker was found dead in his home due to strangulation or poisoning. Despite the suspicious nature of his death and the fact that Jeudy had received several death threats months before, the authorities did not launch a formal investigation (Lavietes 2019).

Epistemological factionalism is not exclusive to Haiti. Disciplinary boundaries elsewhere, a consequence of "institutional arrangements and struggles for power" (Massey 1999, 5), have created hierarchies of knowledge and specialized skills that do not correspond with a world in which "problems do not present themselves as distinct subjects but increasingly within trans-disciplinary contexts" (Kreber 2010, xvii). Moreover, ideological and political silos have increased despite (or because of) social-media-driven global interconnectivity, limiting dialogue across differences and fueling nationalism, xenophobia, homophobia, racism, and sexism (see Kuehn and Salter 2020).

For Ralph, moving beyond epistemological factionalism required transdisciplinary dialogical critique informed by local epistemologies—which he saw as a mark of "true intellectualism." When I asked Ralph what he thought constituted an intellectual, he took in the question as one does a complicated riddle. Taking a long drag from a newly lit cigarette, he rattled off prevailing definitions of "the intellectual." He then followed up with this deeply introspective and philosophical retort:

> The intellectual is a sensibility, a particular orientation to the present. For example, someone who loves to engage in dialogue is an intellectual. Discussion is an essential aspect of intellectualism. It's not because someone went to university—you might not have, but you like to engage in dialogue and exchange ideas. Today, what should the role of the intellectual be in Haiti? If you asked me the question this way, I would be more comfortable providing an answer. I think the most significant problem in the country is that the "intellectual" is no longer local; the intellectual has been "globalized." It's frustrating. That's why I am interested in postcolonial studies. I read Achille Mbembe, Homi Bhabha, and Gayatri Spivak and am reading Edward Said right now. I am concerned with epistemological reconfiguration regarding the representations of occidental knowledge. Historically, we thought that "valid knowledge" was occidental. I don't think this at all! I believe that people construct knowledge locally. I even think that an "ethnophilosophy" is possible.

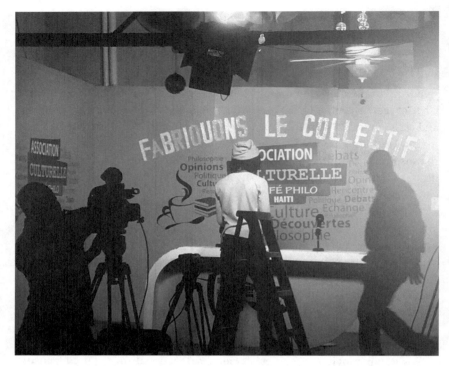

Figure 4.1. Café Philo Haïti, March 27, 2018. Photo by author.

> I am not very Cartesian. For example, I don't believe in universal knowledge but in local knowledge production.

Here, Ralph suggests that the globalization of occidental or Western knowledge forms presents a problem for local epistemologies. Thus, to decolonize knowledge or reconfigure epistemologies, we must valorize "particular" or "local" knowledge, as well as dismantle the boundaries between "valid" and subaltern epistemologies. Ralph's commitment to reconfiguring epistemologies led him to help shape Café Philo Haïti (figure 4.1).

I attended a few Café Philo debates during fieldwork. In the dimly lit outdoor bar-café, peopled by a diverse public, I witnessed an epistemological assembly where scholars, activists, and artists gathered to discuss historical and contemporary issues within a framework of Haitian Atlantic humanism and through transdisciplinary lenses. Each debate began with the Haitian national anthem, "La Dessalinienne," and a video montage of Che Guevara played to Cuban composer Carlos Puebla's "Hasta Siempre, Comandante"—a 1965 song written in honor of the Argentine Marxist intellectual and revolutionary who played a pivotal role in the Cuban Revolution. The Haitian national anthem, for its part, was composed by Nicolas Geffrard and written by Justin Lhérisson in

1903 in honor of Haiti's revolutionary hero, Jean-Jacques Dessalines. Both pieces speak of national freedom and self-determination, framing each Café Philo debate as an exercise of national sovereignty by validating local knowledges. Moreover, that l'Association Café Philo Haïti filmed the discussions, broadcasted them on Radio Television Caraibes, and uploaded them on YouTube was perhaps meant to place these debates on a larger platform that extended beyond Haiti.

Librairie La Pléiade

Founded in 1962 by the late Daniel Lafontant, Librairie La Pléiade was a longstanding bookstore that survived intellectual repression, political turmoil, and natural disasters. I spoke with Monique, Daniel Lafontant's daughter, at the bookstore in Pétionville. We conversed in the middle of the afternoon lag as contemporary jazz music played in the background. Monique was a cheerful woman with buoyant braids and beaded jewelry who described herself as a lifelong reader. We began by discussing the challenges of running a bookstore during the Duvalier dictatorship:

> My father was very much interested in literature, culture, and politics. Still, he could not sell the books he wanted because there was censorship back then. Many intellectuals and professors frequented the bookstore because, here, they could find books that they were unable to find elsewhere. My father was able to find political texts that didn't explicitly use "forbidden words" like "communism," "Marx," etc. However, it was a constant struggle to maintain a large and diverse book inventory that didn't contain these specific words. Understand, it wasn't *easy* back then.
>
> Before 1986, many intellectuals had to leave as Duvalier's government arrested and persecuted them. But my father found a way to function in Haiti without being on the government's radar. He had to purchase books in a way that wasn't apparent. One or two times, the police brought him to the police station to interrogate him. Even so, there had to be people who lived in the country; *everyone* couldn't leave [*laughs amusedly*]. Those who left had no choice. The government arrested them, and people lost their lives. If you were someone whose husband the government had killed, you wouldn't be comfortable staying in the country. But for us, although we had family who engaged in politics, we never envisioned leaving the country.
>
> I spent all my time in the bookstore back then. My fondest memories were the Saturdays when people gathered to exchange ideas with my father. They would talk about *foutbòl* [soccer], literature, and politics. They were people whom my father knew and in whom he could confide. Here [at the bookstore], there was freedom of speech. The meetings became a weekly ritual. And it

wasn't just intellectuals. Sure, scholars came like Jacques Roumain's brother and Jean Dominique. That's how I remember the bookstore. Yes, people came in to buy books, but there was this *social* aspect, too. My father's friends often came by to converse, sit, and drink coffee [laughs indulgently].

Monique moved to Montreal in the 1970s to study literature, intending to help run the family's bookstore one day. However, in 1976, instead of returning home as planned, she decided to go to Mexico for further studies due to the tense political situation under Jean-Claude Duvalier. After Duvalier fell, Monique finally came back and soon began cohosting the cultural program *Entre Nous* [Between us] on Radyo Ayiti with J. J. Dominique (Jean Dominique's daughter) and, at different points, Yanick Lahens and Danièle Magloire, the latter a sociologist and feminist activist. Monique also worked at the bookstore alongside her father and her sister Solange, as she had intended. According to Monique, their work as booksellers was radically more invigorating with the departure of Duvalier. "There was freedom of speech, which made our work more stimulating. We could sell whatever we wanted. There was no more censorship or anything to impede us from buying what we wanted."

In 2001, Monique and Solange took over La Pléiade and expanded its inventory to include Haitian and international journals, novels, and scholarly texts in Kreyòl, French, Spanish, and English. In 2005, political insecurity forced the bookstore to relocate from downtown to Bois Patate, a mixed-class neighborhood in Port-au-Prince. Then, the 2010 earthquake hit and destroyed the bookstore. But Monique and Solange rebuilt the store with the help of patrons and the support of the "entire profession." Monique told me approximately a dozen bookstores existed in Port-au-Prince before the earthquake. By 2018, there were only a handful, including La Pléiade. Monique noted that the quake was not alone in destroying the bookstores. Some bookstores had closed due to family conflicts, and others did not have enough customers to remain open. Conversely, La Pléiade now had two locations, one in Pétionville and the other in Bois Patate (figure 4.2). La Pléiade's success was no small feat in a context where bookstores struggled to stay open, printing presses and book distributors were limited, and one could find used books for cheap on sidewalks alongside items donated to Haiti.

More than a bookstore, La Pléiade was a place of artistic freedom of expression, where regular book readings and live performances brought in various people. Given Haiti's tradition of orality and storytelling (Lahens 1990), the bookstore's incorporation of readings and performances allowed it to expand beyond those who could afford to purchase books and had the time to read. In 2017, La Pléiade hosted performances as part of the fourteenth annual Festival Quatres Chemins: under the direction of Guy Regis Jr., a Haitian director and playwright and the founder of NOUS Théâtre, a contemporary theater movement in Haiti. Festival Quatres Chemins was a two-week-long festival that included

Figure 4.2. La Pléiade, Bois Patate, November 28, 2017. Photo by author.

live performances from dance to music to theater to book readings. During a Festival Quatres Chemins performance at La Pléiade, I witnessed what I now see as an ontological-spiritual assembly:

> A twenty-something guitarist, wearing all-black clothes, skater shoes, and a short afro, sits on a stool with a guitar on his right knee. The author is a 30-something woman with high cheekbones and a single flower in her hair. She is barefooted and wears a black spaghetti-strap camisole and flowy pants. She stands behind the microphone and holds excerpts from the collection, *Ecorchèes vivantes Collectif d'auteurs rèunies*.
>
> She begins reading passionately in French. The phrase "reconstructed brutally" stands out to me. These short stories are the overlapping and distinct voices of women who detail experiences of sexual violence, emotional abuse, and subjugation within the spirit of resistance and self-actualization. I feel a certain kinship with these women. The author becomes each woman as though she's a shapeshifter with the power to assume the form and voice of those she represents. I want to introduce myself to the author but hesitate. My nervousness impedes my ability to speak Kreyòl. With the help of the guitarist,

who speaks English, I explain my research and tell her I appreciate (I mispronounce the word in Kreyòl since it is so close to English) her work. I also inquire about her book. She explains that she's an actress, not the book's author. She was only acting. (Fieldnotes, November 28, 2017)

Perhaps most forms of multiple-character acting are a sort of ontological-spiritual assembly, in that one actor gathers multiple personalities in an exercise of imaginative being and becoming. But something about the realistic and empathic nature of the performance led me to believe that the actor was the author of the multiple women she conveyed. "Belief" is an essential aspect of Karen Barad's (2007) "relational (or performative) ontology"—the idea that "being, existence, is performative and [that] there are only phenomena" (Bryant 2016, 11). Barad (2007) emphasizes the importance of belief in giving phenomena substance or materiality. Writing about the relationship between religious belief, performance, and ontology, Haitian-born U.S. scholar Marie-Jose Alcide Saint-Lot (2004, 52) describes striking parallels between multi-character realist acting and what she calls Vodou's "theatricality of possession." Saint-Lot notes that, just as in specific modes of realist acting, possession in Vodou depends on timing, embodiment, and belief. Saint-Lot (2004, 64) continues that the more remarkable possessions "are the solo sequential performances, where one person performer representing simultaneously a number of gods, reproduces their characteristics: the crawling snake Danbala; the aristocrat, well-dressed Ezili Freda; the aggressive and violent Ezili Danto; Agwetaroyo, the sea god paddling his canoe; the shy, awkward peasant, Kouzen Zaka; the majestic warrior, Ogou Feray; the exuberant, obscene *Gede*. The men incarnate the female deities as brilliantly as the women incarnate the male ones. Young persons show as much flexibility as old ones." In Vodou, gods are given substance and voice through the empathic performances of the possessed. Relatedly, in cognitive psychology, realist acting inspires new ways of teaching empathy, meaning the ability to "feel into" what another is feeling. Psychologists Thalia Goldstein and Paul Bloom (2011, 142) write that the "production and perception of realistic acting poses some daunting cognitive challenges. Actors must convey feelings and actions that do not correspond to their actual selves or their actual situation; they have to 'live truthfully' under imaginary circumstances." They continue that "part of the pleasure one gets from observing acting is . . . the ability of a person to seemingly transform wholly into another person, physically and emotionally" (142). Akin to realist modes of acting, I read ontological-spiritual assembly as a performative and spiritual exercise of empathy where one attempts to see and feel into the experiences of others.[4] Although not a theater, La Pléiade was where such assembly could occur. With its vast selection of books and the varied readings and performances it hosted, the bookstore allowed patrons to become immersed in the lives and stories of different characters, to experience a performative empathy that anticipated the coexistence of multiple narratives of being and becoming.

BUILDING FRACTALS OF BELONGING

Returning to the proverb, "Piti, piti zwazo fè nich li" (little by little, the bird builds its nest): like the bird who makes a fractal nest bit by bit, new worlds are built incrementally, with fragments bound together by a shared desire for belonging despite differences. Thinking with Black and intersectional feminisms, I suggest the concept of "fractals" to envision the broader impact of instances of rasanblaj, like the ones I detailed in this chapter. Coined in the 1960s by mathematician Benoit Mandelbrot to describe objects with irregular geometric shapes, such as nests, conch shells, and ferns, "a fractal is a never-ending pattern. Fractals are infinitely complex patterns that are self-similar across different scales. They are created by repeating a simple process over and over in an ongoing feedback loop" (Fractal Foundation, n.d., para 1, cited in Abetz and Moore 2018, 35). Black and intersectional feminists have mobilized the language and visualization of fractals to represent the "both/and of similarity and difference, where the repetition or recursive construction of patterned privilege/marginalization creates a unique image of repeated, intersectional experiences. Therefore, it is through a simple, similar operation (the operation of privilege/oppression) that multiplicative oppressions come to exist across individuals, groups, and institutions" (Abetz and Moore 2018, 36). Coloniality, conceived in this way, can be seen as a repeating system of privilege/oppression, inclusion/exclusion at multiple scales. Thus, dismantling and remaking the Caribbean world beyond coloniality can occur through the cumulative force of occurrences of rasanblaj, which can "create small changes in the operation of privilege/oppression [that] can result in shifts across scales" (Abetz and Moore 2018, 36; see also Brown 2017). But exactly how to do this would depend on the radical imagination and criticism of "people assembled with others as they, together, face the present, prepare a possible future, and entangle each other in webs they cannot escape" (Varenne 2019, 4). In the next and final chapter, I discuss the interplay between radical imagination and critique in enacting futures beyond coloniality.

CHAPTER 5

Imagining Emancipatory Caribbean Futures

We must remember that the conditions and the very existence of social movements enables participation to imagine something different, to realize that things need not aways be this way. It is that imagination, that I shall call "poetry" or "poetic knowledge."
—Robin D. G. Kelley, Freedom Dreams: The Black Radical Imagination

Les revues ont toujours été un laboratoire et un ferment des movements de transformation sociale et politique; signuliérement dans notre temps et dan ces deux deniers siècles de tribulations, d'espoirs et de bouleversements sociétaux, sigulièrement sur le territorie haïtien.

[Journals have always been a laboratory and a catalyst for movements of social and political transformation; particularly in our time and in these last two centuries of tribulations, hopes, and societal upheavals, particularly in Haiti.]
—Mehdi E. Chalmers, Éditorial, Trois/Cent/Soixante

Since at least the mid-1920s, Antillean *revues* (journals) have been influential sites of "Caribbean critique"—that is, a form of "immanent criticism" grounded in the principle of universal emancipation (Nesbitt 2013a)—helping to inspire and uphold anticolonial, anti-imperialist, and other social movements throughout the Caribbean region through what Robin D. G. Kelley (2002) calls "radical imagination." For instance, *La Revue Indigéne* (1927–1928), "published in Port-au-Prince, and appearing under the slogan, 'Les Arts et La Vie,' . . . expressed the efforts of a small but committed group of young Haitian writers to develop a self-conscious literary movement that would be simultaneously national, regional, and cosmopolitan. Foremost among the social forces driving this movement was a desire to resist the cultural and political domination of the U.S. Occupation, which had been maintained forcibly in Haiti since 1915"

(Meehan and Léticée 2000, 1377). *La Revue Indigéne* was a precursor to similar literary projects that "were taking shape throughout the Caribbean in the late 1920s and early 1930s," including "*Lucioles* in Martinique, *Trinidad* and *The Beacon* in Trinidad, the *West Indian Review* in Jamaica, and the column 'Ideales de una Raza' that appeared in the Cuban daily paper *El Diario de la Mariana*" (Meehan and Léticée 2000, 1377). *Tropiques* (1941–1945), edited by Suzanne Césaire, Aimé Césaire, and René Ménil, represents another exemplar of the Antillean revue. Founded during the repressive Vichy regime, *Tropiques* was "an important voice of decolonization, Black surrealism, Caribbean studies, and anti-racist Nazi repressions of freedom in Martinique and the Black world" (Diawara 2021, 202). Let us also recall how the Haitian journal *La Ruche* contributed to the 1946 revolution against a fascist dictatorship in Haiti (chapter 1). As the second epigraph to this chapter suggests, an intimate relationship exists between Antillean revues and social and political transformation, particularly during times of crisis. Despite their continued relevance to questions of coloniality and global crises, Antillean revues have been sidelined in a contemporary context where journal rankings and dissemination are products and reproducers of colonial hierarchies of knowledge. Relatedly, the criticisms emanating from Haiti have been set apart from international and even Antillean knowledge production. Against this dual marginalization, I forefront two journals produced in postearthquake Haiti: *Trois/Cent/Soixante°* (henceforth *Trois/Cent/Soixante*) and *DO KRE I S*. But before turning to an analysis of these two revues, I illuminate what I see as a link between radical imagination and Caribbean critique.

Radical Imagination and Caribbean Critique

Robin D. G. Kelley's (2002) *Freedom Dreams* makes visible the radical imagination or "poetry" (á la Aimé Césaire) of Black liberation movements. Poetry, in this case, "is not what we simply recognize as the formal 'poem,' but a revolt: a scream in the night, an emancipation of language and old ways of thinking" (Kelley 2002, 10). For Kelley (2002), radical imagination is not only destroying oppressive systems of thought but also dreaming of new worlds. As such, it is akin to what Paul Ricoeur (1986) termed "productive imagination"—that is, the conception of "a place that, unlike an image, is not duplicative of, not determined by, an original" (Taylor 2006, 96). Ricoeur (1986) forwards "utopia"—translated as "nowhere"—to apprehend the revolutionary potential of productive imagination. He writes that "the utopia is 'the possibility of [the] nowhere in relation to [our] social condition.' At its best, the utopia is not only an escape from reality, but it points to a new kind of reality. It expands our sense of reality and reality's possibilities" (cited in Taylor 2006, 96). In effect, radical or productive imagination emerges from a conflict between the world as it is and the world as it should be. But realizing new worlds requires merging thought and action, dreaming and futuring. This merger, I extend, is encapsulated in what Nick Nesbitt (2013a) termed "Caribbean critique."

In his book, *Caribbean Critique: Antillean Critical Theory from Toussaint to Glissant*, Nesbitt describes Caribbean critique as Antillean writings "that cry out in insubordination and aversion to the state of their world (above all, that of plantation slavery and colonialism), and that seek to articulate the promise that another world is possible" (Nesbitt 2013a, xi). This critique is not "mere criticism" or criticism for its own sake that accepts and operates within the given terms of a debate. Instead, Caribbean critique constitutes "immanent criticism" or criticism for change that "seeks to destroy ideological illusion by demonstrating the fundamental non-coincidence of a world with its own professed criteria and self-understanding" (Nesbitt 2013a, 5) and that refuses "to allow the abstract separation of theory and practice" (15). These complementary preoccupations become evident in a founding document of Caribbean critique: the letter Jean François, Biassou, and Toussaint Louverture, signing as his teenaged nephew Charles Bélair, wrote in June 1792, months after the start of the Haitian Revolution. The letter cuts open the contradictions of enlightenment ideology and advances the Idea that "universal emancipation" should naturally extend to Blacks and the enslaved. Louverture, through his actions, would "force reality to conform to the Idea" (Nesbitt 2013a, 4). But the violent continuance of Empire would wrest away Haiti's hard-won freedom. Likewise, in the wider Caribbean, (post)colonial countries have seen their sovereignty and development prospects eroded by the continuation of coloniality through capitalist globalization and neoliberalism (see Sheller 2020). In this light, Antillean writers since Toussaint Louverture have continued to forward immanent critiques grounded in the Idea or "principle" of universal emancipation (Nesbitt 2013a).

Caribbean critique's defining characteristic is its indexification to a "politics of principle." Nesbitt (2013a, 15) writes:

> A politics of *principle* shares with the concept of critique [a] dual commitment to holding together theory and practice; in its very definition, the concept of *principle* itself unites a *practical* dimension . . . that points to the transformation of the world, with a reflective abstract and theoretical element. . . . At the same time, *principle* carries a third moment in common with critique—understood as the process of sorting . . . or judging—insofar as the *principle* stands as a rule orienting action within a given situation, allowing one to articulate a response to the question "What is to be done?"

Nesbitt, here, gestures toward the dialectic between crisis and criticism, a dialectic inscribed into the etymological roots of the word "crisis." Historians have traced the origins of the crisis concept to the ancient Greek verb krinō: "to 'separate' (part, divorce), to 'choose,' to 'judge,' to 'decide;' [a] means of 'measuring oneself,' to 'quarrel,' or to 'fight'" (Koselleck and Richter 2006, 358). In classical Greek, crisis carried different meanings in law, theology, and medicine (Koselleck 1988). In the judicial sense, the term covered both objective and subjective critique since a crisis (or "quarrel" between parties) was settled often through a crisis ("decision" or verdict) made by a judge. Once translated into the Judeo-Christian perspective, crisis became linked to God as the judge of humankind and to the apocalyptic "expectation of the Last Judgement" (Koselleck and Richter 2006, 359). In medicine, crisis referred both to the symptoms of an illness and to its prognosis. At the point of a medical crisis, a doctor could perceive whether a patient would live or die (Koselleck 1988). "With its adoption into Latin, the concept subsequently underwent a metaphorical expansion into the domain of social and political language. There it is used as a transitional or temporal concept," or to indicate "that point in time in which a decision is due but has not yet been rendered" (Koselleck and Richter 2006, 361). In this view, Caribbean critique illustrates David Scott's (1999, 7) "practice of strategic criticism," which "is concerned . . . with reading the present with a view to determining whether (and how) to continue with it in the future." As a strategic practice that is as intellectual as it is political, Caribbean critique engages the present to take up the most "difficult task of thinking fundamentally against the normalization of the epistemological and institutional forms of our political modernity" (Scott 1999, 20), always with an aim toward actuating and actualizing new horizons. In other words, Caribbean critique is an imaginative political project that seeks to move beyond the crises of coloniality toward emancipatory futures in the present.

CARIBBEAN CRITIQUE AFTER THE 2010 HAITIAN EARTHQUAKE

Given the dialectic between crisis and criticism (see also Benhabib 1986; Cordero 2016), the 2010 quake in Haiti inspired a robust wave of Caribbean critique. In the decade following the earthquake, diasporic and international scholars forwarded analyses that, among other concerns, decried neoimperialism and humanitarianism and called for new understandings and narratives of Haiti (e.g., Beckett 2019; Fatton 2014; Polyné 2013a and b; Schuller 2012; 2016, Ulysse 2015a). In Haiti, scholars and artists produced various special issues, essays, poems, and novels that grappled with the embodied experiences of postdisaster recovery and humanitarian occupation, critiqued Haitian social divisions and global marginalization, envisioned love and radical change, etcetera (e.g., Buteau, Saint-Éloi, and Trouillot 2010; Chalmers 2019; Lahens 2010; 2013; Trouillot 2011). Yet, the unequal placement of intellectuals in the global knowledge economy meant that the criticisms that gained the most widespread attention came from critics living outside of Haiti, those at an analytical distance from the experiences of those they wrote about.

130 SUTURES

This body of work's two sides exemplify the two simultaneous modes of criticism animating Caribbean critique: objective and subjective.

> The first is designed to reveal the objective contradictions of colonialism and to locate the potential for the concrete political transformation of that society in moments of systemic crisis. Its modality is primarily analytical, exploring the functional contradictions of slavery and colonialism. The second mode focuses on the subjective experience of exploitation and crisis, and its preferred mode is literary: poetry, novel, play, or manifesto. This division inevitably leads every critical thinker to a crisis of their own mode of production. Will they adopt an objective position external to the suffering of the exploited, to take advantage of their distance to gain quasi-scientific insight into the function of a system, at the risk of speaking in the place of the exploited, and without direct lived experience of the world, or will they seek to speak as the exploited? (Nesbitt 2013a, 9–10)

Now, I am not professing one mode to be more authentic or better than another. Like Nesbitt (2013a), I recognize the necessity of both forms of criticism; however, I emphasize the importance of foregrounding the critiques shaped by and in collaboration with those producing on the margins of the global knowledge economy.

I focus my analysis on *Trois/Cent/Soixante* and *DO KRE I S* not only because of their production in Haiti but also because they effectively gather objective and subjective critique in a "move from the abstract opposition of distanced analysis and poetic description to an understanding of how historical transformations arise out of a necessary mediation of these two positions" (Nesbitt 2013, 10). Indeed, the journals are acts of rasanblaj that assemble older and newer generations of Haitian intellectuals, local and international perspectives, art and science, poetry and prose, and Creoles and European languages to analyze the present and offer the "promise that another world is [still] possible" (Nesbitt 2013a, xi). Both journals are informed by social and cultural movements on the ground in Haiti and across the Black diaspora and are actants in an ongoing process of Caribbean, and thus, universal emancipation.

The balance of this chapter draws on ethnographic interviews and textual and visual analysis to show, on the one hand, how *Trois/Cent/Soixante* forwards a criticism of globalization toward realizing a world hospitable to diverse perspectives, and on the other, how *DO KRE I S* challenges Creole and Haitian exceptionalism to dream of and create Pan-Creole futures. More centrally, I argue that the revues are spaces of Caribbean critique that interrogate present realities to imagine and, thus, enact emancipatory Caribbean futures.

Revue Trois/Cent/Soixante: *From a Haitian Place*

The idea for *Revue Trois/Cent/Soixante* emerged spontaneously during a conversation poet-writer Mehdi Chalmers had with a group of friends one night in

IMAGINING EMANCIPATORY CARIBBEAN FUTURES   131

2015 over drinks at Yanvalou, a café-bar-restaurant in the historic Pacot district of Port-au-Prince. Named after the sacred Vodou dance, Yanvalou's identity as a pillar of Haitian cultural, artistic, and intellectual life found embodiment in the larger-than-life black-and-white mural of Jean Price-Mars prominently painted on its patio walls. In the image, Price-Mars appears deep in thought, with his eyebrows furrowed, gaze downward, and cheek resting in a cupped palm of his hand. Yanvalou, with its dark plum exterior, eclectic décor, and mosaic floors, witnessed myriad art and film festivals, music and dance performances, and vibrant discussions among artists and thinkers conspiring for change.

That night at Yanvalou, Mehdi and his friends were lamenting the decline of revues within a decade after the 2010 earthquake. Mehdi explained, "There were several revues before 2010, ten to twenty. Some went bankrupt, and others were discontinued. We couldn't find them here anymore and had to order them from abroad. It took months for them to arrive. But the writers were still here, and we wanted to read them, so we decided to publish them ourselves." Indeed, various revues (many of which members of jenerasyon 86 had helped establish and maintain) quietly went on hiatus or ceased production in the years following the earthquake. For example, *dEmanbrE: Revue haïtienne de littérature, de la critique et de théorie sociale*—a product of Lyonel Trouillot's *Atelier Jeudi Soir*—published its last edition in 2015; *Revue Conjonction*, founded in 1946, the year of the Revolution that deposed Haitian President Élie Lescot and relaunched in 2002 with Guy Maximilien as editor-in-chief, halted in 2016; and *Chemins Critiques: Revue Haïtiano-Caraïbéenne*, established in 1989 by Laënnec Hurbon, Georges Castera, Francklin Midi, and others, released its last volume in 2017. In Haiti, the revue has been an essential site of intergenerational dialogue toward social transformation (see Dalembert and Trouillot 2010). According to Mehdi, he and his friends desired to create a journal to continue that intergenerational dialogue.

Thus, in 2016, Mehdi—a postearthquake returnee—collaborated with State University of Haiti (UEH) alums Hurbert Muscade and Ricarson Dorcé, as well as European expats Maude Malengrez, Giovanna Salome, and Carine Schermann, to found *Revue Trois/Cent/Soixante: Haïti de l'intérieur, de l'autre bord et sur le fil* (Three hundred and sixty degrees: Haiti from the inside, the outside, and on the border). As its title signals, the journal proposes the metaphor of a "circle" to center Haiti in a critique of globalization. In one of our conversations, Mehdi explained that the circle suggests a concentricity wherein Haiti is the focal point of multiple interrelated but ultimately incomplete perspectives. Evoking the image of a retracting camera lens, he described the circle as a way of "seeing"— of zooming in and out, of playing with proximity and distance. Along these lines, the journal's inaugural editorial reads in part:

TROIS/CENT/SOIXANTE veut abolir dans le domaine de l'information culturelle et scientifique toute caricature idéalisée d'une soi-disant Insularité, tout en remettant en cause l'illusion d'un monde sans frontières spatiales, culturelles et sociales. Le partage véritable reconnait les distances et les lieux, TROIS/CENT/SOIXANTE est du lieu haïtien.

Nous vivons toujours des éponges de changements. Distinguer dans le changement ce qui détruit de ce que nous améliore, c'est l'affaire d'un regard averti et implacable. La revue a pour humble but de rassembler un kaléidoscope de perspectives, haïtiennes ou qui selon nous important aux haïtiens— et qui important donc universellement—de sorte que nous puissions voir et agir en connaissance de cause. (Chalmers 2016, 3)

[*TROIS/CENT/SOIXANTE* wants to abolish in the field of cultural and scientific information any idealized caricature of a so-called Insularity while questioning the illusion of a world without spatial, cultural, and social borders. True sharing recognizes distances and places. *TROIS/CENT/SOIXANTE* is from the Haitian place.

We are still living sponges of change. Distinguishing in change what destroys from what improves us is the business of a discerning and implacable gaze. The journal has the humble goal of bringing together a kaleidoscope of perspectives, whether Haitian or that we think matters to Haitians—and therefore matters universally—so that we can see and act with full knowledge of the facts.]

The journal troubles the notion of "deterritorialization" (the severed relationship between social and cultural identity and geographic territory), highlighting a productive interplay between the local and global. Describing itself as "from the Haitian place," the journal embraces interdisciplinarity and diverse (read: kaleidoscopic) perspectives to examine how Haitian realities shed light on our planetary condition and vice versa. From 2016 and 2019, *Trois/Cent/Soixante* would publish three volumes—*Colére*, *Extravagance*, and *La Merchandise*—each with a theme related to this critique of globalization. In the remainder of this subsection, I draw on samples from *Colére* and *La Merchandise* to show how the journal performs its identity as "a Haitian place," while attending to global interconnections. Whereas *Colére* finds grounding in the transnational Black Lives Matter movement, *La Merchandise* locates itself within Haitian social movements fighting against capitalist globalization, neoliberalism, and government corruption.

Published a few years into the Black Lives Matter movement, *Colére* asserts the humanity of Black people in an anti-Black world. In this inaugural volume, we find the short essay "*L'Image Révélée*" ("The Image Revealed"), written by Assédius Bélizaire—a UEH alum whose undergraduate thesis explores the iconography of the U.S. Occupation of Haiti. Bélizaire's piece analyzes the iconic photo of the "crucifixion" of Charlemagne Péralte, Haiti's renowned *caco* rebel leader, whom U.S. Marines assassinated (see chapter 1). The photograph—taken in 1919 by an anonymous U.S. Marine and circulated by the Marines as a warning to other *cacos*—depicts Péralte's lifeless body tied to a door, his privates covered with a loin cloth, and the Haitian flag mounted on a cross behind him (Alexis 2021). Underscoring the anti-Black violence that produced the photo, Bélizaire (2016, 39) writes, "Un procéde stylistique d'antithéses met en valeur ce rapport de force démesuré entre occupants et occupés: le cadaver nu versus les marines en vie et bien équiés, les machettes contre les armes à fue. Cette image du chef caco suggère à la fois l'humiliation, le danger et l'avertissement." (A stylistic process of antitheses highlights this disproportionate balance of power between occupiers and occupied: the naked corpse versus the living and well-equipped marines, the machetes against the firearms. This image of the *caco* leader suggests humiliation, danger, and warning at the same time.) Bélizaire (2016, 39) later adds that "L'historie de cette photo—qui a été rapidement réappropriée et est devenue un symbole de la resistance—, fait allusion aux engagements puissants grâce auxquels une politique d'espoir, pour la démocrate et pour l'automonie, s'est perpétuée au sein des communautés haïtiennes." (The story of this photo—which was quickly reappropriated and became a symbol of resistance—alludes to the powerful commitments through which a politics of hope, for democracy and for autonomy, was perpetuated within Haitian communities.) The "politique d'espoir" or "politics of hope" of which Bélizaire speaks alludes to the sort of "horizoning work" (Petryna 2018) that Black people have long engaged in making visible and challenging the banality of Black death while apprehending and enacting the possibilities of Black life and futurity. In this view, Haitians' repurposing of the photo prefigures a similar strategy among Black Lives Matter activists, who employed the circulation of Black people's killings by police to underscore the value of Black lives against a context where images of Black people's suffering and death have served to further their dehumanization (see also Dubuisson 2022b).

Within the same volume, there is a similar move of reappropriation in Saul Williams's (1998) *Sha-Clack-Clack*, which Mehdi Chalmers and Ricarson Dorcé (2016, 55) translate into Kreyòl for the first time. The first lines of the poem read:

Si m te ka jwenn kote verite kònen
M tap kanpe la pou m rakonte tout dousman souvni lavni pitit mwen yo
M tap kite lavi yo drive nan pase m
Konsa m ta ka viv yon tan prezan miyò
Tan prezan an se nannan bitasyon m kote w jwenn
tout sa ki te la ak tout sa k ap vini
Epi sa mwen ye a, se sa m te ye epi se sa map ye pake m se
Epi map toujou nèg sa a
M se nèg sa a
M se nèg sa a

. . .

If I could find the spot where truth echoes
I would stand there and whisper memories of my children's future
I would let their future dwell in my past
So that I might live a brighter now
Now is the essence of my domain and it contains
All that was and will be
And I am as I was and will be because I am and always will be
That n—a
I am that n—a
I am that a—a

. . .

The conditional "If/Si" that begins the poem situates the speaker in an alternate reality where he can retrieve the "truth" of his existence to repair his past by living in the promise of his children's tomorrow. The poem defiantly collapses temporalities to affirm a timeless self that is both "n—a" and human. Chalmers and Dorcé expressly translate "n—a" into *nèg:* derived from and rejecting the French equivalent of the English racial slur, *nèg* in Kreyòl translates to (hu)man. The translators, therefore, illuminate how African diasporic languages—Black English on the one hand and Kreyòl on the other—confront European epistemologies by transforming the words meant to dehumanize. As Mark Anthony Neal (2013, 557–558), referencing Helen Jackson Lee, notes: there is a possibility of seeing "n—a" "not simply as a word entrenched in racist discourse, but as the basis for a hybrid black identity—one that speaks to the meta-identities that define most (if not all) people of African descent who live in the United States." Thus, through this translation, Chalmers and Dorcé create a dialogue between U.S. Blacks and Haitians that appreciates Black people's hybridity while recognizing their shared temporalities in the wake of slavery (see Sharpe 2016).

Whereas *Colére* provides a global perspective of anti-Black racism, the latest volume of *Revue Trois/Cent/Soixante, La Merchandise,* refutes the idea of globalization as a type of cultural leveling, highlighting the inequitable ways that local people feel and experience the global. Kanellos Cob—an illustrator and comic artist based in Athens, Greece—crafted the volume's cover art in collaboration with the journal editors. Mehdi described providing Kanellos with several articles and critical essays on the political situation in Haiti and urging him to forefront Pòtoprens in the illustration. The cover art (shown in figure 5.1) is an apocalyptic rendering of downtown Pòtoprens. From symbols of international corporations like the McDonald's arch and Starbucks logo (businesses that do not operate in Haiti) to local fixtures like the Maggi season cube, Digicel, and Natcom (transnational companies with an overwhelming presence in Haiti) to indistinguishable machine parts and prescription pills, we get the sense of Pòtoprens submerged under a sea of brutal capitalism.

IMAGINING EMANCIPATORY CARIBBEAN FUTURES   135

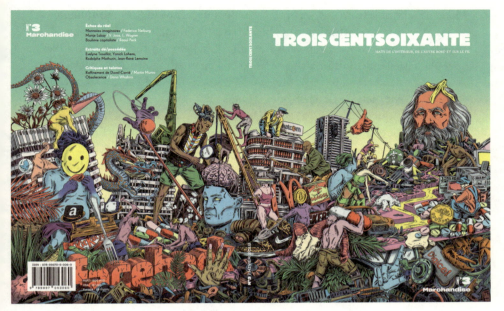

Figure 5.1. Kanellos Cob, *Revue Trois/Cents/Soxiante* cover art, June 2018. Photo courtesy of Mehdi Chalmers.

The cover art is also a critique of the right-wing Pati Ayisyen Tèt Kale (PHTK) or "baldheaded party" and Jovenel Moïse, a PHTK political newcomer who won the 2016 presidential bid on a platform of international commerce and economic development. The cover art references Moïse via the banana peel atop Karl Marx's head. Dubbed *"nèg bannan nan"* (or "the banana man") "because of his mostly failed export agribusiness venture with USAID funding, [Jovenel Moïse] was named victor in a foreign-financed election founded on fraud" (Schuller 2021a, 35). After taking office on February 7, 2017, Moïse betrayed the Haitian people to accumulate personal wealth through what is now known as the PetroCaribe scandal.

The PetroCaribe scandal unfolded as follows. In 2006, Haiti entered Venezuela's PetroCaribe program, which allowed Haiti to borrow fuel from its oil-producing neighbor and defer payments for up to twenty-five years. The Haitian government pledged to extend the savings from the deal to the Haitian people through social and development programs. Yet, a 2017 report by a Haitian senate commission revealed that various government officials, including President Moïse, had mishandled and embezzled at least $2 billion in PetroCaribe funds (Payton 2019). In response, "a loosely coordinated cross-class, cross-sectorial, and transnational movement pushing different tactics erupted under the banner of #KòtKòbPetwoKaribeA? Where are the PetroCaribe funds?" (Dougé-Prosper and Schuller 2021, 3). In March 2018, after experiencing years of economic decline bolstered by U.S. embargos and sanctions, Venezuela broke its commitment to

136   SUTURES

Haiti, leading to a fuel shortage in Haiti. In the summer of 2018, Moïse announced a gas hike imposed by the International Monetary Fund, thus adding to people's outcries against Moïse's repressive regime. Challenging the proposed hikes, people nationwide declared a general strike, compelling Moïse to back down (Schuller 2021a). Then in 2019, Moïse—a President Donald Trump ally—broke ties with Venezuela. "In exchange for Haiti's decisive vote against Venezuela in the Organization of American States (OAS), the Trump administration rewarded Moïse with ongoing support" (Dougé-Prosper and Schuller 2021, 1). Protests continued amid state-sanctioned violence, and by November 2019, the Kreyòl term *peyi lòk* (country lockdown) emerged to describe nearly three months with schools, universities, businesses, and the public sector shut down.

La Merchandise, published in 2019 around this period of political and economic turmoil, forwards a rejection of the epistemological and institutional assumptions of capitalist globalization and neoliberalism that helped create the conditions for the unrest. The volume's cover art effectually encapsulates how unequal global entanglements and the persistent continuation of Empire produced chaos that became inscribed on the physical landscape of Pòtoprens—a receptacle of the material and immaterial waste of "*merchandise*." But within the dizzying and dystopic cover image and the essays, poems, and research articles comprising the volume, we see possibilities of new horizons through analyses of people's everyday acts of future-making: *machann* who sell food and used goods to *chachè lavi,* creators who repurpose and reuse refuse to make art. *La Merchandise* thus shows that even while marginalized Haitians are disproportionately affected by the brutal fissures of globalization and neoliberalism, they are also able to refashion extant fractures toward fulfilling their needs and aspirations, pointing a way out of these seemingly intractable global processes.

DO KRE I S: *Dreaming of Pan-Creole Futures*

On an afternoon in February 2018, in the pebble-covered courtyard of a Pòtoprens apartment complex, I conversed with Jean Erian Samson (or Samson) and Samuel Suffren, cofounders of the bilingual (Creole/French) journal *DO KRE I S: La Revue Haïtienne des Cultures Créoles*.[1] Samson was a pensive poet in his mid-twenties, who wore short free-formed locs and a patchy beard, and Samuel was a photographer and visual artist in his early twenties who smiled often and laughed easily. They met as students at UEH, Institut d'Études et Recherches Africaines (IERAH), where Samuel was still an undergraduate studying *patrimwàn*, or Haiti's African heritage. There, they discussed their desire to create a journal to bring Haiti into conversation with other Creole-speaking countries.[2] As Samson explained:

> We need help encountering other Creole cultures like ours. For example, in school, we learned about France and some about the U.S. But we didn't learn

about Guadeloupe, nor did we gain a geographic imaginary of Guadeloupe. Today, you can talk to people about the Eiffel Tower, and even if they have never been, they will have a picture of it in their minds. When you meet at Guadeloupean and tell them about the *Sitadèl Laferrière, Chan Mas*, or the *Grand Simityè* in Port-au-Prince—sites symbolic in Haiti—will they know what these sites are? The symbolic landmarks in other Creolophone countries are also foreign to us. But when Guadeloupeans speak to us in their Creole, we understand them. We are not geographically or linguistically distant, but we are *significantly* disconnected. So, the journal aimed to create a space to highlight Creole languages and serve as a meeting place for Creolophone countries.

Founded in 2017, *DO KRE I S* confronts two discourses of exceptionalism that have lent to what Samson saw as the disconnection, or fracturing, of the Creolophone world amid the primacy of Western powers like France and the United States: Creole exceptionalism and Haitian exceptionalism. I discuss each discourse in turn.

"Creole exceptionalism," coined by Haitian American linguist Michel DeGraff (2005, 533), refers to the widespread belief among linguists and non-linguists that Creole languages "form an exceptional class on phylogenetic and/or typological grounds." This discourse reads Creole languages as "pseudo languages" that cannot express complex or abstract thought. Creole exceptionalism extends from racist ideas of the so-called inferiority of Black and African diasporic people—the principal speakers of Creole languages (DeGraff 2005; see also Bond and Kleifgen 2009). Historically, Creole languages have been denied official status and marginalized in legal and educational settings (Schieffelin and Doucet 1994). The marginalization of Creole and degradation of Creole-language speakers has hindered the development of a Pan-Creole consciousness. In recent decades, however, Creole-language speakers and advocates have fought for Creole linguistic enfranchisement, particularly in the Creole-speaking Caribbean (Dubuisson 2022a). In 1987, Haiti became the first country to have Creole as a co-official language (followed by Curaçao in 2007). Haitian Kreyòl is also the most widely spoken Creole in the Americas and the second in the world. Despite the country's linguistic status, Haiti has been largely set apart from other Creole-speaking Caribbean countries. This distancing is an outgrowth of "Haitian exceptionalism," a particular outcropping of Caribbean "Otherness" turned inward (see Trouillot 1990b).

In his pathbreaking essay, "The Odd and the Ordinary: Haiti, the Caribbean, and the World," Michel-Rolph Trouillot (1990b, 3) explicates what he terms "Haitian exceptionalism"—that is, recursive representations of Haiti as a uniquely bizarre place "unlike any other." As Yarimar Bonilla (2013, 152) writes in reference to Trouillot's essay: such "representations obscure Haiti's place in the world, casting it beyond the realm of analysis and comparison." Haitian exceptionalism, which persists today, finds its origins in the racist response to the Haitian Revolution. Immediately after Haitian independence, colonial powers sought to limit Haiti's radical influence in the slave-holding Americas by portraying Haiti's singular achievement as a threat to modernity (Trouillot 1995). Throughout the nineteenth century, "Haitian intellectuals rightly saw theories of Haitian exceptionalism that were spreading in Europe and North America as implicitly—and often explicitly—racist" (Trouillot 1990b, 7). In the early twentieth century, with the rise of U.S. imperialism in the Caribbean and Latin America, U.S. journalists and writers cast Haiti under a veil of ignorance and backwardness—turning it into a harbinger of the alleged dangers of Black political rule and a justification for U.S. dominance in the region (Dash 1988). After the 2010 Haitian earthquake, dehumanizing images of the quake victims circulated, fueling notions of Haitian "Otherness" amid global climate change (Pierre 2013).

Haitian exceptionalism also informs negative perceptions of Haiti/ans in the wider Caribbean, even in the French Antilles, which share a "comparable colonial trajectory until 1804, similar racial characteristics, and analogous linguistic origins" (Zacaïr and Reinhardt 2010, 3). Caribbean countries have lauded Haiti as the first Black Republic and the "Pearl of the Caribbean." In 2002, Haiti became the first Francophone Caribbean country to gain full membership in CARICOM (The Caribbean Community and Common Market), which was established in 1973 with the signing of the Treaty of Chaguaramas between Barbados, Jamaica, Guyana, and Trinidad and Tobago. Nevertheless, Caribbean countries have been careful to distance themselves from Haiti, the "ultimate 'Other.'" This distancing is an effect of coloniality inscribed in discourses of otherness that both homogenize and divide the Caribbean. What Stuart Hall (2003, 238) writes in this regard merits a lengthy quotation:

> Vis-à-vis the developed West, we are very much "the same." We belong to the marginal, the underdeveloped, the periphery, the "Other." We are the outer edge, the "rim," of the metropolitan world—always "South" to someone else's El Norte. At the same time, we don't stand in the same relation of the "otherness" to the metropolitan centers. Each has negotiated its economic, political, and cultural dependency differently. And this "difference," whether we like it or not, is already inscribed in our cultural identities. In turn, it is this negotiation of identity which makes us, vis-à-vis other Latin American people, with a very similar history, different—Caribbeans, les Antilliennes ('islanders' to their mainland). And yet, vis-à-vis one another, Jamaican, Haitian, Cuban, Guadeloupean, Barbadian, etc.

Today, "while scholars have become increasingly committed to the critical cultivation of a regional unity among the various islands of the Americas, and particularly among those connected by a common colonial language, Haiti stands apart" (Glover 2010, 15). Therefore, the discourse of Haitian exceptionalism supports Haiti's sequestering not only from comparative analyses but effectively from projects of collective Caribbean consciousness.

In confrontation to Creole and Haitian exceptionalism, *DO KRE I S* was created as "une plateforme permettant aux créateurs et scientifiques des cultures créoles de se regarder, de se découvrir singuliers ou pareils, donc humains" (a platform allowing creators and scientists of Creole cultures to recognize each other, to discover themselves as different or similar, and therefore, human) (Wêche 2017, 5). In this way, the journal not only addresses the fracturing of the Creolophone world and the dehumanization of Creole speakers but also forwards a dream of Pan-Creole futures that includes Haiti. In the rest of this subsection, I draw on the editorial of the journal's inaugural issue—*Vwayaj/Voyage (Passage)*—to further elucidate how the journal's critique of the two discourses of exceptionalism lends toward Pan-Creole futures.

The inaugural editorial essay, written by Evains Wêche (2017, 5)—a prolific writer from southwestern Haiti—begins with the proposition that language brought the colonized together. The editorial states: "Sur les plantations, dans les mines, dans les ateliers, maitres et esclaves ont dû communiquer, mais c'est en voulant se rapprocher de ses pairs que l'esclave a inventé le créole." (On the plantations, mines, and workshops, enslavers and enslaved had to communicate, but it was by wanting to get closer to their peers that the enslaved invented Creole.) The editorial, here, evokes the fact that Creole languages developed outside of/ against the norms of European languages when contact between European enslavers and African enslaved populations decreased with the intensification of the forceful "importation" of African peoples to the Americas (see DeGraff 2001; 2009; Mufwene 1990).

Throughout the editorial, *DO KRE I S* implicitly and explicitly situates itself within *créolité*—a Francophone Caribbean literary movement that rejects notions of racial purity and monolithic "Blackness" in praise of "Creoleness," a neologism that seeks to define the linguistic and cultural heterogeneity of the Caribbean, particularly of the French Antilles. Founded in the 1980s by Martinican writers Patrick Chamoiseau, Jean Bernabé, and Raphaël Confiant in conversation with Eduard Glissant's work, *créolité* challenges what its founders saw as Négritude's binarism, African fetishization, and lack of original aesthetics (McCusker 2003).[3] Hence, although *DO KRE I S* celebrates the African roots of Creole languages and cultures, it follows créolité in (re)defining Creoleness as an identity formed through *passage*, encounter, and the resulting creolization. Indeed, as Hall (2015, 20) observes: "The créolité theorists argue that creolization has produced, not the debased, hybrid, vulgar, vernacular culture incapable of sustaining great work of literature and art, but a potential new basis from which a popular creativity which is distinctive, original to the area itself, and better adapted to capture the realities of daily life in the postcolony, can be, and is being, produced." The editorial moves from this premise and postulates as follows:

> S'il existe une sensibilité créole, propre aux cultures de peuples, pour la plupart d'anciens colonisés (marcorix ou autres langues autochtones, fon ou autres langues africaines, espagnol, français, anglais, ou autres langues européennes), s'il existe une vision du monde créole, s'il existe une esthétique créole, s'il existe une vérité intérieure, une conscience commune créole, nous pouvons l'exprimer dans la langue qui nous convient le mieux. (Wêche 2017, 5)

> [If there is a Creole sensibility, peculiar to the cultures of peoples, for the most part colonized, having forged a language in the crucible of that of the invader (in our case French) and those of the colonized (Macorix or other Indigenous languages, Fon or other African languages, Spanish, French, English, or other European languages). If there is a Creole worldview, a Creole aesthetic, an inner truth, and a Creole shared consciousness, then we can express it in the language that suits us best.]

DO KRE I S offers a space for Creole cultures to (re)encounter one another through the Creole language, which—as créolité thinkers rightly assert—is "capable of sustaining a distinctive 'vernacular' literature of its own" (Hall 2015, 15). Thus, the journal includes an array of Haitian poetry, literature, and essays written in Kreyòl, alongside writings in other Antillean Creoles and French.

The journal's inclusion of Haitian writers within the créolité corpus contradicts the broader créolité movement, which has sidelined Haitian writers despite the early contribution of such writers to the movement's formation. Indeed, whereas Glissant's influences on créolité are well-documented, lesser known are the contributions of Haitian Spiralism—a Haitian surrealist literary movement founded in the 1960s by Frankétienne, Jean-Claude Fignolé, and René Philoctète (see Glover 2010). In the founding document of créolité, *Eloge de la créolité* (In Praise of Creoleness), Bernabé, Chamoiseau, and Confiant note the direct influence of Franketienne's *Dézafi*—the first novel to be published entirely in Kreyòl—on the movement.[4] Bernabé, Chamoiseau, and Confiant (1990, 890) write: "Haitian writer Franketienne, taking part in the first buddings of a Creoleness centered around its native depths, proved, in his work *Dézafi*, (Port-au-Prince 1975), to be both the blacksmith and the alchemist of the central nervure of our authenticity: Creole re-created by and for writing. So that *Malemort* [Glissant's novel] and *Dézafi*—strangely published in the same year, 1975—were the works which, in their deflagrating interaction, released for new generations the basic tool of this approach of self-knowledge: interior vision." This "interior vision" draws inspiration from the Caribbean as opposed to looking outward toward France or Africa. Scholar Ama Mazama (1994) argues, however, that there still exists as "latent Eurocentrism of the Creolist project" due to the Creolist's "premature relegating of Césairean Negritude to a socio-historical moment past/ passed in the interest of establishing themselves globally as the modern-day bearers of Antillean cultural values" (cited in Glover 2010, 11). This latent Eurocentrism has contributed to the marginalization of Haitian writers. As Kaiama Glover (2010, 14) maintains, "Haiti's writers have been quite explicitly set apart by their Antillean compatriots. That is, writer-intellectuals of the French Caribbean departments have exhibited a decided uneasiness as far as Haitian literature is concerned. As Francophone scholar Régis Antoine points out, Haiti's creative reliance on elements characterized as non-Cartesian by early twentieth-century discourses of Antillean resistance has in the past kept the island republic somewhat on the outskirts of a regional francophone affiliation." In other words, the non-dualism of Vodou and folklore found in Haitian literature butt against the philosophical (mind-body) dualism central to French and underlying in French Antillean literature. The fact that various Haitian writers since Jean Price-Mars have venerated Haiti's African heritage through their incorporation of Vodou ontology and folklore in works of fiction, as well as in sociopolitical and cultural analyses, produces an apprehension for Antillean writers seeking to position themselves (however unconsciously) within the philosophical tradition of Western Europe, and France specifically. More broadly, the general disregard of Haitian writers in créolité and French Antillean literature reflects a variant of Haitian exceptionalism that has placed Haiti "outside" Caribbean geo-political and literary imagination (see Glover 2010).

By including Haitian writers in créolité, *DO KRE I S* forwards an alternate geographical imaginary where Haiti is neither exceptional nor alien but part of a vast cultural and linguistic community with its own "interior vision." Since its founding, the journal has brought together over a hundred contributors from Haiti, Guadeloupe, Trinidad and Tobago, Martinique, La Reunion, and other countries, and in 2018, the journal hosted a Creole festival where Creolophone writers traveled to Haiti to encounter one another—some for the first time. *DO KRE I S*, thus, actively fulfills its ambition to "'faire archipel', en offrant un lieu de réflexion, d'épanouissement et surtout de rencontres, aux voix indociles, isolées, marginalisée" ("make an archipelago," by offering a place of reflection, self-actualization and above all of encounters, to unruly, isolated, marginalized voices) (Association Vagues Littéraires 2023). Extrapolating from this vision of Pan-Creole futures, *DO KRE I S* offers the world an alternative to divisiveness and chaos, which is to "*devenir Créole*"—to "become Creole" through anticolonial encounter (Wêche 2017, 5).

Toward Emancipatory Caribbean Futures

Considering the Antillean revue as a site of Caribbean critique, I explored in this chapter how two revues formed in postearthquake Haiti—*Trois/Cent/Soixante* and *DO KRE I S*—forwarded critiques of globalization and Creole and Haitian exceptionalism, respectively, to envision and thus, enact Caribbean liberatory futures. The journals participate in this politics of change through their very form. Samson described it this way:

> In Haiti, revues were always . . . a space of publication and creation, a space that intellectuals and writers put in place to allow multiple people to share their ideas with others. In terms of particular struggles, I often discuss *Revue La Ruche*. . . . *La Ruche* was as literary as it was political. It was a literary journal that was explicitly against the dictatorship in Haiti at the time. . . . So, I would say that the revue is a space—a public space—to share one's creative works, ideas, and critiques—critiques of society, literature, etcetera. The revue is a *"platform"*—it is a platform in Haiti that allows us to liberate ourselves of all that we've come across and to share with others.

As Samson indicates in the quote, the revue in Haiti and the Caribbean remains an essential platform for revolutionary change because it offers a space of suturing, of bringing together theory and activism, intellectuals and "the public" to critique and (re)imagine the world.

———

The 2010 Haitian earthquake exposed the fault lines and contradictions in our global present: despite being in an era of post-s (postemancipation, postimperialism, postcolonialism, postmodernity), the afterlives of slavery and colonialism continue to produce proliferating fractures that seek to enclose the futures of those existing on the global (outer) periphery and on the margins of international centers (see Fatton 2014; Sharpe 2016). Indeed, Haiti's position on the outer edge permitted the tremendous loss of life and houselessness that corresponded with the 2010 quake. Over a decade after the earthquake, political instability, socioeconomic insecurity, and ecological vulnerability in the country have continued the displacement of Haitian citizens, reflecting massive inter- and extra-regional Caribbean migration (see Sheller 2020). And beyond the Caribbean, coloniality and its various manifestations are actively threatening our collective futures through global inequalities, climate disasters, and every day and exceptional violence. As *Trois/Cent/Soixante* and *DO KRE I S* illuminate, the reclamation of Haiti's futures must therefore be approached within broader regional and global perspective.

Coda

RECLAIMING HAITI'S FUTURES:
A CALL FOR PLANETARY SUTURING AND REPAIR

Another devastating earthquake struck Haiti on August 14, 2021, precisely 230 years after the Vodou ceremony at Bwa Kayiman that initiated the Haitian Revolution. The quake, registering a magnitude 7.2 in southwestern Haiti, killed over 2,000 people. Days later, Tropical Storm Grace flooded the earthquake-affected area. This seismic event and storm were the latest in an onslaught of environmental and manufactured assaults on the republic, including the presidential tenure and assassination of Jovenel Moïse.

The presidential tenure of Jovenel Moïse (2017–2021), backed and upheld by foreign powers, was marked by state corruption and violence. Despite Moïse's promise to improve living conditions in the country through international commerce and economic development, he continued the government's entrenchment with local gangs—an entrenchment started under his predecessor, President Michel Martelly (a former musician who performed under the moniker "Sweet Micky"). In their 2021 NACLA report, "End of Empire? A View from Haiti," Mamyrah Dougé-Prosper and Mark Schuller (2021, 2) contend that the U.S.-backed election of Michel Martelly in 2011 and Martelly's "subsequent consolidation of power in his Haitian Tèt Kale Party (PHTK) gave rise to a *bandi legal* or 'legal bandit' toxic masculinist state." Under Moïse, Haitian citizens witnessed the continued "gangsterization" of the country as armed gangs killed, kidnapped, and violated people with impunity (Dougé-Prosper and Schuller 2021, 5). In response to the country's rapid slide into dictatorship, Haitian citizens from all walks of life took to the streets in protest, calling for Moïse's ouster and an end to Empire.

Then, on July 7, 2021, Jovenel Moïse was gunned down at his private residence. The presidential assassination—the first in 102 years—was not an act of vigilante citizens or even the local gangs but of an alleged group of over twenty Colombian mercenaries hired by an alleged conspiracy of translocal actors.[1] A week later, the Core Group and the United Nations Integrated Office in Haiti (BINUH) declared that Ariel Henry—whom Moïse had hand-picked as Haiti's new prime minister—would assume the role of prime minister on July 20, 2021 (Pierre 2023). In her 2023 NACLA report, "Haiti as Empire's Laboratory," Jemima Pierre (2023, 246) writes that: "The 'new'—and completely unelected—government and cabinet was composed mostly of members of the Haitian Tèt Kale Party (PHTK), the neo-Duvalierist political party of Moïse and his predecessor Michel Martelly. In the wake of the devastating 2010 earthquake, the PHTK, with Martelly at the helm, was put in place by the United States and other Western powers without the support of the Haitian masses." In the wake of Moïse's assassination, the capital fell under the control of the local gangs as homicide rates, kidnappings, and sexual assaults continued to rise. These events coincided with global inflation due to the COVID-19 pandemic, increasingly dangerous weather patterns across the Caribbean, and a devastating seismic event in Haiti on August 14, 2021.

Countless Haitian citizens have subsequently emigrated. Among my interlocutors and friends, Mehdi and Samson (chapter 5) left the country to seek doctoral education abroad. As of this writing, Samson is pursuing a doctorate in France, where he continues the production of *DO KRE I S*, and Mehdi is pursuing a doctorate in the United States. Mehdi explained, however, that *Revue Trois/Cents/Soixante* halted production given the dispersal of its editorial board. While Mehdi said he desired to return to Haiti once it was safe, Samson admitted that he might never return to live in the country. Dani, my former student (chapter 3), moved to Brooklyn in 2021, where she continues to work on her master's thesis for her degree at Fakilte Etnoloji.

While many have left, others have stayed. Various returned scholars in the two generational cohorts, and those in-between, are still forging livability in Haiti, continuing to teach, create, and agitate for change. Concurrently, "Since Moïse's 2021 assassination, Haitians have protested foreign support for the illegitimate and corrupt de facto government, rising inflation and fuel prices, illegal weapons dumping, and a dizzying rise in violence. In response, the United States and its allies have continued to push for foreign military intervention in the country" (Pierre 2023, 250). In short, even as Empire continued to shape Haiti's present, people continued to stay and resist the foreclosing of their futures.

Beyond Haiti

Contemporary manifestations of coloniality have created proliferating fractures worldwide, threatening places of inhabitability for those on the margins. Throughout the Caribbean region, the afterlives of colonialism and trans-Atlantic chattel slavery have contributed to socioeconomic and political instability, which, along with climate change, has lent to increasing waves of external and internal displacements (see Sharpe 2016; Sheller 2020; Werner 2015). Regarding external

CODA   145

displacements, as of 2020, "there were a total of 9.08 million migrants from the Caribbean living outside their country or territory of origin. This represents an increase of 117 per cent compared to 1990, in which the total number of Caribbean emigrants reached 4.19 million" (MDP 2023, n.p.). Most of these migrants ended up in the United States or Western Europe (MDP 2023). While extra-regional Caribbean migration significantly outpaces intra-regional migration, "the intra-regional migrant population has continued to increase each year, almost doubling over the last 30 years, with an increase from 437,177 in 1990 to 859,403 in 2020 (UN-DESA 2020). The majority—66 per cent, or 567,956—of intraregional Caribbean migrants originate from Haiti. Of these, 87.4 per cent, or 496,112, lived in the Dominican Republic in 2020" (cited in MDP 2023, n.p.). Haitians in the Dominican Republic have experienced increased violence fueled by anti-Haitian racism, compelling many Haitian immigrants and Dominicans of Haitian ancestry to flee the Dominican Republic (see Pinto and Rodríguez 2023). In the year 2020, "several large-scale displacement events occurred in the region, and a total of 694,035 new displacements were recorded, caused mostly by Tropical Storm/ Hurricane Laura, as well as the devastating Hurricanes Eta (category 4) and Iota (category 5) that hit the region in November 2020" (MDP, 2023, n.p.). The year 2020 thus brought into sharp relief how climate change—propelled by capitalist globalization and neoliberalism—has left the Caribbean particularly vulnerable to ecological disasters, with deadlier and more destructive hurricanes year by year. Pacific Islander and African populations have been similarly dislocated due to rising sea levels, wildfires, and other climate change–related disasters (e.g., Magadza 2000; Perkiss and Moerman 2018; Weatherill 2022). Indigenous, Native Americans, and First Nations people worldwide continue to experience violent displacement on their ancestral lands as capitalist regimes seek new extraction zones (e.g., Castellanos 2020; Urzedo and Chatterjee 2021; 2022). Former colonial metropoles, neocolonial empires, and settler colonies like France and the United States have also experienced the adverse ecological, political, and economic consequences of their global ascendancy. In this view, "Haiti . . . is not exceptional but one piece of [a] fractal puzzle, spiraling out into wider processes that ripple across the entire Caribbean and into the transatlantic and transpacific worlds" (Sheller 2020, 20). In short, we all live in times of fracture (Ulysse 2017), calling for planetary suturing and repair.

Theorizing from Ex-Centric Sites

In this book, I have taken up Black feminist anthropologist and theorist Faye Harrison's (2016, 170) call to theorize from "ex-centric sites"—"Southern" locations, "particularly the peripheral zones where critical intellectual trajectories have been sustained despite trends toward erasure." As Nadève Ménard (2013, 55) asserts: "Rather than viewing Haitian writers as voices of authority, literary scholars [and anthropologists] have a tendency to regard them as naïve informants." This tendency has served coloniality by reinforcing the authority of Northern epistemologies and deepening the inequality of the global knowledge economy and neoliberal university system. This book has instead foregrounded the theorizations of Haitian scholars to "redress disciplinary coloniality, level the 'landscape of knowledge production' and '[unsettle] the megastructre of the academy'" (Escobar, 2008: 306, cited in Harrison 2016, 126), and thereby "operate against the grain of the current neoliberalization of the academy" (126). In this vein, I here conclude by extrapolating from interlocutor's emplacement strategies—improvisation, rasanblaj, and radical imagination—to suggest these approaches as a framework for collective suturing and repair

In chapter 3, I sought to disrupt the "Haitian perpetual crisis" notion by revealing the transnational processes contributing to a roughly two-year crisis at the State University of Haiti (UEH). I argued that neoliberal operations and UEH's articulation as a state/non-state entity in a U.N.-defined yellow zone (site of insecurity) contributed to ongoing crises at the university. I showed how UEH professors, administrators, and students engaged in a "habitus of improvisation" to navigate structural ambivalence and demand change. But, as Dean Vaval posited, without a shared vision, people's improvisational tactics tended to create cacophony—reinforcing the crisis. Building from Vaval's insight, I contended that improvisation could be central to realizing social change to the extent people move toward a shared vision through what Daniel Fischlin and others (2013) termed an "ethics of cocreation," that is, an ethos recognizing how "the permutations of interconnection that bind people together enable a multitude of potential practices that can give rise to new lived, embodied, material realities" (Fischlin et al. 2013, xi). The question remained: How can improvisation be employed to realize new worlds?

In times of crisis, uncertainty forces an attunement to the present, which is necessary for moment-to-moment survival. This attunement, or "rifference" (Fischlin et al. 2013), also forms the basis of improvisational "cocreation"—wherein people actively listen to one another to create a space of agency for creative world-making. Fischlin et al. (2013, 58) define rifference as "the capacity of improvised music to invoke differential ways of being in the world across multiple contingencies that include politics, ideology, history, spirituality, ethnicity, and alternative forms of social and musical practice." But the musicians must agree beforehand to "lock into uncompromised improvisational dialogue" (58). In grassroots activism and other collective mobilizations for social transformation, actors must also commit themselves to improvisational dialogue (Fischlin et al. 2013). Indeed, collective actions such as peyi lòk and Black Lives Matter required people to coordinate movement and messages through impromptu conversation and sensing.

CODA   147

In chapter 4, I looked at how various interlocutors created gathering places that instantiated multiple belongings in the present. These gathering places were alternatives to UEH that allowed instances of rasanblaj to emerge. As a decolonial praxis, rasanblaj prefigures prospects by rearranging existing generational, social, epistemological, and ontological arrangements—arrangements constructed around binaries of inclusion/exclusion, belonging/non-belonging (see Ulysse 2015b; 2017). Since, as Trinidadian scholar-activist and spiritualist M. Jacqui Alexander (2005; 2015) contends, colonization has created physical and psychic fragmentation and de-memberment, the work of decolonization is re-memberment and defragmentation through reassembly—that is, the reclamation and reintegration of the ways of knowing, interacting, and being with others and the world that colonialism sectioned off and discarded as inferior (see Ulysse 2015b). The decolonial project of rasanblaj requires assemblages beyond colonial fractures. As academics, the project of rasanblaj would include bridging the academe/public divide by inviting public critiques of our work, producing work that is accessible to those outside of academe and our disciplinary fields, transgressing disciplinary and ideological boundaries to address shared problems, and fostering empathy through performative and spiritual embodiment and play.

Chapter 5 centered on two Haitian revues: *Trois/Cents/Soixante* and *DO KRE I S. Trois/Cent/Soixante* considers Haiti's geopolitical marginalization while envisioning a world where plurality and mutuality can abound. For its part, *DO KRE I S* imaginatively repositions Haiti within the Creolophone world, challenging long-standing tropes of Creole and Haitian exceptionalism. The journal connects Haiti linguistically and culturally to other places and affirms the contribution of Haitian writers and creators to contemporary Caribbean thought. In the chapter, I argued that in forwarding immanent criticism to reimagine Haiti and its place in the world, these revues—as sites of Caribbean critique (Nesbitt 2013a)—acted in an ongoing struggle for Caribbean and, thus, universal emancipation. Imagination is central to the ways human beings create new realities. But such creation requires both critique and new visions. As Robin D. G. Kelley (2002, xii) writes: "Trying to envision 'somewhere in advance of nowhere' . . . is an extremely difficult task, yet it is a matter of urgency. Without new visions, we don't know what to build, only what to knock down."

An Audacious Hope

Radical visions of Haiti's futures continue to circulate in Haiti and the dyaspora. One such vision was told to me by my maternal aunt/second mother. This small yet stocky woman—gentle and generous as she was stern and strong-minded—still lived in her home in Delmas (a commune in Port-au-Prince) despite growing gang violence. Although she had permanent residence in the United States, was retired from her decades-long employment as a civil engineer for the Haitian government, and experienced failing health due to daily stress and sequestering in her home, she explained that she intends to stay in Haiti. The last time she visited me, she said that against a narrative of Haitian perpetual crisis, various Haitians, particularly those whom she called "mystics" (spiritual clairvoyants), saw a new Haiti rising from the ocean as the old one—the one produced through coloniality's processes—was submerged. As she shared this vision with me, I gleaned the glisten of hope in her aging and decerning face. "You must include this perspective in your book," she insisted. And so, I have—not only because of her insistence but because this sort of visioning is an example of the "somewhere in advance of nowhere" (Kelley 2002, xii) that stirs a "momentum into a future that navigates the otherwise-than-actual" (Bryant and Knight 2019, 134).

Haiti was once commonly viewed as a beacon of Black liberatory futures, inspiring the hope of emancipation across the Caribbean and greater Americas. Yet, today, Haiti is often depicted as a place with no future, where people have no choice but to leave. Against Empire, many Haitians in Haiti and the dyaspora refuse this foreclosing of Haiti's horizons, holding onto an "audacious hope" that the country's futures can still be reclaimed. Audacious hope, here, may be read as a stubborn momentum toward a horizon that is not yet visible but destined to be. In a conversation with Gina Athena Ulysse, M. Jacqui Alexander (2015a, n.p.) contends: "As human beings, we are constantly making and remaking our destiny. There is really no abrogation or suspension of will, because these acts of creation require consciousness." Navigating consciously and willfully toward open futures amid systems of enclosure requires a boldness to action to topple Empire.

Repair is imperative to decoloniality, to the upending of Empire (see also Corwin and Gidwani 2024; Figueroa 2015; Kabel 2022). In the case of Haiti, repair would include the rejection of the imperialist and white supremacist demonization of Vodou and pathologizing of Haiti and its peoples, the restitution of the billions upon billions of dollars and natural resources stolen by foreign powers and state elites, the cancellation of all foreign debts, the creation and sustainment of increased livelihoods for the Haitian youth systematically disenfranchised by neoliberal processes, the suturing of societal divides, and the foregrounding of the voices, perspectives, and desires of Haitian peoples in shaping their own futures. In this book, I have contended that Haiti's futures relate to those of the rest of the world, suggesting that coloniality, in its myriad manifestations, has made it such that our futures—although felt and experienced differently in an unequal world (see also Appadurai 2013; Trouillot 2003)—are already inextricably bound. So, either we stand by while coloniality's fractures continue to displace those on the (outer) periphery until no inhabitable places are left, or we join in the reclamation of emancipatory futures started long ago at Bwa Kayiman and other similar sites of decolonial assembly.

Acknowledgments

This book would not have been possible without the community of family, colleagues, and friends who inspired, supported, advised, and encouraged me. I first want to acknowledge my immediate family, my son Kingston Lennan and partner Nthando Thandiwe, who witnessed and endured the most intimate aspects of the writing process. Kingston was my fieldwork partner and grounded me through field research, dissertation writing, a divorce, and a pandemic. He believed in me with a child-like faith that kept me going. I met Nthando in the first few months of moving to Pittsburgh for my first faculty position. Nthando has been a partner in life and thought. He read various versions of chapters and assumed childcare and household responsibilities to free me to write at the most ungodly hours. His love and support are unmatched, and for that, I am grateful.

I am eternally thankful to my mother, Chrismene Dubuisson, and my maternal aunt, Marie-Suze Gesse. My mother was a constant presence who rooted for me. My aunt, who lives in Port-au-Prince, was endlessly generous with her time, resources, and wisdom. These two women lent me their strength when I felt tired and pushed me when I wanted to give up.

I am grateful for my professors, advisors, and mentors—George C. Bond, Lambros Comitas, Hervé Varenne, Mark Schuller, Claudio Lomnitz, David Scott, Vanessa Agard-Jones, Lesley Bartlett, Lila Abu-Lughod, and Nicolas Limerick. Dr. George Bond helped set me on this path, and I am so humbled that our paths crossed when they did. He was an inspiration and a guide whom I miss dearly. I give special thanks to Hervé Varenne, who provided clear expectations and evoked Bond when I needed it the most. I am also grateful to Claudio Lomnitz and Vanessa Agard-Jones who joined my dissertation committee in the final stages and provided astute and critical feedback that I worked to incorporate in the book. Although I did not work with David Scott on the dissertation or book writing phase, he shaped my work in unparalleled ways through the graduate seminars I took with him: *Third World after Sovereignty* and *The Black Radical Tradition*. The theories and ideas I only grazed during the seminars continued to shape and reshape my thinking years later. Finally, I could not have written this book, let alone completed my dissertation, if it were not for the steady and unmatched mentorship, encouragement, and support of Mark Schuller. More than a mentor, Mark is a friend who was always available to listen. I cannot express what Mark's friendship has meant to me.

While any shortcomings of the book are my own, the manuscript greatly benefited from several scholars who reviewed individual chapters or the entire manuscript and provided substantive feedback: Aaron Kamugisha, Alessandra Benedicty-Kokken, Amira Pierce, Armond Towns, Celucien Joseph, Eddy M. Souffrant, Gina Athena Ulysse, Mark Schuller, and Myron M. Beasley. I give special thanks to Ulysse, who read the manuscript with a critical eye toward poetics and politics. I am also grateful to former and current UEH Professors Lewis Clormeus and Jean Mozart Feron, who read the entire manuscript and participated in a constructive Zoom book discussion. I also want to acknowledge the anonymous peer-reviewers from Rutgers University Press. The peer reviews were thoughtfully written and helped shape the structure and tone of the book.

I give special thanks to the Rutgers University Press editorial director, Kimberly Guinta, who believed in this project from the beginning and encouraged me to keep the book readable and accessible. I also greatly acknowledge the Critical Caribbean Studies series editors Yolanda Martínez San Miguel, Kathleen López, and Carter Mathes. I am honored to have my book in a series that effectively centers the Caribbean within critical questions of our time.

I wrote this book in the first years of my faculty position at the University of Pittsburgh. Despite a difficult transition from New York to Pittsburgh, my colleagues in the Department of Anthropology provided a rigorous and collegial environment that helped me write this book. I want to acknowledge especially Nicole Constable, Tomas Matza, Heath Cabot, Emily Wanderer, Gabby Yearwood, Gabriella (Gabi) Lukacs, Stephanie Love, Zachary Sheldon, Tanzeen Rashed Doha, Joe Alter, Claire Ebert, and Dela Kuma. I am particularly grateful to my faculty advisor, Nicole Constable, whose attention to clarity and ethnographic writing helped me craft a successful book proposal. I received advisement from other senior colleagues in sociocultural anthropology, including Heath Cabot (now at Bergen University), Tomas Matza, Gabi Lukacs, Gabby Yearwood, and Emily Wanderer. My friendships with archeologists Claire Ebert and Dela Kuma also greatly benefited my scholarship. I also want to thank the Anthropology Department Chair, Margaret Judd, for guiding me through my third-year review.

ACKNOWLEDGMENTS

I am grateful to early advisors in Africana studies: Michele Reid-Vazquez, currently endowed chair in Race, Racism, and Racial Justice and E. Frederic Morrow Associate Professor of Latin American, Caribbean, and Latinx Studies and Africana Studies at Bowdoin College, and Felix Germain, associate professor and chair of Africana Studies at University of Pittsburgh. I give special thanks to Felix Germain for organizing my first book talk and being a steadfast ally and collaborator.

I am appreciative of my circle of dear friends and colleagues with whom I exchanged ideas as well as mundane and essential life moments: Amelia Herbert, Astar Lambert, Bruce Burnside, Christina Mohmmad, Crystal Eddins, Frank Myers, Gabrielle Oliveira, Heather Prentice Walz, Irene Brisson, Jessica Hsu, Jill Seigel, Keisha Stephenson, Kiran Jayaram, Laura Neitzel, Letia Knight, Mamyrah Dougé-Prosper, Pisey Noun, Prashanth Kuganathan, Sarah Glinski, Sonia Erlich, Sophonie Joseph, Tara Bahl, Tiana Bakić Hayden, Toni Cela, and Virginia Ravenscroft. I am incredibly thankful for Amelia and Tiana, my sisters-colleagues-friends. Despite living in separate countries for most of our friendship, Tiana is one of my closest friends. We met in Professor Claudio Lomnitz's impactful graduate seminar, *Borders and Boundaries*. We would go on to write our dissertations, become parents, and acquire our first faculty positions in close succession to one another. I met Amelia in the second year of my Ph.D. studies, and we would go on to see each other through the program and other early hurdles in our academic careers. Amelia challenged me to stand in my truth and claim my voice. For that, I am grateful. I remain heartbroken over the loss of my longest and dearest friend, Keisha. In our very last conversation, when she called to say that the cancer had returned, she turned from her devastating prognosis and asked with genuine interest: "How's the book going?" That was her way: turning from herself to inquire about the details of the lives of those she loved.

I want to express special gratitude to my interlocutors, mentors, and friends in Haiti: to name a few, Camille Chalmers, Evelyn Trouillot, Jean Erian Samson, Josue Vaval, Jhon Picard Byron, Lyonel Trouillot, Mehdi Chalmers, Nadève Ménard, Laënnec Hurbon, Suzy Castor, Ilionor Louis, and Yanick Lahens. I am so grateful and honored that they entrusted me with their stories, perspectives, and theorizations. Special thanks to Mehdi Chalmers and Jean Erian Samson, who worked with me through the later phases of the book project. I am also thankful to my students at the State University of Haiti for their patience and grace. Finally, I am grateful to the State University of Haiti (UEH), the Interuniversity Institute for Research and Development (INURED), and the Fondation Connaissance et Liberté/Fondasyon Konesans Ak Libète (Foundation for Knowledge and Liberty) (FOKAL) for facilitating my ethnographic field research.

The writing phase of this book was generously supported by the Wenner-Gren Hunt Post-Doctoral Fellowship (#Gr. 10370) and the University of Pittsburgh

Summer Stipend for Untenured Faculty. A portion of chapter 2 was published in "There Is a Real Generational Problem in This Country": Haitian Intellectual Exile and Academic Diaspora Returns," *Transforming Anthropology* 2023 31:1, 3–14. And a portion of chapter 3 was published in "The (State) University of Haiti: Toward a Place-Based Understanding of Kriz," *Political and Legal Anthropology Review* 2022 45:8–25.

Notes

PREFACE

1. For critiques of the anthropological "Other," see Abu-Lughod 1991, Fabian 1983, Harrison 1991, and Trouillot 2003.

2. See also Hurston's 1928 essay "How It Feels to Be Colored Me."

3. In *Tell My Horse*, Hurston's "use of the phrase *blood brothers* suggests her perception of both an ideological and a racial connectedness between race men and Haitian patriots. In so doing, she communicates her conception of the two communities/societies as not just parallel to each other but as kin. The belief in the racial and ideological sameness apparent in the phrase blood brothers is reinforced throughout the Haiti section with comparable details" (Nwankwo 2003, 68).

4. Hurston praised the nineteen-year U.S. Occupation of Haiti in the section "Politics and Personalities in Haiti" (see also Nwankwo 2003; Trefzer 2000).

5. For discussions of Vodou cosmology, see Bellegarde-Smith and Michel 2006; Hurbon 1972; 1995. For critiques of Euro-American perversions of Vodou that proliferated during the U.S. Occupation of Haiti, see Dash 1988; Renda 2001.

6. The term "outsider within" comes from Patricia Hill Collins's (1986) "Learning from the Outsider Within: The Sociological Significance of Black Feminist Thought." The term "insider without" comes from Mark Schuller's (2014) "Being an Insider Without: Activist Anthropological Engagement in Haiti after the Earthquake."

CHRONOLOGY

1. CNN 2022, n.p.

2. Vega Ocasio et al. 2023.

INTRODUCTION

1. By the late 1980s and early 1990s, the term "dyaspora" entered Haitian parlance, reflecting the ever-growing influence of Haitian populations living outside the country (Laguerre 1998). In the late 1980s, interim Haitian president Henri Namphy created The Office of Diaspora Affairs, which operated under the aegis of the Ministry of Foreign Affairs. In 1994, the Aristide administration established *Ministère des Haïtiens Vivant à l'Étranger* (the Ministry of Diaspora) as "the official unit responsible for the coordination of the relations of the diaspora and Haitian government" (Laguerre 1998, 163). Aristide saw the dyaspora

as Haiti's Tenth Department, conceptualizing it "as an extra-territorial unit of the republic" (Laguerre 1998, 162).

The global Haitian dyaspora population has grown exponentially since the 1980s and 1990s. A 2023 Migration Policy Institute article reports that:

> The Haitian diaspora in the United States was comprised of more than 1.2 million individuals who were either born in Haiti or reported Haitian ancestry or race, according to MPI tabulation of data from the U.S. Census Bureau 2021 ACS. People born in the United States accounted for 508,000 individuals (42 percent) of the U.S.-based Haitian diaspora. The United States was the top destination for Haitians living internationally, followed by the Dominican Republic (496,000), as of the most recent, mid-2020 United Nations Population Division estimates. Other top destinations included Chile (237,000), Canada (101,000), France (85,000), and Brazil (33,000). These figures are likely to be an underestimate of the number of Haitians abroad because of the significant postpandemic migration of Haitians in the Americas. (Dain and Batalova 2023, n.p.).

2. The "occupation" I reference here was the presence of MINUSTAH (the International United Nations Mission for the Stabilization of Haiti) military forces, which occupied Haiti to "restore order" after a coup ousted President Jean-Bertrand Aristide in 2004. The operation lasted from 2004 to 2017 and was marked by corruption and violence against Haitian citizens (see Beeton 2012; Parra 2020).

3. Plastic waste, deforestation, and clothing donations from abroad have contributed to environmental pollution in Haiti. Jennifer Haney and John E. Bodenman (2017, 17) discuss the growing issue of plastic and other municipal solid waste (MSW) in Port-au-Prince. They call the problem of MSW in Haiti "overwhelmingly complex and inextricably linked to the geographic context: political instability, weak governance, inadequate human and financial resources, and insufficient disposal procedures." Kelsey Gasseling (2017, 1279) discusses how the trade of second-hand clothing from the United States to Haiti has fostered neoliberalism in Haiti by "justifying inequitable trade programs and allowing well-intentioned donors to unwittingly foist unmanageable burdens" onto the Haitian people.

4. Diaspora denotes a particular transnational formation that depends on dispersal, homeland orientation, and boundary conservation (Daswani 2013). In the case of the U.S.-based Haitian diaspora, Haitian American scholar Michel Laguerre (1998, 12) examines how political and socioeconomic engagements with Haiti fostered "diasporic citizenship"—that is, the "subjective reality of belonging" to two or more nation-states. Similarly, Nancy Glick Schiller and Georges Fouron (1999) use the concept "transnational social field" to explore how the "vision" of Haiti as a transnational nation-state builds on the needs and experiences of Haitians living in the United States. "Transnational social field" defines "the broader social, economic and political processes through which migrating populations are embedded in more than one society and to which they react" (Glick Schiller and Fouron 1999, 344).

5. See Alessandra Benedicty's 2015 article, "Male Protagonists and Haitian (Un)inhabitability in Ketly Mars's *L'Heure hybride* and *Aux fronières de la soif*," for a discussion of Haitian uninhabitability and its counter-concept, inhabitability.

6. Modernity and its formations are premised on anti-Blackness. Anti-Blackness is a form of racism particular to phenotypically "Black" persons. It operates on a global scale with regional and local contours. In their book, *Antiblackness*, scholars João H. Costa Vargas and Moon-Kie Jung (2021, 7) use a framework of anti-Blackness to stress "the uniqueness of Black positionality and experiences relative to those of non-black social groups. It proposes that the defining antagonism of modernity is Black-nonblack . . . Deriving from theoretical efforts and historical and sociological analyses, such perspective suggests that Black people (a) are not only exceptionally and systematically excluded socially . . . but (b) are the nonbeing that

NOTES TO PAGES 5–12

underpins and engenders modern non-black subjectivities. These propositions assume a logic of social and ontological abjection, rather than domination or subjection, of Black people."

7. Nadève Ménard is the daughter of acclaimed writer and educator Évelyne Trouillot and the niece of award-winning writer and poet Lyonel Trouillot (both of whom live in Haiti). She is also the niece of the late Haitian anthropologist Michel-Rolph Trouillot.

8. This notion of "conscription" is a nod to David Scott's (2004) *Conscripts of Modernity*.

9. In *Refashioning Futures*, Scott (1999, 11) explains how unraveling anticolonial efforts propelled "a new field of cognitive-political discourse about colonialism": postcoloniality.

10. In *Humanitarian Aftershocks in Haiti*, Mark Schuller (2016, 3) notes that it was "United Nations Office of Special Envoy Bill Clinton [appointed in May 2009 by U.N. Secretary-General Ban Ki-moon] [who] pledged that the world would help Haiti 'build back better.'" Clinton and Jean-Max Bellerive, then prime minister of Haiti, cochaired the Interim Haiti Recovery Commission (IHRC). The IHRC, comprised of government officers and donor representatives, "only had an eighteen-month mandate, which was, arguably, too short to deal with the situation on the ground. There was also criticism of its effectiveness; a report by the U.S. Government Accountability Office found that over a year after its creation, IHRC was still not fully operational" (Ramachandran and Walz 2015, 35).

11. In their 2015 article, "Haiti: Where Has All the Money Gone?" Vijaya Ramachandran and Julie Walz document where the billions of dollars of aid went. They write that

> some $3 billion was spent by the government of the United States; another $3 billion was spent by foreign governments, and an estimated 13 billion was donated by private citizens. [N]ongovernmental organizations (NGOs) and private contractors were the intermediate recipients of most U.S. government funds. The government of Haiti received just 1 percent of humanitarian aid and somewhere between 15 and 21 percent of longer-term relief aid. As a result, NGOs and private contractors in Haiti built an extensive infrastructure for the provision of social services. Yet, these entities appear to have limited accountability; despite the use of public funds, there are few evaluations of the services delivered, the lives saved, or the mistakes made. Most importantly, Haitians are disillusioned with the overall lack of progress, and with the lack of transparency and accountability. (Ramachandran and Walz 2015, 27)

12. Funded by the International Development Research Centre (IDRC), the cross-case study was a collaboration between INURED, George Washington University, Oxford University, and the Peace Research Institute Oslo (PRIO) that investigated how diasporas affect political, economic, and social recovery in postdisaster and postconflict contexts. The project posited that diaspora-homeland interactions are profoundly affected by major "threshold events" (e.g., natural disaster or an election). The project focused on four countries—Haiti, Liberia, Sri Lanka, and Somaliland—that had in common a significant diaspora and a recent experience of a major threshold event. The project consisted of four individual yet overlapping case studies and benefited from the cumulative expertise of researchers with experience working in each of these societies and with their diasporas as well as South-North institutional partnership. Each case shared a common conceptual framework and set of hypotheses, yet each had different empirical and, hence, distinct methodological priorities. INURED explored the impact of Haitian diaspora on higher education in postearthquake Haiti; George Washington University investigated diasporic influence on postconflict transition in Liberia; Oxford University examined diaspora agency in postwar Sri Lanka; and PRIO evaluated diaspora influence on conflict and reconciliation in Somaliland. This innovative, cross-case approach enabled broader generalizations and theoretical development of diaspora-homeland relations. (Adapted with tense changes. Source: INURED 2012 Annual Meeting Special Issue, *Haiti's Recovery:*

Democratizing Access through Research and Policy, http://www.inured.org/uploads/2/5/2 /6/25266591/special_issue_newsletter_2012_english.pdf.)

13. For example: Brodwin 2003; Cela 2016; Glick Schiller and Fouron 1999; Glick Schiller, Basch, and Blanc 1995; Glick Schiller and Fouron 1990; Jackson 2010; Laguerre 1984, 1998; Mooney 2009; Pierre-Louis 2006; Zacaïr 2010.

14. My use of Caribbean im/mobilities is in the vein of Mimi Sheller's definition. In her book, *Island Futures: Caribbean Survival in the Anthropocene,* Sheller (2020, 18) defines im/ mobilities as "the intertwined coproduction of mobility for some and immobility for others, as well as the ways in which disempowered groups also experience forced displacements, evictions, deportations, and expulsions."

15. Founded over thirty-five years ago by Haitian diaspora academics, the Haitian Studies Association (HSA) is a scholarly association that "provides a forum for the exchange and dissemination of ideas and knowledge in order to inform pedagogy, practice, and policy about Haiti in a global context. To this end, we work to infuse scholarship with new ideas, and to make it relevant to Haitian reality; to advance to its rightful place the historical and potential contributions of Haiti to a pluralistic world; to celebrate the achievements of Haitians while affirming the inherent dignity of their history; to bridge the gap between the Haitian Diaspora, Haiti, and Caribbean; and to recognize the diversity that exists among Haitians" (HSA 2023, n.p.).

16. As of this writing, UEH included nineteen schools/colleges: École Normale Supérieure; Faculty of Agronomy and Veterinary Medicine; Faculty of Human Sciences; Faculty of Sciences; Faculty of Law and Economic Sciences; Faculty of Ethnology; Faculty of Applied Linguistics; Faculty of Medicine and Pharmacy; Faculty of Odontology; Institute of African Studies and Research; National Institute of Administration, Management and Advanced International Studies; Center for Planning Techniques and Applied Economics; School of Law and Economics of Port-de-Paix; Hinche Law School; Jacmel Law School; Les Cayes School of Law and Economic Sciences; Fort-Liberté School of Law and Economic Sciences; Gonaïves School of Law and Economic Sciences; and Faculty of Law, Economic Sciences and Management.

17. Please see http://bri.univ-antilles.fr/corpuca/ for a list of CORPUCA members.

18. In total, I conducted numerous conversational interviews and over sixty (60) audio-recorded discussions with three different groups—returned scholars (40); professors, administrators, and intellectuals who had not lived abroad (14); and university students (10)—and led two (2) focus group interviews with student activists.

19. Reparations—as in financial compensation for wrongs done—is one form of repair that I read as crucial to projects of decoloniality. Other forms of decolonial repair include linguistic justice, land restitution, and restorative justice. For recent analyses on repair and decoloniality, see Bruno, Tianna et al. (2023), "The Work of Repair: Land, Relation, and Pedagogy," *Cultural Geographies* 0 (0); Twitchin, Mischa (2021), "On Repair," *Performance Research* 26 (6): 54–61; Corwin, Julia E., and Vinday Gidwani (2024), "Repair Work as Care: On Maintaining the Planet in the Capitalocene," *Antipode,* https://doi.org/10.1111/anti.12791.

CHAPTER 1 — COLONIAL RUPTURES IN THE CARIBBEAN AND THE
DISPLACEMENT OF HAITIAN INTELLECTUALS

1. Various anthropologists have sought to "reveal the agency of intellectuals in the projects and operations of states and nations" (Boyer and Lomnitz 2005, 105), positioning intellectuals vis-à-vis hegemonic and counter-hegemonic processes (Feierman 1990; Lomnitz 2001; Said 1997; Verdery 1995).

2. Forming part of the Greater Antilles and situated between the Caribbean Sea and the North Atlantic Ocean, Hispaniola is the second-largest island (after Cuba) in the Caribbean

NOTES TO PAGES 25–46

Sea. The Republic of Haiti occupies the western third of the island of Hispaniola with the Dominican Republic. Haiti's size is 10,714 mi², and it is located 47.8 miles (77 km) southeast of Cuba.

3. In *Awakening the Ashes*, historian Marlene Daut (2023, 31) writes: "Nineteenth-century Haitians did not call the inhabitants of fifteenth-century Ayiti collectively by the erroneous name of "Taínos." Instead, they called them the "first Haitians." In this vein, I refer to Ayiti's original inhabitants as Indigenous Ayitians.

4. "The town gave its name to the Spanish colony of Santo Domingo, which, centuries later, would become the Dominican Republic" (Dubois 2012, 17).

5. The inhumanity of enslavement continues through what Saidiya V. Hartman (2008, 6) calls the "afterlife of slavery"—that is, the "skewed life chances, limited access to health and education, premature death, incarceration, and impoverishment" that seek to enclose the futures of Black peoples throughout the Americas and global Black diaspora.

6. This translated excerpt of the Haitian Constitution of 1805 is found in *Caribbean Political Thought*, edited by Aaron Kamugisha. It is a reprint of the Haitian Constitution of 1805 found in the edited volume *Slave Revolution in the Caribbean 1789–1804: A Brief History with Documents*, edited by Laurent DuBois and John D. Garrigus.

7. See L. M. Alexander 2022; Daut 2015; Ferrer 2009; 2014; Gaffield 2015; Horne 2015a; 2015b; Trouillot 2005; Wilkins, Martin, and West 2009.

8. "Milat" is the translation of French term *mulâtre* and is also a postindependence equivalent to gens de couleur.

9. The Monitorial System, or Lancastrian System, was a colonial education model that spread during the early nineteenth century.

10. President Boyer also invaded colonial Santo Domingo (current-day Dominican Republic) and unified the entire island of Hispaniola from 1822 to 1843. "Under the pretext of reorganization, he closed the University of Santo Domingo, which had been established in 1528 by the Spanish in the eastern portion of the island" (Clément 1979a, 166).

11. For a more nuanced analysis of the French indemnity and its consequences, see *Rethinking the Haitian Revolution* (2019) by Alex Dupuy.

12. General Fabre-Nicholas Geffrard sought to undermine Haitian Vodou and signed the country's first concordat, making Catholicism the official religion in 1860. Before 1860, the Vatican had refused to recognize Haiti until it signed what some argued was a thirdclass concordant (Baur 1954; Concordato fra Pio IX e la Repubblica di Haiti [28.03.1860]; Dayan 1995).

13. Demesvar Delorme (1831–1901) was a writer, theoretician, and rebel who joined an attempt to depose President Geffrard in 1865 (Daut 2016). My decision to focus on Janvier and Firmin here is not to diminish Delorme's contributions to Black radical thought.

14. "Despite the international political success of his *Inequality of Races*, de Gobineau was never admitted to any scientific academy in France" (Fluehr-Lobban 2000, 460).

15. Anna Julia Cooper wrote her dissertation, *L'attitude de la France à l'égard de l'esclavage pendant la revolution*, on the Haitian Revolution.

16. Informed by a conversation with Aaron Kamugisha on February 15, 2024.

17. A noted recipient of the Island Scholarship was Eric Williams, the first prime minister of Trinidad and Tobago. In his autobiography *Inward Hunger*, Williams (1969, 30) describes the Island Scholarship as his father's dream for him, a *"summum bonum* goal" that was "made both more difficult and more limited."

18. "Russell personally selected George F. Freeman for the job. He found Freeman through an advertisement that began with three qualification requirements that captured an unintended irony: 'White, no racial prejudice, agricultural expert.'" (Angulo 2011, 5).

19. Rayford Logan examined U.S. relations with Haiti in his book *The Diplomatic Relations of the United States with Haiti, 1776–1891.*

158   NOTES TO PAGES 48–55

20. François Duvalier first used the nickname "Papa-Doc" himself: "As an ethnohistorian and a country doctor, he knew that it evoked positive echoes in Haitian political symbolism" (Trouillot 1990a, 194).

CHAPTER 2 — INTERNAL DISPLACEMENTS

1. Although I use a pseudonym, here, Carole could have been named. The choice to give her a pseudonym is for purposes of consistency. Also, those familiar with her life history will likely recognize her in these pages.

2. "In demographic terms, Haiti is a young nation. Almost 60 percent of people living in Haiti are under 25 years of age. One-third of the population is aged between 10 and 24 and defined as 'youth' in the Haiti Youth Survey" (Lunde 2010).

3. I first encountered Karl Mannheim's concept of "location" in David Scott's 2014 essay, "The Temporality of Generations," in which Scott draws from Mannheim's "The Problem of Generations" to propose his concept of "temporality." Scott (2014, 162) assesses Mannheim's essay "as offering a conceptual portrait, from the inside, of the self-conscious experience of a particular *conjuncture* of generational disillusionment and displacement."

4. See McCarthy and Prudham (2004).

5. Complicating Carole's claim, the Haitian government did create insurance (1965 law) and pensions (1976 law) for "*Ti Gran Moun*" (economically poor old people), although the amount of coverage was often meager compared to living costs. For an overview of social welfare programs and retirement assistance in Haiti, see "Social Security Programs Throughout the World: The Americas, 2019," Social Security Office or Retirement and Disability Policy, https://www.ssa.gov/policy/docs/progdesc/ssptw/2018-2019/americas/haiti.html.

6. In *Stuart Hall's Voice: Intimations of an Ethic of Receptive Generosity*, David Scott (2017, 7) describes what he calls the "relational sentiments and virtues we commonly think of as internal to friendship: among them (and in no particular order), affection, loyalty, indulgence, sympathy, complementarity, tolerance, equality, stability, candor, respect, truthfulness, liberality, trustworthiness."

7. In *Architextual Authenticity*, Jason Herbeck reflects on the Haitian gingerbread house in an analysis of French Caribbean identity and authenticity. Herbeck summarizes Anghelen Arrington Phillips in her 1975 book *Gingerbread Houses: Haiti's Endangered Species*:

> Gingerbread architecture is arguably, with the possible exception of King Henri Christophe's Citadel, the country's most impressive feature (7). Ranking the colorful houses as more significant than Haiti's internationally renowned art tradition in terms of both charm and beauty, Phillips supports her claim on three distinct levels: historical, cultural, and ornamental. The turn-of-the-century structures, she asserts, represent post-revolution, independent Haiti's efforts to stimulate cultural development and expressions of individuality. Noting that the term "gingerbread" derives from the intricate lace trim that adorns the mansions' roof ledges, the author adds: "The houses, with their turrets, cornices, balconies and lacy lattice work, are works of art—reflecting many places and styles; yet remaining uniquely Haitian" (7). (cited in Herbeck 2017, 34–35)

8. After Duvalier came to power, poets and young professionals Marcel Numa and Louis Drouin fled to New York in the 1950s. "There, they had joined a group called Jeune Haiti, or Young Haiti, and were two of the thirteen Haitians who left the United States for Haiti in 1964 to engage in a guerrilla war that they hoped would eventually topple the Duvalier dictatorship" (Danticat 2011, 2).

9. The Food for Work program was implemented by The Cooperative for American Relief Everywhere (CARE), "one of the oldest NGOs in Haiti. It began to operate in the country after the 1954 Hurricane Hazel, which destroyed the country's cash crops of cof-

NOTES TO PAGES 55–60

fee, cocoa, and plantains in the southeast. In 1966 CARE moved to the northwest of Haiti, where it began to implement community development activities (www.care.org). The development activities that CARE mentioned were primarily called Food for Work" (Pierre-Louis 2011, 195–196).

10. My maternal grandmother who lived in the countryside in Petite Rivière de l'Artibonite—a commune in the Dessalines Arrondissement—had herself kept a team of creole pigs to help provide for the family. My grandparents would relocate to Pòtoprens in 1964 to secure better educational opportunities for their children.

11. Haitian-born feminist scholar Carolle Charles (1995, 153) notes that the Women's March in Port-au-Prince on April 3, 1986, included more than 30,000 women. These women "took to the streets of Port-au-Prince, reiterating their demands for jobs, full political rights, and the elimination of all forms of prostitution and gender discrimination. At least fifteen women's groups and organizations, representing quite different perspectives, social backgrounds, and world outlooks, participated in the demonstration."

12. A gourde is the basic monetary unit of Haiti.

13. As Laura Wagner (2017, 2), the former digital archivist for Radyo Ayiti, writes:

When Jean Dominique, the outspoken and charismatic director of Radio Haïti-Inter, and his professional partner and wife, Michèle Montas, landed at the airport in Port-au-Prince on March 4, 1986, an estimated sixty thousand people were there to greet them. Photographs and video from that day show Dominique—a man ever unflappable—looking stunned.

They had been away, along with the rest of Radio Haiti's team, since Jean-Claude Duvalier famously declared, "*Le bal est fini*" (The party is over), and cracked down on the independent press and human rights activists on November 28, 1980. Dominique took refuge in the Venezuelan embassy, since Jean-Claude Duvalier had issued an order that he be killed on sight. The other journalists of Radio Haiti were arrested, imprisoned at the Casernes Dessalines, and then exiled with nothing more than the clothes on their backs. They were able to return to Haiti only after the regime fell in 1986. That March day at the airport, the crowd lifted Dominique onto their shoulders and virtually carried the car to Radio Haiti's old station building, on Rue du Quai in downtown Port-au-Prince.

14. Haitian American artist Leyla McCalla's 2022 album, *Breaking the Thermometer to Hide the Fever*, captures this "energy" in the form of a "multi-disciplinary music, dance, and theatre work, which follows her personal journey as she uncovers the history of Radio Haiti, the first radio station in Haiti to report news in Haitian Kreyol—the voice of the people." https://propermusic.com/products/leylamccalla-breakingthethermometer.

15. "The *chef seksyon* [section chief] . . . acted as the sole representative of the three branches of government [executive, legislature, and judiciary] in the deep countryside" (Trouillot 1994, 48).

16. For instance, "the Regan administration granted $2.8 million in military aid for the CNG's first year. A joint letter from human rights organizations to then U.S. Secretary of State George Schultz asserted later that the aid has only served 'to strengthen the tendency of the CNG to violate the rights of the citizens'" (Trouillot 1990a, 222).

17. According to Dupuy (2007, 90–91),

Aristide could not run for office without the cover of a political organization. . . . The recently formed Front National pour le Changement et la Démocratie (FNCD, National Front for Democracy and Change) had asked Aristide to run under its banner. The FNCD, which regrouped fifteen left-of-center organizations (including KONAKOM and the KID [Komité Inité Démokratik]), had initially chosen Victor Benoit, the leader

160 NOTES TO PAGES 62–75

of KONAKOM, as its presidential candidate. However, it became evident that Benoit lacked the popular appeal to defeat the other well-known candidates. . . . Pressured by the KID, the FNCD apparently went over Benoit's head to nominate Aristide and compelled Benoit to agree (reluctantly, if not angrily) to withdraw his candidacy. . . . Though he became the candidate of the FNCD, Aristide never considered himself beholden to that organization. . . . For Aristide, the FNCD served merely as a conduit and legal cover for his candidacy, and nothing more. His allegiance was only to the people and to his soon-to-be baptized Opération Lavalas (OL, Operation Lavalas, meaning "cleansing flood") movement, which he believed was more significant than the FNCD (or any other political organization then in place) and of which he was the self-proclaimed leader.

18. Castor 1978.

19. See Said 1994 and Ignatieff 1997 for discussions on the decline of the public intellectuals.

20. Launched on May 20, 1979, by Joseph C. Bernard—Haiti's then-minister of education—la Réforme Bernard or the Bernard Reform was a "a series of dramatic measures aim at reforming Haiti's educational system, outlining five major goals: (1) establishment of basic education for all school-age children by the year 2000; (2) introduction of Kreyòl as an official language of instruction; (3) restructuring of primary and secondary grades; (4) revamping of pedagogy; (5) adaptation of curricula to students' reality as a catalyst for social and economic development" (Prou 2009, 39). Prou (2009, 38) maintains, however, that the implementation of the Bernard Reform was due in part to Jean-Claude Duvalier regime's attempt to "respond to pressure from the funding agencies of donor countries to raise educational standards and increase access to schooling. . . . [In effect], la Réforme Bernard allowed the Duvalier regime to buy time while securing international aide under incoming U.S. President Ronald Regan's Caribbean Basin Initiative (CBI), and—at the same time—to remain in power by appeasing the growing number of opposition and international critics."

21. See the funding detail for the UEH Faculty of Science at https://www.iadb.org/en/whats-our-impact/HA-T1283.

22. To read the complete *Horizon 2020: Strategic Plan 2011–2020*, see https://www.ueh.edu.ht/admueh/pdf/planstrategique2011.pdf.

23. In Haiti, "grimo" is often used to denote light skin and straight or curly hair texture. As Carolyn Fluehr-Lobban (2005a, 215) writes, "Many complex categories of phenotype operate in Haiti today that are best negotiated and understood by Haitians themselves. They include: nèg/nèges, nwa (all meaning black); marabout, brin, grimo/grimèl, grifonn, wouj (red); jonn (yellow); milat/milatrès (mulatto); and blan (white) (Avril 1997, 5). In everyday usage, these terms are used descriptively and not pejoratively, but they do connote class, status, and position that privilege light skin, straight hair, and fine features, especially among the upper classes, who control access to jobs and resources." Being called "ti grimo," therefore, can function as a form of exclusion based on perceived (and actual) class differences.

24. The tenure process at many Northern higher education institutions is also notoriously unclear. In their 2022 article, "Strategic Ambiguity: How Pre-Tenure Faculty Negotiate the Hidden Rules of Academia," higher education scholars Leandra Cate, LaWanda Ward, and Karly S. Ford use the term "academic ambiguity" to describe the lack of clarity surrounding tenure and promotion. They argue that: "The tenure evaluation process is strategically ambiguous, governed by criteria that are unclear in ways that benefit the institution but at the same time are an important part of the racialization of higher education organizations" (Cate, Ward, and Ford 2022, 796). Among the pre-tenured faculty in their

NOTES TO PAGES 82–136

study, "minoritized faculty articulate critiques of the ways ambiguity maintains the status quo and sustains the exclusion of people of color from positions of power within the academy" (796).

CHAPTER 3 — THE "CRISIS FACTORY"

1. Constructed in the early nineteenth century, Le Habitation LeClerc was the home of Pauline Bonaparte, the sister of Napoleon and the wife of Gen. Victoire-Emmanuel LeClerc, the French governor of Haiti. In 2012, the Haitian cultural organization FOKAL (Fondation Connaissance et Liberté / Fondasyon Konesans Ak Libète (Foundation for Knowledge and Liberty) bought Habitation Leclerc and turned it into a botanical garden.

2. I place "State" in parentheses to indicate the university's liminal status as a state–nonstate entity.

3. See Dispositions Transitoires: Relatives à l'Organisation de l'Administration Centrale de l'Université d'État d'Haïti, 1997, https://www.ueh.edu.ht/admueh/pdf/Dispositions_transitoires.pdf.

4. When I inquired about who had create the mural, I was told it was a collective effort, perhaps by UEH students.

CHAPTER 4 — *RASANBLAJ*

1. "You send your father to buy three bombs/To bombard the youth of Haiti/Who declares that the uprooting isn't over/The government council/Has Régala in it/The uprooting isn't over/The government council/Has thieves in it." The "you" addressed in the first stanza is Michèle Bennett, Jean-Claude Duvalier's ex-wife and former first lady of Haiti. "Régala" in the fifth stanza refers to Colonel Williams Régala, a macoute and Conseil National de Gouvernement (CNG) member. The song is about the unfinished campaign of dechoukaj. Special thanks to Laura Wagner for helping me contextualize this song.

2. In 2006, UEH's academic press, Éditions de l'Université d'État d'Haïti, was launched by the late scholar Hérard Jadottee, a jenerasyon 86 member who had returned from Montreal, Canada, in 1986. Since its founding, the press published or reissued nearly one hundred academic titles.

3. "Masisi" is a derogatory and reappropriated Kreyòl term for gay men and women.

4. See Mark Schuller's discussion of "radical empathy" in his 2021 book, *Humanity's Last Stand: Confronting Global Catastrophe*.

CHAPTER 5 — IMAGINING EMANCIPATORY CARIBBEAN FUTURES

1. The journal's title is a neologism that captures its mission and scope: "DO: comme dominos. Jeu d'idées qui se suivent de manière logique; KRE: parce qu'il faut creuser pour créer, même á partir du vide, du creux; I: comme dans Illustres. Portraits et entretien de personnalités créoles les unes plus illustres que les autres; and S: comme une marque du pluriel dans beaucoup de langues" (DO: like dominoes, a game of ideas that follow each other logically; KRE: because you have to dig to create, even from the void, from the hollow; I: as in Illustrious. Portraits and interviews of Creole personalities, some more well-known than the others; and S: as a plural mark in many languages) (Wêche 2017, 6).

2. Creole languages refer "to the speech varieties that developed in many of the newly created communities—the 'Creole' communities—in and around the colonial and slave-based plantations of the New World in the 17th through 19th centuries. In the Caribbean, these Creole communities emerged relatively abruptly as the result of Europe's colonization efforts, subsequent to Columbus's expeditions. Caribbean Creole languages thus developed among Europeans and Africans as restructured versions of some (erstwhile) 'target' language" (DeGraff 2005, 542).

3. Créolité extends Édouard Glissant's work, which "heralded an epistemological break [from] over-simplifying binary opposition" (McCusker 2003, 114). Following the provocation of Glissant's *Poetics and Relation*, the créolité movement rejects "notions of ancestral purity and racial authenticity, proposing the mobile and horizontally proliferating rhizome as a more appropriate metaphor of Antillean identity than the unitary root" (McCusker 2003, 114).

4. Written under the Duvalier dictatorship, Frankétienne sets the novel—*Dézafi* ("cock fight" in Kreyòl)—in a fictional Haitian village: Bouanèf. It tells the story of an uprising against a Sintil, a *houngan* (a Vodou priest). Sintil enslaved inhabitants of Bouanèf, turning them into *zonbis*. The story ends with the awakening and emancipation of the zonbis, who violently overthrow Sintil. The coded language used throughout the novel may have been a reference to the immanent overthrow of Jean-Claude Duvalier (Franklin 2019).

CODA

1. See recent updates on President Jovenel Moïse assassination at https://www.bbc.com/news/world-latin-america-57762246 and https://www.aljazeera.com/news/2024/2/20/haiti-president-moises-widow-ex-pm-among-50-charged-in-his-assassination.

References

Abetz, Jenna, and Julia Moore. 2018. "Visualizing Intersectionality through a Fractal Metaphor." In *Transgressing Feminist Theory and Discourse*, edited by Jennifer Dunn and Jimmie Manning, 31–43. London: Routledge.

Abu-Lughod, Lila. 1986/2016. *Veiled Sentiments Honor and Poetry in a Bedouin Society*. Berkeley: University of California Press.

———. 2006/1991. "Writing against Culture." In *Anthropology in Theory: Issues in Epstemology*, edited by Henrietta Moore and Todd Sanders, 466–479. Oxford: Blackwell.

Acacia, Michel. "Janvier, Louis-Joseph," translated by Carol Macomber. In *Dictionary of Caribbean and Afro–Latin American Biography*, Vol. 3, edited by Franklin W. Knight and Henry Louis Gates Jr., 380–382. Oxford, UK: Oxford University Press.

Agamben, Giorgio. 1995. *Homo Sacer: Sovereign Power and Bare Life*. Translated by Daniel Heller-Roazen. Stanford, CA: Stanford University Press.

Agard-Jones, Vanessa. 2013. "Bodies in the System." *Small Axe* 17 (3): 182–192.

Alexander, Leslie M. 2021. "Black Utopia: Haiti and Black Transnational Consciousness in the Early Nineteenth Century." *William and Mary Quarterly* 78 (2): 215–222.

———. 2022. *Fear of a Black Republic: Haiti and the Birth of Black Internationalism in the United States*. Champaign: University of Illinois Press.

Alexander, M. Jacqui. 2005. *Pedagogies of Crossings: Meditations on Feminism, Sexual Politics, Memory and the Sacred*. Durham, NC: Duke University Press.

———. 2015. "Groundings on Rasanblaj with M. Jacqui Alexander." *Caribbean Rasanblaj* (emisférica) 12 (1–2): n.p. https://hemisphericinstitute.org/en/emisferica-121-caribbean-rasanblaj/12-1-essays/e-121-essay-alexander-interview-with-gina.html.

Alexander, William. 2018. "Francophone Identity and Price Mars." In *Between Two Worlds: Jean Price-Mars, Haiti, and Africa*, edited by Celucien L. Joseph, Glodel Mezilas and Jean Eddy Saint Paul, 117–132. New York: Lexington Books.

Alexis, Yveline. 2021. *Haiti Fights Back: The Life and Legacy of Charlemagne Péralte*. New Brunswick, NJ: Rutgers University Press.

Altglas, Véronique. 2014. "'Bricolage': Reclaiming a Conceptual Tool." *Culture and Religion* 15 (4): 474–493.

REFERENCES

Amit, Vered. 2003. *Constructing the Field: Ethnographic Fieldwork in the Contemporary World*. London: Taylor & Francis, 2003.

Angulo, A. J. 2011. "Education during the American Occupation of Haiti, 1915–1934." *Historical Studies in Education / Revue d'histoire de l'éducation* 22 (2). https://doi.org/10.32316/hse/rhe.v22i2.2357.

Appadurai, Arjun. 2013. *The Future as Cultural Fact: Essays on the Global Condition*. Brooklyn, NY: Verso.

Aquilanti, Alessandra. 2011. "DLCL Writer in Residence, Lyonel Trouillot, Discusses Haitian Literature and Identity." https://dlcl.stanford.edu/news/dlcl-writer-residence-lyonel-trouillot-discusses-haitian-literature-and-identity.

Aristide, Marx, and Laurie Richardson. 1995. "Haiti's Popular Resistance." In *Haiti: Dangerous Crossroads*, edited by Deidre McFadyen, 181–194. New York: North American Congress on Latin America.

Association Vagues Littéraires. 2023. "DO KRE I S Revue Haïtienne Des Cultures Créoles." https://www.associationvagueslitteraires.org/revue-dokreis.

Barad, Karen. 2007. *Meeting the Universe Halfway Quantum Physics and the Entanglement of Matter and Meaning*. Durham, NC: Duke University Press.

Barcan, Ruth. 2013. *Academic Life and Labour in the New University: Hope and Other Choices*. Farnham, UK: Ashgate.

Baron, Amelie. 2014. "Nine Charged in 2000 Murder of Haitian Journalist Jean Dominique." January 18. https://www.reuters.com/article/us-haiti-murder-dominique/nine-charged-in-2000-murder-of-haitian-journalist-jean-dominique-idUSBREA0H0G020140118.

Barrios, Roberto. 2017. "What Does Catastrophe Reveal for Whom? The Anthropology of Crises and Disaster at the Onset of the Anthropocene." *Annual Review of Anthropology* 46:151–166.

Barthélémy, Gérard.1989. *Le pays en dehors, Essai sur l'univers rural haïtien*. Quebec City and Port-au-Prince: CIDIHCA and Éditions Henri Deschamps.

Bastide, Roger. 1970. "Mémoire collective et sociologie du bricolage." *L'Année sociologique* 65–108.

Bastien, Remy. 1961. "Haitian Rural Family Organization." *Working Papers in Caribbean Social Organization* 10 (4): 478–510.

———. 1960/2006. "The Role of the Intellectual in Haitian Plural Society." *Annals of the New York Academy of Sciences* 83:843–849.

Bauer, Andrew M., and Mona Bhan. 2018. *Climate without Nature: A Critical Anthropology of the Anthropocene*. Cambridge: Cambridge University Press.

Baur, John E. 1954. "The Presidency of Nicolas Geffrard of Haiti. *The Americas* 10 (4): 425–461.

Beasley, Myron. 2017. "Rasanblaj, Same-Sex Desire, and the Archive in Haiti." *Women and Performance*. https://www.womenandperformance.org/ampersand/myron-beasley-27-2.

Beauvoir-Dominique, Rachel. 2016. "Castor, Suzy." In *Dictionary of Caribbean and Afro-Latin American Biography*, Vol. 2, edited by Franklin W. Knight and Henry Louis Gates Jr., 86–87. Oxford: Oxford University Press.

Beckett, Greg. 2013. "Rethinking the Haitian Crisis." In *The Idea of Haiti: Rethinking Crisis and Development*, edited by Millery Polyné, 27–50. Minneapolis: University of Minnesota Press.

REFERENCES

———. 2019. *There Is No More Haiti: Between Life and Death in Port-au-Prince.* Stanford: University of California Press.

Beeton, Dan. 2012. "Soldiers without a Cause: Why Are Thousands of UN Troops Still in Haiti?" *NACLA Report on the Americas* 45 (1): 6–11.

Bélizaire, Assédius. 2016. "L'Image Revelee." *Revue Trois/Cent/Soixante: Haïti de l'intérieur, de l'autre bord et sur le fil* 1:38–39.

Bell, Marvin. 1997. "About the Dead Man Poems ("The Book of the Dead Man #70")." In *Introspections: American Poets on One of Their Own Poems,* edited by Robert Pack and Jay Parini, 42–47. Hanover, NH: Middlebury College Press.

Bellegarde-Smith, Patrick. 2013. "Dynastic Dictatorship: The Duvalier Years, 1957–1986." *Haitian History: New Perspectives,* 273–284.

Bellegarde-Smith, Patrick, and Claudine Michel, eds. 2006. *Haitian Vodou: Spirit, Myth, and Reality.* Bloomington: Indiana University Press.

Benedicty, Alessandra. 2015. "Male Protagonists and Haitian (Un)inhabitability in Ketly Mars's *L'Heure hybride* and *Aux fronières de la soif.*" *Francosphères* 4 (1): 105–120.

Benhabib, Seyla. 1986. *Critique, Norm, and Utopia: A Study of the Foundations of Critical Theory.* New York: Columbia University Press.

Benjamin, Harold R. W. 1964. "Higher Education in Latin America." *Phi Delta Kappan* 45 (4): 178–182.

Bernabe, Jean, Patrick Chamoiseau, and Raphael Confiant. 1989. *Éloge de la créolité.* Paris: Gallimard.

———. 1990. "In Praise of Creoleness." Translated by Mohamed B. Taleb Khyar. *Callaloo* 13 (4): 886–909.

Bernard, Jacob Jean. 1989. *Higher Education in Haiti, 1958–1988: An Analysis of Its Organization, Administration and Contributions to National Development.* Ph.D. diss., University of North Texas.

Blackledge, Adrian, and Angela Creese. 2022. "The Potential of Ethnographic Drama in the Representation, Interpretation, and Democratization of Sociolinguistic Research." *Journal of Sociolinguistics* 26 (5): 586–603.

Boisvert, Jayne. 2001. "Colonial Hell and Female Slave Resistance in Saint-Domingue." *Journal of Haitian Studies* 7 (1): 61–76.

Bond, George C. 1976. *The Politics of Change in a Zambian Community.* Chicago: University of Chicago Press.

Bond, George C., and Jo Anne Kleifgen, eds. 2009. *The Languages of Africa and the Diaspora: Educating for Language Awareness.* London: Multilingual Matters.

Bonilla, Yarimar. 2013. "Ordinary Sovereignty." *Small Axe* 42:152–165.

———. 2015. *Non-Sovereign Futures: French Caribbean Politics in the Wake of Disenchantment.* Chicago: University of Chicago Press.

———. 2019. *Aftershocks of Disaster: Puerto Rico Before and After the Storm.* Chicago: Haymarket Books.

Bourdieu, Pierre. 1997. "The Forms of Capital." In *Education: Culture, Economy, Society,* edited by A. H. Halsey, Hugh Lauder, Phillip Brown, and Amy Stuart Wells, 46–58. Oxford: Oxford University Press.

Bolles, Lynn Augusta. 2022. *Women and Tourist Work in Jamaica: Seven Miles of Sandy Beach.* New York: Lexington Books.

Boyer, Dominic, and Claudio Lomnitz. 2005. "Intellectuals and Nationalism: Anthropological Engagements." *Annual Review of Anthropology* 34 (1): 105–120.

Braithwaite, Lloyd. 1958. "The Development of Higher Education in the British West Indies." *Social and Economic Studies* 7 (1): 1–64.

Britannica, T. Editors of Encyclopaedia. 2022. "Jean Price Mars." *Encyclopaedia Britannica.* https://www.britannica.com/biography/Jean-Price-Mars.

Brodwin, Paul. 2003. Marginality and Subjectivity in the Haitian Diaspora. *Anthropological Quarterly* 76 (3): 383–410.

Brown, Adrienne Maree. 2017. *Emergent Strategy: Shaping Change, Changing Worlds.* Chino, CA: AK Press.

Brown, Elspeth H., and Thy Phu. 2014. *Feeling Photography.* Durham, NC: Duke University Press.

Bruno, Tianna, Andrew Curley, Mabel Denzin Gergan, and Sara Smith. 2023. "The Work of Repair: Land, Relation, and Pedagogy." *Cultural Geographies* 31 (1): 5–19.

Bryant, Levi R. 2016. "Phenomenon and Thing: Barad's Performative Ontology." *Rhizomes* 30 (1): 1–14. http://www.rhizomes.net/issue30/bryant.html.

Bryant, Rebecca, and Daniel M. Knight. 2019. *The Anthropology of the Future.* Cambridge: Cambridge University Press.

Buchanan, Ian. 2010. "Bare Life (nuda vita)." *A Dictionary of Critical Theory.* Oxford: Oxford University Press.

Buteau, Pierre, Rodney Saint-Éloi, and Lyonel Trouillot. 2010. *Refonder Haïti?* Montreal, Quebec: Mémoire d'encrier.

Butler, Philip, ed. 2021. *Critical Black Futures: Speculative Theories and Explorations.* New York: Springer Nature.

Byron, Jhon Picard. 2010. "La pansée de Jean Price-Mars: Entre construction politique de la nation et affirmation de l'identité culturelle haïtienne." In *Production du sovoir et construction sociale: L'ethnologie en Haïti,* edited by Jhon Picard Byron, 47–82. Port-au-Prince: Éditions de l'Université d'État d'Haïti.

Cable News Network (CNN). 2022. "Editorial Research. Haiti Fast Facts." October 19. https://www.cnn.com/2013/10/17/world/americas/haiti-fast-facts/index.html.

Carter, Donald Martin. 2010. *Navigating the African Diaspora: The Anthropology of Invisibility.* Minneapolis: University of Minnesota Press.

Casimir, Jean. 2020. *The Haitians: A Decolonial History.* Translated by Laurent Dubois. Durham, NC: University of North Carolina Press.

Casimir, Jean, Eglantine Colon, and Michelle Koerner. 2011. "Haiti's Need for a Great South." *The Global South* 5 (1), Special Issue: *The Global South and World Dis/Order,* 14–36.

Castellanos, M. Bianet. 2020. *Indigenous Dispossession: Housing and Maya Indebtedness in Mexico.* Stanford, CA: Stanford University Press.

Castor, Suzy. 1978. *La ocupacion norteamericana de haiti y sus consecuencias 1915–1934.* Havana, Cuba: Casa de las Americas.

———. 1987. *Les origines de la structure agraire en Haïti.* Port-au-Prince: Centre de Recherche et de Formation Economique et Sociale pour le Développement (CRESFED).

———. 1988. *L'Occupation américaine d'Haïti.* Port-au-Prince: Centre de Recherche et de Formation Economique et Sociale pour le Développement (CRESFED).

———. 1994. *Les femmes haïtiennes aux élections de 1986.* Port-au-Prince: Centre de Recherche et de Formation Economique et Sociale pour le Développement (CRESFED).

Castor, Suzy, Monique Brisson, and Morna McLeod. 1998. *Femme: Société et legislation.* Port-au-Prince: Centre de Recherche et de Formation Economique et Sociale pour le Développement (CRESFED).

REFERENCES

Cate, Leandra, LaWanda Ward, and Karly S. Ford. 2022. "Strategic Ambiguity: How Pre-Tenure Faculty Negotiate the Hidden Rules of Academia." *Innovative High Education* 47:795–812.

Cela, Toni. 2016. *(Re)conceptualizing Higher Education in Post-disaster Contexts: A Processual Analysis of Diaspora Engagement in Haiti's Reconstruction.* [Dissertation] ProQuest.

———. 2021. "Higher Education Reform and Diasporic Engagement in Post-earthquake Haiti." *International Studies in Sociology of Education* 32 (2): 239–266.

Chalmers, Mehdi E. 2016. "Editorial." *Revue Trois/Cent/Soixante: Haïti de l'intérieur, de l'autre bord et sur le fil* 1:3.

———. 2019. *Mer libre et autres lieux imaginaires.* Paris: Le Temps des Cerises.

Chalmers, Mehdi. Chantal Kenol, Jean-Laurent Lhérisson, and Lyonel Trouillot. 2015. *Anthologie bilingue de la poésie créole haïtienne de 1986 à nos jours.* Atelier jeudi soir (Haiti). Paris: Coédition Actes Sud.

Chancy, Myriam J. A. 1997. *Framing Silence: Revolutionary Novels by Haitian Women.* New Brunswick, NJ: Rutgers University Press.

———. 2012. *From Sugar to Revolution: Women's Visions of Haiti, Cuba, and the Dominican Republic.* Canada: Wilfrid Laurier University Press, 2012.

Charlemagne, Manno. 1990. "Ayiti Pa Forè." Track 6 on *Oganizasyon Mondyal*, Mini Records, digital recording, 3:47. https://open.spotify.com/album/3nwosSVAxrmUSwotyg B28Z.

Charles, Asselin. 2016. "Firmin, Joseph Anténor." In *Dictionary of Caribbean and Afro-Latin American Biography*, Vol. 2, edited by Franklin W. Knight and Henry Louis Gates Jr., 27–30. Oxford, UK: Oxford University Press.

Charles, Carolle. 1995. "Gender and Politics in Contemporary Haiti: The Duvalierist State, Transnationalism, and the Emergence of a New Feminism (1980–1990)." *Feminist Studies* 21 (1): 135–164.

Chattoraj, Diotima. 2022. *Displacement among Sri Lankan Tamil Migrants: The Diasporic Search for Home in the Aftermath of War.* Singapore: Springer Nature Singapore.

Clément, Job B. 1979a. "History of Education in Haiti: 1804–1915 (First Part)." *Revista de Historia de América* 87:141–181.

———. 1979b. "History of Education in Haiti: 1804–1915." *Revista de Historia de América* 88:33–74.

Clifford, James. 1994. "Diaspora." *Cultural Anthropology* 9 (3): 302–338.

Clifford, James, and Marcus, George E., eds. 1986. *Writing Culture: The Poetics and Politics of Ethnography.* Berkeley: University of California Press.

Clitandre, Nadège T. 2011. "Haitian Exceptionalism in the Caribbean and the Project of Rebuilding Haiti." *Journal of Haitian Studies* 17 (2): 146–153.

Coates, Chad O. 2012. "Educational Developments in the British West Indies: A Historical Overview." Bulgarian Comparative Education Society, 347–352. https://files.eric.ed .gov/fulltext/ED567093.pdf.

Cobley, Alan. 2000. "The Historical Development of Higher Education in the Anglophone Caribbean." In *Higher Education in the Caribbean: Past, Present and Future Directions*, edited by Glenford D. Howe, 1–23. Kingston, Jamaica: University of the West Indies.

Cocco, Massimo, Stefano Aretusini, Chiara Cornelio, Stefan B. Nielsen, Elena Spagnuolo, Elisa Tinti, and Giulio Di Toro. 2023. "Fracture Energy and Breakdown Work during Earthquakes." *Annual Review of Earth and Planetary Sciences* 51 (1): 217–252.

"The Code Noir (The Black Code)." 1685. *Liberty, Equality, Fraternity: Exploring the French Revolution*. https://revolution.chnm.org/d/335/.

Collins, Patricia Hill. 1986. "Learning from the Outsider Within: The Sociological Significance of Black Feminist Thought." *Social Problems* 33 (6): S14–32.

Collyer, Fran M. 2018. "Global Patterns in the Publishing of Academic Knowledge: Global North, Global South." *Current Sociology* 66 (1): 56–73.

Concordato fra Pio IX e la Repubblica di Haiti (28.03.1860). http://canonlaw.byethost7 .com/k/haiti-1860.pdf?i=1.

Cordero, Rodrigo. 2016. *Crisis and Critique on the Fragile Foundations of Social Life*. London: Taylor & Francis.

Corwin, Julia E., and Vinay Gidwani. 2024. "Repair Work as Care: On Maintaining the Planet in the Capitalocene." *Antipode*. https://doi.org/10.1111/anti.12791.

Courouve, Claude. 1998. "Démocratie et anarchie dans les cafés de philosophie." *Esprit* 239:200–205.

Cox, Aimee Meredith. 2015. *Shapeshifters: Black Girls and the Choreography of Citizenship*. Durham, NC: Duke University Press.

Crawley, Ashon T. 2016. *Blackpentecostal Breath: The Aesthetics of Possibility*. New York: Fordham University Press.

Crichlow, Michaeline A. 2012. "Making Waves: (Dis)Placements, Entanglements, Movements." *The Global South* 6 (1): 114–137.

Dain, Beatrica, and Jeanne Batalova. 2023. "Haitian Immigrants in the United States." Migration Policy Institute. https://www.migrationpolicy.org/article/haitian-immigrants -united-states.

Dalembert, Louis-Philippe, and Lyonel Trouillot. 2010. *Haïti, une traversée littéraire*. Paris: Éditions Philippe Rey.

Daniel, Valentine E. 1997. *Charred Lullabies: Chapters in an Anthropography of Violence*. Princeton, NJ: Princeton University Press.

Danticat, Edwidge. 2011. *Create Dangerously: The Immigrant Artist at Work*. New York: Knopf Doubleday Publishing Group.

Dash, J. Michael. 1981. *Literature and Ideology in Haiti, 1915–1961*. London: Palgrave Macmillan.

———. 1988. *Haiti and the United States: National Stereotypes and the Literary Imagination*. New York: St. Martin's Press.

———. 1992. "Engagement, Exile and Errance: Some Trends in Haitian Poetry 1946–1986." *Callaloo* 15 (3): 747–760.

Daswani, Girish. 2013. "The Anthropology of Transnationalism and Diaspora." In *A Companion to Diaspora and Transnationalism*, edited by Ato Quayson and Girish Daswani. New York: Wiley-Blackwell.

Daut, Marlene. 2015. *Tropics of Haiti: Race and the Literary History of the Haitian Revolution in the Atlantic World, 1789–1865*. Liverpool, UK: Liverpool University Press.

———. 2016. "Caribbean 'Race Men': Louis Joseph Janvier, Demesvar Delorme, and the Haitian Atlantic." *L'Esprit Créateur* 36:9–23.

———. 2021. "When France Extorted Haiti—The Greatest Heist in History." *The Conversation*. June 30. https://theconversation.com/when-france-extorted-haiti-the-greatest -heist-in-history-137949.

———.2023. *Awakening the Ashes: An Intellectual History of the Haitian Revolution*. Chapel Hill: The University of North Carolina Press.

REFERENCES

Dayan, Joan. 1995. *Haiti, History, and the Gods*. Berkeley: University of California Press.

Decena, Carlos Ulises. 2023. *Circuits of the Sacred: A Faggotology in the Black Latinx Caribbean*. Durham, NC: Duke University Press.

DeGraff, Michel 2001 "On the Origin of Creoles: A Cartesian Critique of Neo-Darwinian Linguistics." *Linguistic Typology* 5 (2–3): 213–310.

———. 2005. "Linguists' Most Dangerous Myth: The Fallacy of Creole Exceptionalism." *Language in Society* 34:533–591.

———. 2009. "Language Acquisition in Creolization and, Thus, Language Change: Some Cartesian-Uniformitarian Boundary Conditions." *Language and Linguistics Compass* 3 (4): 888–971.

———. 2005. "Linguists' Most Dangerous Myth: The Fallacy of Creole Exceptionalism." *Language in Society* 34:533–591.

Delgado, Richard. 1984. "The Imperial Scholar: Reflections on a Review of Civil Rights Literature." *University of Pennsylvania Law Review* 132:561–578.

DeLuca, Kevin. 1999. "Articulation Theory: A Discursive Grounding for Rhetorical Practice." *Philosophy & Rhetoric* 32 (4): 334–348.

Denis, Watson R. 2006. "Reviewed Work: The Equality of the Human Races. (Positivist Anthropology) by Anténor Firmin, Asselin Charles." *Caribbean Studies* 32 (1): 325–334.

Denzin, Norman K. 1997. *Interpretive Ethnography: Ethnographic Practices for the 21st Century*. Thousand Oaks, CA: Sage Publications.

Deshommes, Fritz. 2010. *Salaire minimum et sous-traitance en Haïti*. Port-au-Prince: Éditions Cahiers Universitaires.

———. 2011. *Et si la Constitution de 1987 était porteuse de refondation?* Port-au-Prince: Éditions Cahiers Universitaires.

Désir, Charlene. 2011. "Diasporic Lakou: A Haitian Academic Explores Her Path to Haiti Pre-and Post-Earthquake." *Harvard Educational Review* 81 (2): 278–387.

Diament, Jacques. 2003. *Les "Cafés De Philosophie" une forme inédite de socialisation par la philosophie*. Paris: L'Harmattan.

Diawara, Manthia. 2021. "Tropiques and the Surrealist Movement in Martinique." *Nka: Journal of Contemporary African Art* 49: 202–208.

Dirksen, Rebecca. 2019. *After the Dance, the Drums Are Heavy: Carnival, Politics, and Musical Engagement in Haiti*. Oxford: Oxford University Press.

Dirlik, Arif. 2002. "Rethinking Colonialism: Globalization, Postcolonialism, and the Nation." *Interventions* 4 (3): 428–448.

Dougé-Prosper, Mamyrah, and Mark Schuller. 2021. "End of Empire? A View from Haiti." *NACLA Report on the Americas* 53 (1): 1–6.

Douglas, Rachel. 2022. "Futures in the Presents: Decolonial Visions of the Haitian Revolution." *Interventions* 24 (7): 1029–1052.

Downie, Andrew. 2012. "Haitian Universities Struggles to Rebound." *Chronicle of Higher Education* 58 (18): A8.

Drumhiller, Casey, and Nicole K. Skvorc. 2018. "A Psychological and Political Analysis of a 20th Century 'Doctator': Dr. François Duvalier, President-for-Life of Haiti." *Global Security & Intelligence Studies* 3 (1): 9–32.

Dubois, Laurent. 2004. *Avengers of the New World: The Story of the Haitian Revolution*. Cambridge, MA: Harvard University Press.

———. 2012. *Haiti: The Aftershocks of History*. New York: Henry Holt and Company.

Dubois, Laurent, Kaiama L. Glover, Nadève Ménard, Millery Polyné, and Chantalle F. Verna. 2020. *The Haiti Reader: History, Culture, Politics.* Durham, NC: Duke University Press.

Dubuisson, Darlène Elizabeth. 2020. "'We Know How to Work Together': Konbit, Protest, and the Rejection of INGO Bureaucratic Dominance." *Journal of Haitian Studies* 26 (2): 54–80.

———. 2022a. "Ethnography In-Sight and Sound: Rasanblaj and the Poetics of Creole Orality." *The Journal of Latin American and Caribbean Anthropology* 27 (3): 220–226.

———. 2022b. "The Haitian Zombie Motif: Against the Banality of Antiblack Violence." *Journal of Visual Culture* 21 (2): 255–276.

Dupuy Alex. 2001. "Haiti: Social Crisis and Population Displacement." *WRITENET Paper* (18).

———. 2007. *The Prophet and the Power: Jean-Bertrand Aristide, the International Community, and Haiti.* New York: Rowman and Littlefield.

———. 2012. "The Neoliberal Legacy in Haiti." In *Tectonic Shifts: Haiti Since the Earthquake*, edited by Mark Schuller and Pablo Morales. 23–27. New York: Kumarian Press.

———. 2013. "From François Duvalier to Jean-Bertrand Aristide: The Declining Significance of Color Politics in Haiti." In *Politics and Power in Haiti. Studies of the Americas*, edited by Kate Quinn and Paul Sutton. 44–63. New York: Palgrave Macmillan.

———. 2019. *Rethinking the Haitian Revolution: Slavery, Independence, and the Struggle for Recognition.* Lanham, MD: Rowman and Littlefield.

Eastmond, Marita. 2006. "Transnational Returns and Reconstruction in Post-war Bosnia and Herzegovina." *International Migration* 44:141–166.

Eddins, Crystal Nicole. 2021. *Rituals, Runaways, and the Haitian Revolution: Collective Action in the African Diaspora.* Cambridge: Cambridge University Press.

Egerton, Douglas R. 2005. "Caribbean Dreams, Haitian Nightmares." *Atlantic Studies* 2 (2): 111–128.

Eller, Anne. 2021. "Skirts Rolled Up: The Gendered Terrain of Politics in Nineteenth-Century Port-au-Prince." *Small Axe* 25 (1 (64)): 61–83.

Fabian, Johannes. 1983/2014. *Time and the Other: How Anthropology Makes Its Object.* New York: Columbia University Press.

Fagg, John E. 2022. "Toussaint Louverture." *Encyclopedia Britannica.* https://www.britannica.com/biography/Toussaint-Louverture.

Fass, Simon. 1988. *Political Economy in Haiti: The Drama of Survival.* New Brunswick, NJ: Transaction Publishers.

Fatton, Robert. 2014. *Haiti: Trapped in the Outer Periphery.* Boulder, CO: Lynne Rienner Publishers.

Faubert, Carrol. 2004. *Case Study Haiti: Evaluation of UNDP Assistance to Conflict-Affected Countries.* New York: United Nations Development Programme Evaluation Office. https://www.oecd.org/countries/haiti/44826404.pdf.

Feierman, Steven. 1990. *Peasant Intellectuals: Anthropology and History in Tanzania.* Madison: University of Wisconsin Press.

Felima, Crystal. A. 2022. "Teaching Haitian Studies and Caribbean Digital Humanities: A Rasanblaj of Critical Pedagogical Approaches and Black Feminist Theory in the Classroom." *Taboo: The Journal of Culture and Education* 21 (1): 14–28.

REFERENCES

Ferrer, Ada. 2009. "Speaking of Haiti: Slavery and Freedom in Cuban Slave Testimony." In *The World of the Haitian Revolution*, edited by David Geggus and Norman Fiering. Bloomingston: University of Indiana Press.

———. 2014. *Freedom's Mirror: Cuba and Haiti in the Age of Revolution*. Cambridge: Cambridge University Press.

Figueroa, Yomaira C. 2015. "Reparation as Transformation: Radical Literary (Re)imaginings of Ruturities through Decolonial Love." *Decolonization: Indigeneity, Education & Society* 4 (1): 41–58.

Firmin, Anténor. 1885. *De l'égalité des races humaines: Anthropologie positive*. Paris: F. Pichon.

Fischer, Sibylle. 2013 "Haiti Fantasies of Bare Life." In *The Idea of Haiti: Rethinking Crisis and Development*, edited by Millery Polyné, 68–86. Minneapolis: University of Minnesota Press.

Fischlin, Daniel, Ajay Heble, and George Lipsitz. 2013. *The Fierce Urgency of Now: Improvisation, Rights, and the Ethics of Cocreation*. Durham, NC: Duke University Press.

Fluehr-Lobban, Carolyn. 2000. "Anténor Firmin: Haitian Pioneer of Anthropology." *American Anthropologist* 102:449–466.

———. 2002. "Introduction." In *The Equality of the Human Races: Positivist Anthropology* by Anténor Firmin. Translated by Charles Asselin. Champaign: University of Illinois Press.

———. 2005a. *Race and Racism: An Introduction*. New York: AltaMira Press.

———. 2005b. "Anténor Firmin and Haiti's Contribution to Anthropology." *Gradhiva* (December): 95–108.

Frankétienne.1975/2018. *Dézafi*. Translated by Asselin Charles. Charlottesville: University of Virginia Press.

Franklin, Jocelyn. 2019. "Review of Dézafi, by Frankétienne." *Journal of Haitian Studies* 25 (2): 282–284.

Gacel-Ávila, Jocelyne. 2007. "The Process of Internationalization of Latin American Higher Education." *Journal of Studies in International Education* 11 (3–4): 400–409.

Gaffield, Julia. 2015. *Haitian Connections in the Atlantic World: Recognition after Revolution*. Chapel Hill: University of North Carolina Press.

Gasseling, Kelsey. 2017. "The Threads of Justice: Economic Liberalization and the Second-hand Clothing Trade between the United States and Haiti." *Boston College Law Review* 1279–1319.

Gill, Lyndon K., and Gina Athena Ulysse. 2023. "Bwapin Rasanblaj: A Curated Conversation." *Feminist Studies* 49 (2): 328–351.

Gilles, Alain. 1990. *Popular Movements and Political Development in Haiti*. New York: Columbia University-New York University Consortium.

Gilroy, Paul. 1993. *The Black Atlantic: Modernity and Double-Consciousness*. Cambridge, MA: Harvard University Press.

———. 1994. "Diaspora." *Paragraph* 17 (3): 207–212.

Girard, Philippe. 2009. "Rebelles with a Cause: Women in the Haitian War of Independence, 1802–04." *Gender & History* 21:60–85.

Giroux, Henry A. 2002. "Neoliberalism, Corporate Culture, and the Promise of Higher Education: The University as a Democratic Public Sphere." *Harvard Educational Review* 72 (4): 425–463.

Glick Schiller, Nancy, Linda Basch, and Christina S. Blanc. 1995. "From Immigration to Transmigrant: Theorizing Transnational Migration." *Anthropological Quarterly* 68 (1): 48–63.

Glick Schiller, Nancy, and Georges E. Fouron, G. 1990. "'Everywhere We Go, We Are in Danger:' Ti Manno and the Emergence of Haitian Transnational Identity." *American Ethnologist* 17 (2): 329–347.

———. 1999. "Terrains of Blood and Nation: Haitian Transnational Social Fields." *Ethnic and Racial Studies* 22 (2): 340–367.

———. 2001. *Georges Woke Up Laughing: Long-Distance Nationalism and the Search for Home.* Durham, NC: Duke University Press.

Glissant, Edouard.1989. *Caribbean Discourse.* Charlottesville: University of Virginia Press.

Glover, Kaiama L. 2010. *Haiti Unbound: A Spiralist Challenge to the Postcolonial Canon.* London, UK: Liverpool University Press.

———. 2013. "'Black' Radicalism in Haiti and the Disorderly Feminine: The Case of Marie Vieux Chauvet." *Small Axe* 17 (1 (40)): 7–21.

Goldstein, Thalia R., and Bloom, Paul. 2011. "The Mind on Stage: Why Cognitive Scientists Should Study Acting." *Trends in Cognitive Sciences* 15 (4): 141–142.

Green, Paula Patricia. 2016. *The Impact of Internationalization on the Regionalization of Higher Education in the English Speaking Caribbean: A Case Study of the University of the West Indies.* University of Toronto (Canada). Dissertation.

Greenburg, Jennifer. 2016. "'The One Who Bears the Scars Remembers': Haiti and the Historical Geography of US Militarized Development." *Journal of Historical Geography* 51:52–63.

Gros, Jean-Germain. 2000. "Haiti: The Political Economy and Sociology of Decay and Renewal." *Latin American Research Review* 35 (3): 211–226.

Guo, Fei, Robyn R. Iredale, and Santi Rozario. 2003. *Return Migration in the Asia Pacific.* London: Edward Elgar.

Guruz, Kemal. 2011. *Higher Education and International Student Mobility in the Global Knowledge Econom.* Albany: State University of New York Press.

Gwaltney, John Langston. 1993. *Drylongso: A Self Portrait of Black America.* New York: New Press.

Hackl, Andreas. 2017. "Key Figures of Mobility: The Exile." *Social Anthropology* 25:55–68.

Haitian Constitution 1805. In *Caribbean Political Thought: The Colonial State to Caribbean Internationalisms,* edited by Aaron Kamugisha (2013), 1–4. Kingston, Jamaica: Ian Randle Publishers.

Haitian Constitution rev. 1987. https://pdba.georgetown.edu/Constitutions/Haiti/haiti1987.html.

Haitian Studies Association. 2024. *Mission and Vision.* https://www.haitianstudies.org/about/mission-and-vision/.

HaïtiLibre. 2015. "Haiti-Security: BOID, a New Specialized Police Brigade," June 25. https://www.haitilibre.com/en/news-14314-haiti-security-boid-a-new-specialized-police-brigade.html.

———. 2016. "Illegal Occupation, UEH Announces First Sanctions," November 15. https://www.haitilibre.com/en/news-19229-haiti-education-illegal-occupation-ueh-announces-first-sanctions.html.

REFERENCES 173

Hall, Stuart. 2003. "Cultural Identity and Diaspora." In *Theorizing Diaspora: A Reader*, edited by Jana Evans Braziel and Anita Mannur, 233–246. Oxford: Blackwell.

———. 2015. *Creolité and the Process of Creolization.* Vols. 12–25, In *Creolizing Europe: Legacies and Transformation*, edited by Encarnación Gutiérrez Rodríguez and Shirley Anne Tate. Liverpool, UK: Liverpool University Press.

Haney, Jennifer, and John Bodenman. "Creating Markets for Recylable Materials: Municipal Solid Waste in Haiti." *Middle States Geographer* 50:17–27.

Harrison, Faye V, ed. 1991. *Decolonizing Anthropology: Moving Further Toward an Anthropology for Liberation.* Arlington, VA: Association of American Anthropology.

———. 2008. *Outsider Within: Reworking Anthropology in the Global Age.* Champaign: University of Illinois.

———. 2016. "Theorizing from Ex-centric Sites." *Anthropological Theory* 16 (2–3): 160–176.

Harrison, Ira E., and Faye V. Harrison, eds. 1999. *African-American Pioneers in Anthropology.* Champaign: University of Illinois Press.

Harrison, Ira E., Deborah Johnson-Simon, and Erica Lorraine Williams, eds. 2018. *The Second Generation of African American Pioneers in Anthropology.* Champaign: University of Illinois.

Harrison, Nicholas. *Our Civilizing Mission: The Lessons of Colonial Education.* Liverpool, UK: Liverpool University Press.

Hartman, Saidiya. 2008. *Lose Your Mother: A Journey Along the Atlantic Slave Route.* New York: Farrar, Straus and Giroux.

Heinrich, Bernd. 2014. *The Homing Instinct: Meaning and Mystery in Animal Migration.* Boston: Houghton Mifflin Harcourt.

Herbeck, Jason. 2017. *Architextual Authenticity: Constructing Literature and Literary Identity in the French Caribbean.* Liverpool, UK: Liverpool University Press.

Hickling-Hudson, Anne. 1989. "Education in the Grenada Revolution: 1979-83." *Compare: A Journal of Comparative and International Education* 19 (2): 95–114.

Horne, Gerald. 2015a. *Confronting Black Jacobins: The U.S., the Haitian Revolution, and the Origins of the Dominican Republic.* New York: Monthly Review Press.

———. 2015b. "The Haitian Revolution and the Central Question of African American History." *The Journal of African American History* 100 (1): 26–58.

Horst, Heather. 2007. "'You can't be in two places at once': Rethinking Transnationalism through Jamaican Return Migration." *Identities: Global Studies in Culture and Power,* 14: 63–83.

Howe, Glenford D., ed. 2000. *Higher Education in the Caribean: Past, Present, and Future Directions.* Barbados: Univerity of the West Indies Press.

Hurbon, Laënnec. 1972. *Dieu dans le audoux haïtien.* Paris: M. Palau-Marti.

———. 1987. *Comprendre Haiti: essai sur lètat, la nation, la culture.* Paris: Karthala.

———. 1995. *Voodoo: Search for the Spirit.* New York: Abrams Discoveries

Hurston, Zora Neale. 1928. "How It Feels to Be Colored Me." *World Tomorrow* 11: 215–216.

———. 1935/2009. *Mules and Men.* New York: HarperCollins.

———. 1938/1990. *Tell My Horse: Voodoo and Life in Haiti and Jamaica.* New York: HarperCollins.

Ignatieff, Michael. 1997. "Decline and Fall of the Public Intellectual." *Queen's Quarterly* 104 (3): 394–340.

Interuniversity Institute for Research and Development (INURED). 2010. *The Challenge for Haitian Higher Education: A Post-Earthquake Assessment of Higher Education Institutions in the Port-au-Prince Metropolitan Area.* https://www.inured.org/uploads/2/5/2/6/25266591/the_challenge_for_haitian_higher_education.pdf.

Jackson, Regine, ed. 2010. *Geographies of the Haitian Diaspora.* New York: Routledge.

Jacob, Sergot. 2020. "Massification and the Public Financing of Higher Education in Haiti: Issues and Challenges." *International Review of Administrative Sciences* 86 (2): 349–367.

Jadotte, Evans. 2009. "International Migration, Remittances and Labour Supply: The Case of the Republic of Haiti." *WIDER Research Paper* (2009/28): 1–22.

James, C.L.R. 1938/1989. *The Black Jacobins: Toussaint L'Ouverture and the San Domingo Revolution.* New York: Knopf Doubleday Publishing Group.

James, Erica Caple. 2010. *Democratic Insecurities: Violence, Trauma, and Intervention in Haiti.* Berkeley: University of California Press.

Janvier, Louis-Joseph. 1884/2023. *Haiti for the Haitians.* Edited by Brandon R. Byrd and Chelsea Stieber. Translated by Nadève Ménard. Liverpool, UK: Liverpool University Press.

Jaupart, Pascal. 2023. *International Migration in the Caribbean.* Background paper. Washington, DC: The World Bank.

Jean-Charles, Régine Michelle. 2022. *Looking for Other Worlds: Black Feminism and Haitian Fiction.* Charlottesville: University of Virginia Press.

Joseph, Celucien L. 2016. "Hurbon, Laënnec." In *Dictionary of Caribbean and Afro–Latin American Biography*, Vol. 2, edited by Franklin W. Knight and Henry Louis Gates Jr., 330–332. Oxford: Oxford University Press.

Joseph, Celucien, Glodel Mezilas, and Jean Eddy Saint Paul, eds. 2018. *Between Two Worlds: Jean Price-Mars, Haiti, and Africa.* New York: Lexington Books.

Kabel, Ahmed. 2022. "From Neoliberal to Decolonial Language Rights and Reparative Linguistic Justice." *The Handbook of Linguistic Human Rights* (2022): 159–173.

Kadish, Doris Y., and Deborah Jenson, eds. 2015. *Poetry of Haitian Independence.* New Haven, CT: Yale University Press.

Kamugisha, Aaron. 2019. *Beyond Coloniality: Citizenship and Freedom in the Caribbean Intellectual Tradition.* Bloomington: Indiana University Press.

Kecskemeti, Paul. 1972. "Introduction." In *Karl Mannheim: Essays*, edited, introduced, and translated by Paul Kecskemeti, 22–24. New York: Routledge.

Keeling, Kara. 2019. *Queer Times, Black Futures.* New York: New York University Press.

Kelley, Robin D. G. 2000. "Foreword: Why Black Marxism? Why Now?" In *Black Marxism, Revised and Updated Third Edition: The Making of the Black Radical Tradition* by Cedric J. Robinson. Chapel Hill: University of North Carolina Press.

———. 2002. *Freedom Dream: The Black Radical Imagination.* Boston: Beacon Press.

Khan, Aisha. 2001. "Journey to the Center of the Earth: The Caribbean as Master Symbol." *Cultural Anthropology* 16:271–302.

Knepper, Wendy. 2006. "Colonization, Creolization, and Globalization: The Art and Ruses of Bricolage." *Small Axe* 10 (3): 70–86.

Knight, Franklin W. 2005. "The Haitian Revolution and the Notion of Human Rights." *Journal of the Historical Society* 5:391–416.

Koselleck, Reinhart. 1988. *Critique and Crisis: Enlightenment and the Pathogenesis of Modern Society.* Cambridge, MA: MIT Press.

REFERENCES

Koselleck, Reinhart, and Michael Richter. 2006. "Crisis." *Journal of the History of Ideas* 67 (2): 357–400.

Kreber, Carolin. 2010. *The University and Its Disciplines: Teaching and Learning within and beyond Disciplinary Boundaries.* New York: Routledge.

Kuehn, Kathleen M., and Leon A. Salter. 2020. "Assessing Digital Threats to Democracy, and Workable Solutions: A Review of the Recent Literature." *International Journal of Communication* 1 (14): 2589–2610.

Laguerre, Michel S. 1984. *American Odyssey: Haitians in New York City.* Ithaca, NY: Cornell University Press.

———. 1998. *Diasporic Citizenship: Haitian Americans in Transnational America.* London: Palgrave Macmillan UK.

Lahens, Yanick. 1990. *L'exil entre l'ancrage et la fuite.* Port-au-Prince: Deschamps.

———. 1992. "Exile: Between Writing and Place." Translated by Cheryl Thomas and Paulette Richard. *Callaloo* 15 (3): 735–746.

———. 2010. *Failles.* Paris: Sabine Wespieser Editeur.

———. 2013. *Guillaume et Nathalie: Roman.* Paris: Sabine Wespieser Editeur.

———. 2020. "Faults." In *The Haiti Reader: History, Culture, Politics,* edited by Laurent Dubois, Kaiama L. Glover, Nadève Ménard, Millery Polyné and Chantalle F. Verna, 470–475. Durham, NC: Duke University Press.

Lamour, Sabine. 2021. "The Toxic Masculinity of the 'Legal Bandit.'" *NACLA Report on the Americas* 53 (1): 86–91.

Laraque, Paul. 2001. Introduction to *Open Gate: An Anthology of Haitian Creole Poetry (Creole and English Edition),* edited by Paul Laraque and Jack Hirschman, xiii–xvi. Willimantic, CT: Curbstone.

Laurent, Gérard Mentor. 1949. *Coup d'œil sur la politique de Toussaint-Louverture.* Port-au-Prince: Deschamps.

Lavietes, Matthew. 2019. "Leading LGBT+ Activist Found Dead in Haiti." *Thomson Reuters Foundation News.* November 19. https://news.trust.org/item/20191126215929-83jib/.

Lemay-Hébert, Nicolas. 2018. "Living in the Yellow Zone: The Political Geography of Intervention in Haiti." *Political Geography* 67:88–99.

Le Nouvelliste. 2014. "Zoom sur Café Philo Haïti." December 11. https://lenouvelliste .com/article/137979/zoom-sur-cafe-philo-haiti.

Lévi-Strauss, Claude. 1966. *The Savage Mind.* Chicago: University of Chicago Press.

Li, Wei, Lucia Lo, Yixi Lu, Yining Tan, and Zheng Lu. 2021. "Intellectual Migration: Considering China." *Journal of Ethnic and Migration Studies* 47 (12): 2833–2853.

Logan, Rayford Whittingham. 1941. *The Diplomatic Relations of the United States with Haiti, 1776–1891.* Chapel Hill: University of North Carolina Press.

Lomnitz, Claudio. 2001. *Deep Mexico, Silent Mexico: An Anthropology of Nationalism.* Minneapolis: University of Minnesota Press.

Losier, Toussaint. 2013. "Jean Anil Louis-Juste, Prezan!" *Radical History Review* 115: 213–217.

Louis, Ilionor. 2021. "Repression and Resistance in the Liberal University." *NACLA Report on the Americas* 53 (1): 76–80.

Low, Setha. 2003. "Embodied Spaces: Anthropological Theories of Body, Space, and Culture." *Space and Culture* 6 (1): 9–18.

———. 2009. "Towards an Anthropological Theory of Space and Place." *Semiotica* 175 (1/4): 21–37.

Low, Setha, and Denise Lawrence-Zúñiga. 2003. *The Anthropology of Space and Place: Locating Culture*. Malden, MA: Blackwell Publishing.

Lowenthal, David. 1972. *West Indian Societies*. London: Oxford University Press.

Lunde, Henriette. 2010. *Haiti Youth Survey 2009*. Vol. 2. *Analytical Report*. https://www.fafo.no/en/publications/fafo-reports/haiti-youth-survey-2010.

Lundy, Patricia. 1999. *Debt and Adjustment: Social and Environmental Consequences in Jamaica*. New York: Routledge.

Lussier, Martin. 2009. Review of *The Philosophy of Improvisation* by Gary Peters. *Critical Studies in Improvisation*. https://www.criticalimprov.com/index.php/csieci/article/view/1778/2391.

Luzincourt, Ketty and Jennifer Gulbrandson. 2010. "Education and Conflict in Haiti Rebuilding the Education Sector after the 2010 Earthquake." *United States Institute of Peace*. https://www.usip.org/sites/default/files/sr245.pdf.

Madison, D. Soyini. 1999. "Performing Theory/Embodied Writing." *Text and Performance Quarterly* 19 (2): 107–124.

Magadza, Christopher H. D. 2000. "Climate Change Impacts and Human Settlements in Africa: Prospects for Adaptation." *Environmental Monitoring and Assessment* 61: 193–205.

Magloire, Gérarde. 1997. "Haitian-ness, Frenchness and History." *Pouvoirs dans la Caraïbe* 18–40.

Magloire, Gérarde, and Kevin A. Yelvington. 2005. "Haiti and the Anthropological Imagination." *Gradhiva* 127–152.

Magloire-Danton, Gerarde. 2016. "Price-Mars, Jean." In *Dictionary of Caribbean and Afro–Latin American Biography*, Vol. 5, edited by Franklin W. Knight and Henry Louis Gates Jr., 212–215. Oxford: Oxford University Press.

Maingot, Anthony P. 1987. "Haiti: Problems of a Transition to Democracy in an Authoritarian Soft State." *Journal of Interamerican Studies and World Affairs* 28 (4): 75–102.

Malkki, Liisa. 1995. *Purity and Exile: Violence, Memory, and National Cosmology among Hutu Refugees in Tanzania*. Chicago: Chicago University Press.

Mannheim, Karl. 1952/1972. "The Problem of Generation." In *Karl Mannheim: Essays*, edited, introduced, and translated by Paul Kecskemeti. 276–322. New York: Routledge.

Marcus, George E. 1995. "Ethnography in/of the World System: The Emergence of Multi-Sited Ethnography." *Annual Review of Anthropology* 24:95–117.

Markowitz, Fran, and Anders H. Stefansson. 2004. *Homecomings: Unsettling Paths of Return*. Lanham, MD: Lexington Books.

Massey, Doreen. 1999. "Negotiating Disciplinary Boundaries." *Current Sociology* 47 (4): 5–12.

Maynard, Kent, and Melisa Cahnmann-Taylor. 2010. "Anthropology at the Edge of Words: Where Poetry and Ethnography Meet." *Anthropology and Humanism* 35 (1): 2–19.

Mazama, Ama. 1994. "Critique afrocentrique de la créolité." In *Penser la créolité*, edited by Maryse Conde and Madeleine Cottenet-Hage. Paris: Karthala.

McAfee, Kathy. 1991. *Storm Signals: Structural Adjustment and Development Alternatives in the Caribbean*. London: Zed Books.

McAlister, Elizabeth. 2002. *Rara! Vodou, Power, and Performance in Haiti and its Diaspora*. Berkeley: University of California Press.

REFERENCES

McCarthy, James, and Scott Prudham. 2004. "Neoliberal Nature and the Nature of Neoliberalism." *Geoforum* 35 (3): 275–283.

McClaurin, Irma. 1996. *Women of Belize: Gender and Change in Central America*. New Brunswick, NJ: Rutgers University Press.

———, ed. 2001. *Black Feminist Anthropology Theory, Politics, Praxis, and Poetics*. New Brunswick, NJ: Rutgers University Press.

McCusker, Maeve. 2003. "'This Creole Culture, Miraculously Forged': The Contradictions of 'Créolité.'" In *Francophone Postcolonial Studies: A Critical Introduction*, edited by Charles Forsdick and David Murphy, 112–121. London: Edward Arnold.

Meehan, Kevin, and Marie Léticée. 2000. "A Folio of Writing from La Revue Indigène (1927–28): Translation and Commentary." *Callaloo* 23 (4): 1377–1380.

Ménard, Nadève. 2013. "The Myth of the Exiled Writer." *Transition* 111:53–58.

Messeri, Lisa. 2016. *Placing Outer Space: An Earthly Ethnography of Other Worlds*. Durham, NC: Duke University Press.

Metz, Jeremy. 2016. "Lahens, Yanick." In *Dictionary of Caribbean and Afro–Latin American Biography, Vol. 4*, edited by Franklin W. Knight and Henry Louis Gates Jr., 19–21. Oxford, UK: Oxford University Press.

Mignolo, Walter, and Catherine E. Walsh. 2018. *On Decoloniality: Concepts, Analytics, Praxis*. Durham, NC: Duke University Press.

Migration Data Portal (MDP). 2023. *Migration Data in the Caribbean*. May 31. https://www.migrationdataportal.org/regional-data-overview/migration-data-caribbean.

Mikell, Gwendolyn. 1982. "When Horses Talk: Reflections on Zora Neale Hurston's Haitian Anthropology." *Phylon* 43 (3): 218–230.

Miller, Daniel. 2008. "Migration, Material Culture and Tragedy: Four Moments in Caribbean Migration." *Mobilities* 3 (3): 397–413.

Ministère de l'Education Nationale et de la Formation Professionnelle. 2007. *La stratégie nationale d'action pour l'éducation pour tous*. Port-au-Prince: MENFP. http://planipolis.iiep.unesco.org/upload/Haiti/Haiti_EFA.pdf.

Mintz, Sidney. 1986. *Sweetness and Power: The Place of Sugar in Modern History*. London: Penguin Publishing Group.

———. 1989. *Caribbean Transformations*. New York: Columbia University Press.

Mintz, Sidney, and Sally Price. 1985. *Caribbean Contours*. Baltimore, MD: Johns Hopkins University Press.

Mooney, Margarita. A. 2009. *Faith Makes Us Strong: Surviving and Thriving in the Haitian Diaspora*. Berkeley: University of California Press.

Morrish, Liz. 2020. "Academic Freedom and the Disciplinary Regime in the Neoliberal University." In *Neoliberalism in Context*, edited by Simon Dawes and Marc Lenormand, 235–253. New York: Palgrave Macmillan.

Mufwene, Salikoko. 1990. "Transfer and the Substrate Hypothesis in Creolistics." *Studies in Second Language Acquisition* 12:1–23.

Mukherjee, Sumita. 2009. *Nationalism, Education and Migrant Identities the England-Returned*. London: Taylor & Francis.

Mullings, Leith. 1996. *On Our Own Terms: Race, Class, and Gender in the Lives of African-American Women*. New York: Taylor & Francis.

Munk, Martin D., Panu Poutvaara, and Mette Foged. 2012. "Transnational Cultural Capital, Educational Reproduction, and Privileged Positions." *Munich Reprints in Economics 19333*. University of Munich, Department of Economics.

Munro, Martin. 2007. *Exile and Post-1946 Haitian Literature: Alexis, Depestre, Ollivier, Laferrière, Danticat*. Liverpool, UK: Liverpool University Press.

Mutheu, Juliette, and Ruth Wanjala. 2009. "The Public, Parasites and Coffee: The Kenyan Science Café Concept." *Trends Parasitol* 25 (6): 245–292.

Neal, Mark Anthony. 2013. "NIGGA: The 21st-Century Theoretical Superhero." *Cultural Anthropology* 28:556–563.

Nelson, Carol, and Christine Clarke. 2020. *Contextualizing Jamaica's Relationship with the IMF*. Berlin: Springer International Publishing.

Nesbitt, Nick. 2013a. *Caribbean Critique: Antillean Critical Theory from Toussaint to Glissant*. Liverpool, UK: Liverpool University Press.

———. 2013b. "Haiti, the Monstrous Anomaly." In *The Idea of Haiti: Rethinking Crisis and Development*, edited by Millery Polyné, 3–26. Minneapolis: University of Minnesota Press.

Nicholls, David. 1986. "Haiti: The Rise and Fall of Duvalierism." *Third World Quarterly* 8 (4): 1239–1252.

Nwankwo, Ifeoma Kiddoe. 2003. "Insider and Outsider, Black and American: Rethinking Zora Neale Hurston's Caribbean Ethnography." *Radical History Review* 87 (1): 49–77.

N'Zengou-Tayo, Marie-José. 1998. "'Fanm se poto mitan': Haitian Woman, the Pillar of Society." *Feminist Review* 59:118–142.

———. 2004. "The End of the Committed Intellectual: The Case of Lyonel Trouillot." In *Ecrire en pays assiégé—Haïti—Writing under Siege*, edited by Kathleen M. Balutansky and Marie-Agnes Sourieau, 323–343. Leiden, Netherlands: Brill.

Obregón, Liliana. 2018. "Empire, Racial Capitalism and International Law: The Case of Manumitted Haiti and the Recognition Debt." *Leiden Journal of International Law* 31 (3): 597–615.

Olssen, Mark, and Michael A. Peters. 2005. "Neoliberalism, Higher Education and the Knowledge Economy: From the Free Market to Knowledge Capitalism." *Journal of Education Policy* 20 (3): 313–345.

Olsson, Erik. 2004. "Event or Process? Repatriation Practice and Open-Ended Migration." In *Transnational Spaces: Disciplinary Perspectives*, edited by Maja Povrzanović Frykman, 151–168. Malmö, Sweden: Malmö University Press.

Olsson, Erik, and Russell King. 2014. "Introduction: Diasporic Returns." *Diaspora: A Journal of Transnational Studies* 17 (3): 255–261.

Oliver-Smith, Anthony. 2012. "Haiti's 500-year Earthquake. In *Tectonic Shifts: Haiti Since the Earthquake*, edited by Mark Schuller and Pablo Morales. 18–23. New York: Kumarian Press.

Organization of American Societies. 2002. "Report of the Commission of Inquiry into the Events of December 17, 2001, in Haiti." http://www.oas.org/oaspage/haiti_situation/cpinf4702_02_eng.htm.

Owens, Imani D. 2023. *Turn the World Upside Down: Empire and Unruly Forms of Black Folk Culture in the U.S. and Caribbean*. New York: Columbia University Press.

Padmore, George. 1931. *The Life and Struggles of Negro Toilers*. London: Red International of Labour Union.

Palmié, Stephan. 2006. "Creolization and Its Discontents." *Annual Review of Anthropology* 35 (1): 433–456.

Pamphile, Leon D. 1985. "America's Policy-Making in Haitian Education, 1915–1934." *Journal of Negro Education* 54 (1): 99–108.

REFERENCES

Parra, Mariana Dos Santos. 2020. "Building or Breaking the Polity? International Intervention, Statebuilding and Reproduction of Crisis in Haiti (2004–2019)." *Revista de Ciencia Política* 40 (2): 351–378.

Payton, Claire Antone. 2019. "Building Corruption in Haiti." *NACLA Report on the Americas.* 51 (2): 182–187.

Perkiss, Stephanie, and Lee C. Moerman. 2018. "A Dispute in the Making: A Critical Examination of Displacement, Climate Change and the Pacific Island." *Accounting, Auditing and Accountability* 31 (1): 166–192.

Peters, Gary. 2009. *The Philosophy of Improvisation.* Chicago: University of Chicago Press.

Petit Frère, Dieulermesson. 2021. "Rodolphe Mathurin." *Île en île.* January 3. http://ile-en-ile.org/mathurin/.

Petryna, Adriana. 2018. "Wildfires at the Edges of Science: Horizoning Work amid Runaway Change." *Cultural Anthropology* 33 (4): 570–595

Pierre, Jemima. 2013. "Haiti and the 'Savage Slot.'" *Journal of Haitian Studies* 19 (2): 110–116.

———. 2023. "Haiti as Empire's Laboratory." *NACLA Report on the Americas.* September 26. https://nacla.org/haiti-empire-laboratory.

Pierre-Louis, François. 2006. *Haitians in New York City: Transnationalism and Hometown Associations.* Tampa: University Press of Florida.

———. 2011. "Earthquakes, Nongovernmental Organizations, and Governance in Haiti." *Journal of Black Studies* 42 (2): 186–202.

Pinto, Antonio J., and Nairobi Rodríguez. 2023. "Colonial Roots for Contemporary Xenophobic Attitudes: Dominican Hatred toward The Haitians." In *Xenophobia and Nativism in Africa,Latin America, and the Caribbean,* edited by José de Arimatéia da Cruz, Michael R. Hall, and Sabella O. Abidde, 34–50. New York: Taylor & Francis.

Polyné, Millery. 2013a. *The Idea of Haiti: Rethinking Crisis and Development.* Minneapolis: University of Minnesota Press.

———. 2013b. "Introduction: To Make Visible the Invisible Epistemological Order: Haiti, Singularity, and Newness." In *The Idea of Haiti: Rethinking Crisis and Development,* edited by Millery Polyné, xi–xxxviii. Minneapolis: University of Minnesota Press.

Price-Mars, Jean. 1919. *La Vocation de l'élite.* Paris: Impre. E. Chenet.

———. 1928/1983. *So Spoke the Uncle.* Translated by Magdalene Shannon. Washington, DC: Three Continents Press.

Prou, Marc. 2009. "Attempts at Reforming Haiti's Education System: The Challenges of Mending the Tapestry, 1979–2004." *Journal of Haitian Studies* 15 (1/2): 29–69.

Quashie, Kevin. 2021. *Black Aliveness, Or A Poetics of Being.* Durham, NC: Duke University Press.

Rajan, Rajeswari Sunder. 1997. "The Third World Academic in Other Places; Or, the Postcolonial Intellectual Revisited." *Critical Inquiry* 23 (3): 596–616.

Ramji, Hasmita. 2006. "British Indians Returning 'Home': An Exploration of Transnational Belonging." *Sociology* 40 (4): 645–662.

Ramsey, Kate. 2011. *The Spirits and the Law: Vodou and Power in Haiti.* Chicago: University of Chicago Press.

Ramachandran, Vijaya, and Julie Walz. 2015. "Haiti: Where Has All the Money Gone? *Journal of Haitian Studies* 21 (1): 26–65.

Remy, Anselme. 1974. "The Duvalier Phenomenon." *Caribbean Studies* 14 (2): 38–65.

Renda, Mary A. 2001. *Taking Haiti: Military Occupation and the Culture of U.S. Imperialism, 1915–1940*. Chapel Hill: University of North Carolina Press.

Ricoeur, Paul. 1986. *Lectures on Ideology and Utopia*. New York: Columbia University Press.

Rizvi, Fazal. 2005. "Rethinking 'Brain Drain' in the Era of Globalisation." *Asia Pacific Journal of Education* 25 (2): 175–192.

Robinson, Cedric J. 1983. *Black Marxism: The Making of the Black Radical Tradition*. Chapel Hill: Universty of North Carolina Press.

Rodman, Margaret C. 1992. "Empowering Place: Multilocality and Multivocality." *American Anthropologist* 94 (3): 640–656.

Rodriguez Miranda, Esther I. 2018. "The Role of Price-Mars's Thought in the Haitian Renaissance in the First Half of the Twentieth Century." In *Between Two Worlds: Jean Price-Mars, Haiti, and Africa*, edited by Celucien L. Joseph, Glodel Mezilas, and Jean Eddy Saint Paul, 3–30. New York: Lexington Books.

Rogers, Matthew. 2012. "Contextualizing Theories and Practices of Bricolage Research." *Qualitative Report* 17 (48): 1–17.

Roniger, Luis, Leonardo Senkman, Saúl Sosnowski, and Mario Sznajder. 2018. *Exile, Diaspora, and Return: Changing Cultural Landscapes in Argentina, Chile, Paraguay, and Uruguay*. Oxford: Oxford University Press.

Rose, Euclid A. 2002. *Dependency and Socialism in the Modern Caribbean: Superpower Intervention in Guyana, Jamaica, and Grenada, 1970–1985*. New York: Lexington Books.

Rothenberg, Jerome, ed. 1985. *Technicians of the Sacred: A Range of Poetries from Africa, America, Europe and Oceania*, Vol. 2. Berkeley: University of California Press.

Rowell, Charles Henry. 2015. "Dedication to the Memory of J. Max Bond, Jr." *Callaloo* 38 (4): xiii–xviii.

Rush, Anne Spry. 2011. *Bonds of Empire: West Indians and Britishness from Victoria to Decolonization*. Oxford: Oxford University Press.

Rushdie, Salman. 1988. *The Satanic Verses*. New York: Random House.

Safran, William. 1991. "Diaspora in Modern Societies: Myths of Homeland and Return." *Diaspora* 1 (1): 83–99.

Said, Edward. 1994. *Representations of the Intellectual: The 1993 Reith Lectures*. London: Vintage.

———. 2000. *Out of Place: A Memoir*. New York: Knopf Doubleday Publishing Group.

Saint-Lot, Marie-Jose Alcide. 2004. *Vodou: A Sacred Theatre—The African Heritage in Haiti*. Coconut Creek, FL: Educa Vision.

Sanders Johnson, Grace. 2023. *White Gloves, Black Nation: Women, Citizenship, and Political Wayfaring in Haiti*. Chapel Hill: University of North Carolina Press.

Sargsyan, Nelli. 2022. "Finding a Livable Feminist Academic Life through *Rasanblaj*." *Feminist Anthropology* 2:112–119.

Schieffelin, Bambi B., and Rachelle Charlier Doucet. 1994. "The "Real" Haitian Creole: Ideology, Metalinguistics, and Orthographic Choice." *American Ethnologist* 21:176–200.

Schloss, Rebecca Hartkopf. 2009. *Sweet Liberty: The Final Days of Slavery in Martinique*. Philadelphia: University of Pennsylvania Press.

Schmidt, Hans. 1995. *The United States Occupation of Haiti, 1915–1934*. New Brunswick, NJ: Rutgers University Press.

Schuller, Mark. 2007. "Seeing Like a "Failed" NGO: Globalization's Impacts on State and Civil Society in Haiti." *PoLAR: Political and Legal Anthropology Review* 30:67–89.

REFERENCES

———. 2012. *Killing with Kindness: Haiti, International Aid, and NGOs*. New Brunswick, NJ: Rutgers University Press.

———. 2014. "Being an Insider Without: Activist Anthropological Engagement in Haiti after the Earthquake." *American Anthropologist* 116:409–412.

———. 2016. *Humanitarian Aftershocks in Haiti*. New Brunswick, NJ: Rutgers University Press.

———. 2021a. "Haiti: What Does Solidarity Really Mean?" *Anthropology Now* 13 (3): 31–41.

———. 2021b. *Humanity's Last Stand: Confronting Global Catastrophe*. New Brunswick, NJ: Rutgers University Press.

Schwartz, Stephanie. 2019. "Home, Again: Refugee Return and Post-Conflict Violence in Burundi." *International Security* 44 (2): 110–145.

Scott, David. 1999. *Refashioning Futures: Criticism after Postcoloniality*. Princeton, NJ: Princeton University Press.

———. 2004. *Conscripts of Modernity: The Tragedy of Colonial Enlightenment*. Durham, NC: Duke University Press.

———. 2013. "On the Very Idea of a Black Radical Tradition." *Small Axe* 17:1–6.

———. 2014. "The Temporality of Generations: Dialogue, Tradition, Criticism." *New Literary History* 45 (2): 157–181.

———. 2017. *Stuart Hall's Voice: Intimations of an Ethics of Receptive Generosity*. Durham, NC: Duke University Press.

Segalla, Spencer D. 2009. *The Moroccan Soul: French Education, Colonial Ethnology, and Muslim Resistance, 1912–1956*. Lincoln: University of Nebraska Press.

Seim, Josh. 2021. Participant Observation, Observant Participation, and Hybrid Ethnography. *Sociological Methods & Research* 53 (1): 121–152.

Shahjahan, Riyad. 2014. "From 'No' to 'Yes': Postcolonial Perspectives on Resistance to Neoliberal Higher Education." *Discourse: Studies in the Cultural Politics of Education* 35 (2): 219–232.

Shannon, Magdaline W. "Introduction." In Price-Mars, Jean. 1928/1983. *So Spoke the Uncle*. Translated by Magdalene Shannon, ix–xxviii. Washington, DC: Three Continents Press.

———. 1996. *Jean Price-Mars, The Haitian Elite and the American Occupation, 1915–1935*. London: Palgrave Macmillan UK.

Sharpe, Christina. 2010. *Monstrous Intimacies: Making Post-Slavery Subjects*. Durham, NC: Duke University Press.

———. 2016. *In the Wake: On Blackness and Being*. Durham, NC: Duke University Press.

Shaw, William, and Dilip Ratha. 2007. "South-South Migration and Remittances." *World Bank Working Papers*. https://doi.org/10.1596/978-0-8213-7072-8.

Sheller, Mimi. 2012. *Citizenship from Below Erotic Agency and Caribbean Freedom*. Durham, NC: Duke University Press.

———. 2020. *Island Futures: Caribbean Survival in the Anthropocene*. Durham, NC: Duke University Press.

Sherwood, Marika. 2010. *Origins of Pan-Africanism: Henry Sylvester Williams, Africa, and the African Diaspora*. Oxford: Taylor & Francis Group.

Shevchenko, Olga. 2008 *Crisis and the Everyday in Postsocialist Moscow*. Bloomington: Indiana University Press.

Shore, Cris. 2008. "Audit Culture and Illiberal Governance: Universities and the Politics of Accountability. *Anthropological Theory* 8 (3): 278–298.

Simmons, Kimberly Eison. 2001. "A Passion for Sameness: Encountering a Black Feminist Self in Fieldwork in the Dominican Republic." In *Black Feminist Anthropology Theory, Politics, Praxis, and Poetics*, edited by Irma McClaurin, 77–101. New Brunswick, NJ: Rutgers University Press.

———. 2009. *Reconstructing Racial Identity and the African Past in the Dominican Republic*. Gainesville: University Press of Florida.

Slocum, Karla. 2006. *Free Trade and Freedom: Neoliberalism, Place, and Nation in the Caribbean*. Ann Arbor: University of Michigan Press.

Slocum, Karla, and Deborah A. Thomas. 2003. "Rethinking Global and Area Studies: Insights from Caribbeanist Anthropology." *American Anthropologist* 105:553–565.

Smalls, Krystal A. 2021." Fat, Black, and Ugly: The Semiotic Production of Prodigious Femininities. *Transforming Anthropology* 29 (1): 12–28.

Smith, Matthew J. 2009. *Red and Black in Haiti: Radicalism, Conflict, and Political Change, 1934–1957*. Chapel Hill: University of North Carolina Press.

———. 2020. "On the 1946 Revolution." In *The Haiti Reader: History, Culture, Politics*, edited by Laurent Dubois, Kaiama L. Glover, Nadève Ménard, Millery Polyné, and Chantalle F. Verna. Durham, NC: Duke University Press.

Social Security Office or Retirement and Disability Policy. 2019. "Social Security Programs throughout the World: The Americas, 2019." *Social Security Office or Retirement and Disability Policy*. https://www.ssa.gov/policy/docs/progdesc/ssptw/2018-2019/americas/haiti.html.

Solarz, Stephen. 1995. "Foreword." In Schmidt, Hans. *The United States Occupation of Haiti, 1915–1934*, xi–xvii. New Brunswick, NJ: Rutgers University Press.

Solomon, Marisa. 2019. "'The Ghetto Is a Gold Mine': The Racialized Temporality of Betterment." *International Labor and Working-Class History* 95:76–94.

Special to New York Times. 1960. *Haiti Seek to Halt Strike by Students with Martial Law*. Port-au-Prince, November 23.

Stephenson, Max, and Laura Zanotti. 2019. "Neoliberalism, Academic Capitalism and Higher Education: Exploring the Challenges of One University in Rural Haiti." *International Journal of Educational Development* 65:115–122.

Stack, Carol. 1996. *Call to Home: African Americans Reclaim the Rural South*. New York: Basic Books.

Strathern, Marilyn. 2003. *Audit Cultures: Anthropological Studies in Accountability, Ethics and the Academy*. London: Taylor & Francis.

Sylvain, Patrick. 2013. "The Macoutization of Haitian Politics." In *Politics and Power in Haiti. Studies of the Americas*, edited by Kate Quinn and Paul Sutton. New York: Palgrave Macmillan.

Sylvain-Bouchereau, Madeleine. 1944. *Education des femmes en Haïti*, Port-au-Prince: Imp. de l'Etat.

Sylvester, Megan. 2008. "The Globalisation of Higher Education: Assessing the Response of the University of the West Indies." In *Power, Voice and the Public Good: Schooling and Education in Global Societies (Advances in Education in Diverse Communities)*, Vol. 6, edited by Rodney K. Hopson, Carol Camp Yeakey, and Francis Musa Boakari, 261–284. Bingley, UK: Emerald.

Taleb-Khyar, Mohamed B. 1992. "Interview with Lyonel Trouillot." *Callaloo* 15 (2): 403–406.

REFERENCES

Taussig, Karen-Sue, Klaus Hoeyer, and Stefan Helmreich. 2013. "The Anthropology of Potentiality in Biomedicine: An Introduction to Supplement 7." *Current Anthropology* 54 (S7): S3–S14.

Taylor, George H. 2006. "Ricoeur's Philosophy of Imagination." *Journal of French Philosophy* 16 (1 & 2): 93–104.

Thiong'o, Ngugi Wa. 2023. *The Language of Languages.* Kolkata, India: Seagull Books.

Thomas, Deborah. A. 2022. "What the Caribbean Teaches Us: The Afterlives and New Lives of Coloniality." *Journal of Latin American and Caribbean Anthropology* 27:235–254.

Tozzi, Miche. 2002. "Les enjeux de l'animation d'un café-philo." *Dossier les cafés philosophiques* 13.

Trefzer, Annette. 2000. "Possessing the Self: Caribbean Identities in Zora Neale Hurston's Tell My Horse." *African American Review* 34 (2): 299–312.

Trouillot, Lyonel. 1989. *Les fous de Saint-Antoine.* Port-au-Prince: Les Cahiers du Vendredi, Editions Henri Deschamps.

———. 2011. *La belle amour humaine.* Arles, France / Montréal, Actes Sud: Leméac.

Trouillot, Michel-Rolph. 1977. *Ti difé boulé sou istoua Ayiti.* Brooklyn, NY: Kóleksion Lakensièl.

———. 1982. "Motion in the System: Coffee, Color, and Slavery in Eighteenth-Century SaintDomingue." *Review (Fernand Braudel Center)* 5 (3): 331–388.

———. 1990a. *Haiti, State against Nation: The Origins and Legacy of Duvalierism.* New York: Monthly Review Press.

———. 1990b. "The Odd and the Ordinary: Haiti, the Caribbean, and the World." *Cimarrón* 2 (3): 3–12.

———. 1994. "Haiti's Nightmare and the Lessons of History." *NACLA Report on the Americas* 27 (4): 46–51.

———. 1995. *Silencing the Past: Power and the Production of History.* Boston: Beacon Press.

———. 2001. "The Anthropology of the State in the Age of Globalization." *Current Anthropology* 42 (1): 125–138.

———. 2003. *Global Transformations: Anthropology and the Modern World.* New York: Palgrave Macmillan US.

Tsuda, Takeyuki, ed. 2009. *Diasporic Homecoming: Ethnic Return Migration in Comparative Perspective.* Stanford, CA: Stanford University Press.

Twitchin, Mischa. 2021. On Repair. *Performance Research* 26 (6): 54–61.

Ulysse, Gina Athena. 2007. *Downtown Ladies: Informal Commercial Importers, a Haitian Anthropologist and Self-Making in Jamaica.* Chicago: University of Chicago Press.

———. 2015a. *Why Haiti Needs New Narratives: A Post-Quake Chronicle.* Middletown, CT: Wesleyan University Press.

———. 2015b. "Rasanblaj Continua: A Conversation with Gina Athena Ulysse." *Anthropology Now.* November 14. http://anthronow.com/onlinearticles/rasanblaj-continua.

———. 2017. "Why Rasanblaj, Why Now? New Salutations to the Four Cardinal Points in Haitian Studies." *Journal of Haitian Studies* 23 (2): 58–80.

United Nations Department of Economic and Social Affairs (UN-DESA). 2020. Population Division. International Migrant Stock 2020. https://www.un.org/development /desa/pd/content/international-migrant-stock.

United States Bureau of Citizenship and Immigration Services. 1999. *Haiti: Human Rights Abuses by CIMO.* Washington, DC: USBCIS.

United States Department of State. n.d. "Bandung Conference (Asian-African Conference), 1955." *Milestones in the History of U.S. Foreign Relation*. Accessed January 3, 2024. https://history.state.gov/milestones/1953-1960/bandung-conf.

Urzedo, Danilo, and Pratichi Chatterjee. 2021. "The Colonial Reproduction of Deforestation in the Brazilian Amazon: Violence against Indigenous Peoples for Land Development." *Journal of Genocide Research* 23 (2): 302–324.

———. 2022. "The Colonial Reproduction of Deforestation in The Brazilian Amazon: Violence against Indigenous Peoples for Land Development." In *The Genocide-Ecocide Nexus*, edited by Damien Short and Martin Crook, 146–168. New York: Routledge.

Varenne, Hervè, ed. 2019. *Educating in Life: Educational Theory and the Emergence of New Normals*. New York: Taylor & Francis.

Vargas, João H. Costa, and Moon-Kie Jung. 2021. *Antiblackness*. Durham, NC: Duke University Press.

Vega Ocasio, Denisse, Stanley Juin, David Berendes, et al. 2023. Cholera Outbreak—Haiti, September 2022–January 2023. *MMWR Morb Mortal Wkly Rep*. 72:21–25.

Verdery, Katherine. 1995. *National Ideology under Socialism: Identity and Cultural Politics in Ceausescu's Romania*. Berkeley: University of California Press.

Verna, Chantalle F. 2017. *Haiti and the Uses of America: Post-U.S. Occupation Promises*. New Brunswick, NJ: Rutgers University Press.

Verna, Chantalle F., and Paulette Poujol Oriol. 2011. "The Ligue Feminine d'Action Sociale: An Interview with Paulette Poujol Oriol." *Journal of Haitian Studies* 17, no. 1: 246–257.

Voltaire, Frantz. 1988. *Pouvoir noir en Haïti: L'explosion de 1946*. Mont-Royal, Québec, Canada: V & R éditeurs; Montréal, Québec, Canada: Editions du CIDIHCA; Flushing, NY: Haitian Book Centre.

Wagner, Laura. 2017. "Nou toujou La! The Digital (After-) Life of Radio Haïti-Inter." SxArchipelagos 2. https://archipelagosjournal.org/assets/issue02/nou-toujou-la.pdf.

Wagner, Laura, and Ayanna Legros. 2022. "From the Other Side of the Sea: Rasanblaj/Reassembling Haitian Radio Archives of Exile." *Global South* 15 (2): 154–175.

Wah, Tatiana. 2013. "Engaging the Haitian Diaspora." *Cairo Review of Global Affairs*. https://fount.aucegypt.edu/faculty_journal_articles/3773.

Wang, Bingyu. 2020. "Time in Migration: Temporariness, Precarity and Temporal Labour amongst Chinese Scholars Returning from the Global North to South." *Journal of Ethnic and Migration Studies* 46 (11): 2127–2144.

Warwick, Ozzi. 2022. "The History of Socialism in the English-Speaking Caribbean." *Socialist History* 62:10–36.

Watkins, Rachel. 2018. "George Clement Bond: Anthropologist, Africanist, Educator, Visionary." In *The Second Generation of African American Pioneers in Anthropology*, edited by Ira E. Harrison, Deborah Johnson-Simon, and Erica Lorraine Williams. Champaign: University of Illinois.

Weatherill, Charlotte Kate. 2022. "Sinking Paradise? Climate Change Vulnerability and Pacific Island Extinction Narratives." *Geoforum*. https://www.sciencedirect.com/science/article/pii/S0016718522000884.

Welsh, Richard O. 2012. "Overcoming Smallness through Education Development: A Comparative Analysis of Jamaica and Singapore." *Current Issues in Comparative Education* 15 (1): 114–131.

Werner, Marion. 2015. *Global Displacements: The Making of Uneven Development in the Caribbean*. New York: Wiley.

REFERENCES

Wêche, Evains. 2017. "Editorial." *La Revue DO KRE I S* 1:5–6.

Wilkins, Fanon Che, William G. Martin, and Michael Oliver West, eds. 2009. *From Toussaint to Tupac: The Black International Since the Age of Revolution*. Chapel Hill: University of North Carolina Press.

Williams, Eric. 1969. *Inward Hunger: The Education of a Prime Minister*. Princeton, NJ: Markus Wiener.

Williams, Gershom. 2021. "Anténor Firmin, Pan-Africanism, and the Struggle for Race Vindication." In *Reconstructing the Social Sciences and Humanities*, Vol. 1, edited by Celucien L. Joseph Paul C Mocombe, 123–134. Oxford: Routledge, 2021.

Williams, Raymond. 1977. *Marxism and Literature*. New York: Oxford University Press.

Williams, Roger M. 1971. *The Bonds: An American Family*. Louisville, KY: Atheneum.

Williams, Saul. 2016. "Sha Clack Clack." Translated by Mehdi E. Chalmers and Ricarson Dorcé. *Revue Trois/Cent/Soixante: Haïti de l'intérieur, de l'autre bord et sur le fi*, 54–56.

Wolf-Meyer, Matthew. 2019. *Theory for the World to Come: Speculative Fiction and Apocalyptic Anthropology*. Minneapolis: University of Minnesota Press.

Worlgenson, Noël. 2017. "À l'Ecole normale supérieure, plus rien ne fonctionne à la normale". *Le Nouvelliste*, August 11. https://lenouvelliste.com/article/174640/a-lecole-normale-superieure-plus-rien-ne-fonctionne-a-la-normale.

Yusoff, Kathryn. 2018. *A Billion Black Anthropocenes or None*. Minneapolis: University of Minnesota Press.

Zacaïr, Philippe, ed. 2010. *Haiti and the Haitian Diaspora in the Wider Caribbean*. Gainesville: University Press of Florida.

Zacaïr, Philippe, and Catherine Reinhardt. 2010. "Introduction." In *Haiti and the Haitian Diaspora in the Wider Caribbean*, edited by Philippe Zacaïr, 1–10. Gainesville: University Press of Florida.

Zani, Leah. 2019. *Bomb Children: Life in the Former Battlefields of Laos*. Durham, NC: Duke University Press.

———. 2023. *How to Write Field Poetry*. In *An Ethnographic Inventory: Field Devices for Anthropological Inquiry*, edited by Tomás Sánchez Criado and Adolfo Estalella. 83–91. New York: Taylor & Francis.

Index

Agamben, Giorgio, 5
Agard-Jones, Vanessa, 82
Alex, 61
Alexander, Leslie M., 31–32
Alexander, M. Jacqui, 147, 148
Alexander, William, 31
Antillean revues, 126–127, 130–136
Antoine, Régis, 141
Appadurai, Arjun, 3, 4–5
Aristide, Jean-Bertrand: administration, 153n1; campaign, 62; coup deposing, 1, 60; persecution, 91; presidency, 4; restored to power, 83–84, 114; running for office, 159n17; second term, 72
Aristide, Marx, 57
Aubertin, Ernest, 37
audit culture, 10–11

Bajeux, Jean-Claude, 59
Barad, Karen, 124
Barrios, Roberto, 90
Beaulieu, Christian, 43–44
Beauvoir-Dominique, Rachel, 17
Beckett, Greg, 18, 81–82
Bélair, Charles, 30, 128
Bélair, Sanite, 24, 30
Bélizaire, Assédius, 132
Bell, Marvin, 112
Benjamin, Harold, 28
Bernabé, Jean, 139, 140
Bhabha, Homi, 119
Biamby, Phillipe, 60
Biassou, 128
Bishop, Maurice, 67
Black Lives Matter, 132, 133, 146

Bloom, Paul, 124
Blot, Jean Yves, 88–89
Bonaparte, Napoleon, 29
Bonilla, Yarimar, 137
Borno, Louis, 42
Boukman, Dutty, 29
Boyer, Jean-Pierre, 32–33
Brierre, Jean, 44
Brouard, Carl, 45
Bryant, Rebecca, 3, 57

Carole, 4, 51–52, 53–54, 56–57, 58–59, 76–77
Castera, Georges, 131
Castor, Suzy, 61–62
Cèdras, Raoul, 60
Center for Economic and Social Development (Le Centre de recherche et de formation économique et sociale pour le développement or CRESFED), 62
Césaire, Aimé, 41, 45, 127
Césaire, Suzanne, 127
Chalmers, Mehdi, 72–73, 115, 130–131, 133–134, 144
Chamoiseau, Patrick, 139, 140
Chancy, Myriam, 43
Charlemagne, Manno, 105–106
Charlier, Étienne, 41
Christophe, Henri, 32
Clément, Job B., 24, 26, 28
Cob, Kanellos, 134
Cobley, Alan, 67
Cocco, Massimo, 17
Code Noir, 27–28, 101
Collyer, Fran, 117–118
Columbus, Christopher, 25

187

Confiant, Raphaël, 103, 139, 140
Conseil National de Gouvernement (CNG, National Council of Government), 58, 59, 159n16, 161n1
Cooper, Anna Julia, 37
COVID-19, 144
Crawley, Ashon, 103
Creole: Black-skinned elite, 17; creolization, 103–104; culture, 7, 26, 139; exceptionalism, 19, 130, 137, 139, 142, 147; festival, 141; oral tradition, 112, 115
Creole language: advocacy of, 41; to analyze the present, 130; communities, 161n2; developed outside of/against European norms, 139–140; inhabiting, 64; language of educated and propertied, 59–60; literacy programs, 57; serve as meeting space, 136–137
creolization, 103–104
Crichlow, Michaeline, 9
crisis: Aristide deposed, 1; of authoritarian rule, 54; economic, 68; etymological roots, 128–129; Haitian, 80–82; in the Haitian public university system, 6, 18–19, 79–80, 87–90, 94–96; housing, 74; political, 84–85, 116; ruptures, 3; times of, 127, 146
Cuffe, Paul, 32

Dallas, Duncan, 116
Damien revolt, 42, 44, 46
Dani, 95, 144
Daut, Marlene, 24, 36, 116
David, 95–96
Decena, Carlos Ulises, 103
dechoukaj (political uprooting), 18, 52, 58, 59
de Gobineau, Arthur, 37
Déjoie, Louis, 47
Delorme, Demesvar, 36, 63
Denis, Lorimer, 45
de Ovando, Nicolás, 26
Deshommes, Fritz, 87–88, 94
Dessalines, Jean Jacques, 28, 30, 32, 121
diaspora: academic diaspora members, 12–13, 71, 73; Black diaspora, 38–39, 130; blackness in, 5; diaspora-homeland interactions, 155n12; diasporic scholars, 129; displacements, 8–9; Haitian, 153n1; Haitian diasporic editorials, 48; transnational formation, 154n4
Dirlik, Arif, 25
displacements: Caribbean, 8; coloniality, 3, 6; diasporic populations, 9; external,

144–145; extraction zones, 145; of Haitians, 142; intellectuals, 4; internal, 52, 144; jenerasyon 86, 6, 18; point of rupture, 23; postcolonial subjects, 24; urgency of rasanblaj, 102
DO KRE I S, 127, 130, 136–142
Dominique, Jean, 49, 56–57, 62, 122, 159
Dominique, J. J., 122
Dorcé, Ricarson, 131, 133–134
d'Oregon, Bertrand, 26
Dorsainvil, J. C., 41
Dubois, François Elie, 35
Du Bois, W.E.B., 37
Dumas, Léon, 41
Dupuy, Alex, 59–60
Dutty, Boukman, 24
Duvalier, François: ascension to power, 23–24; control of University of Haiti, 48, 83; dictatorship, 2, 4, 24, 49, 53; fall of, 14; forcing exile, 62, 76; presidency, 47
Duvalier, Jean-Claude: crackdown on journalists, 159n13; fall of, 4, 66, 122; government of, 48, 59; international aid to Haiti, 68; regime, 160n20; repression of opposition, 49; transferring power to, 54

enslavement, 6–7, 8, 24, 26–27, 29, 104
Esper, Gaylord, 51
Estimé, Dumarsais, 47
exile: Bajeux, 59; Caribbean, 8; colonial space, 7; "de-exile" process, 61, 62; definition, 8; fleeing persecution, 48; forced by Duvalier, 53–54, 62, 76; Gérard, 62; Haitian literature, 5–6; intellectual, 4; intellectuals, 51, 58, 60, 62, 64, 115; internal, 63–64; journalists forced into, 49, 159n13; Laraque, 115; Lescot, 47; returning home, 9, 18, 56, 58; Roumain, 44; scholars forced into, 49; Trouillot, 65

Fatiman, Cécile, 24, 29
Fatton, Robert, 81
Fignolé, Jean-Claude, 140
Firmin, Joseph Anténor, 25, 35, 36–38
Fischlin, Daniel, 98, 146
Fouron, Georges, 81, 154n4
François, Jean, 128
François, Michael, 60
Frankétienne, 140
Freeman, George, 43
futures: academic, 96; of belonging, 115; communicability, 52–53; emancipatory,

7–8, 129–130, 148; epistemological and practical implications for, 24; felt and experienced differently, 5; future-making, 97, 136; future-oriented places of belonging, 6, 19; liberatory, 32, 142, 148; Pan-Creole, 130, 139, 141; potentiality, 25, 57; and rasanblaj, 104; studies of, 3

Gacel-Ávila, Jocelyne, 28
Geffrard, Nicholas, 35, 120
Girard, Philippe, 30
Glick Schiller, Nancy, 81, 154n4
Glissant, Eduard, 139, 140
Glover, Kaiama, 141
Goldstein, Thalia, 124
Griots movement, 45, 47
Guevara, Che, 62, 120

Haiti: all citizens legally equal, 31; anti-imperial nationalist movement, 42–43; author's time in, 1–2; colonialism, 18, 24; crises in, 18, 79–80; displacements, 19; earthquakes, 17, 142–143; education sector, 32–33, 35, 38; exceptionalism, 19, 137–139; extant fractures in, 6; feminists, 45, 103; Firmin on, 36–38; fractures throughout academia, 98; Haitian Atlantic humanism, 36; Haitian Revolution, 7, 29–30, 31–32, 80; identity, 41; independence, 33–34; intellectuals, 23–24, 60–61, 64, 81; Lahens on, 60, 63–64; leaving, 107–108; leftist radicalism, 43–44; literature, 5–6, 140–141; neocolonial relations with France, 33, 36; neoliberalism in, 54–55; noirisme, 45–46; north/south division, 32; politics, 47; post-Duvalier, 57, 63, 66, 115; presidency, 4; rejection of African heritage, 34; scholars, 11–16, 50, 146; security mapping, 86; social transformation, 18; storytelling tradition, 122; uninhabitability, 4, 82; U.S. imperialism in, 39–40; Western representations of, 5
Haiti's futures: diaspora's responsibility, 12; doubts about, 96; empowering, 20; multiple belongings, 4; radical visions of, 147; reclamation of, 142, 148; related to rest of world, 148; resistance against foreclosing of, 144; stream-of-consciousness discussion, 111; Western intervention, 5
Hall, Stuart, 138

Harrison, Faye, 116, 145
Heble, Ajay, 98
Henry, Ariel, 144
Holly, Arthur, 41
Hudicourt, Max, 41, 44
Hughes, Langston, 46
Hugot, Héléna, 116
humanism, 36, 116
Hurbon, Laënnec, 13–14, 131

Inginac, M. B., 33
intellectuals: Black futurity, 6; dechoukaj, 58–59; definitions, 119; displacements, 4; elite, 33–34, 38; exile, 51, 58, 60, 62, 64, 115; friendship, 75–77, 111; Griot, 45; Haiti, 23–24, 60–61, 64, 81; imprisonment and state-sanctioned murders of, 23–24, 48; labor, 9–11; public, 9–10, 60–66, 117; restricted, 49
International Monetary Fund (IMF), 67–68, 136
Interuniversity Institute for Research and Development (INURED), 12–13, 70, 155n12

Jacques, 72, 73–74
Janvier, Louis-Joseph, 25, 35–37, 45, 63
Jean-Baptiste, Ralph, 116–117, 118–120
Jean-Charles, Régine, 103
jenerasyon 86: "aging," 87; conflict with jenn doktè, 75–76; displacement of, 6, 18; homecoming of, 52; members of, 66, 75–76, 94, 111, 131; professor, 88; after return of, 4, 77
jenn doktè: conflict with jenerasyon 86, 75–76; displacement of, 6; financial situations, 74–75; higher education reform, 4; homecoming of, 52; intellectual friendship with jenerasyon 86, 111; mouvman jenn doktè, 87; return of, 72–73; struggle for place, 18; student manipulation, 88; and UEH, 66, 71
Jeudy, Charlot, 118–119
Johnson, Lyndon B., 54

Kecskemeti, Paul, 76–77
Kelley, Robin D. G., 126, 127, 147
Kirsthie, 97
Knight, Daniel, 3, 57
Knight, Franklin W., 30
Komite Nasyonal Kongres Oganizasyons Demokratik (National Committee of the Congress of Democratic Organizations, or KONAKOM), 59
kriz, 1, 18, 79–80, 82

Lafontant, Daniel, 121
Lahens, Yanick, 17, 60, 63–64, 122
Lamartinière, Marie-Jeanne, 24, 30
La Pléiade, 122–124
Leclerc, Charles, 29
Lee, Helen Jackson, 134
Lemay-Hébert, Nicolas, 86
Lescot, Élie, 43, 46–47, 101, 131
Lhérisson, Justin, 120
Ligue féminine d'action sociale (Feminine
   League for Social Action), 44–45
Lipsitz, George, 98
Logan, Rayford, 46
Louis-Juste, Jean Anil, 72, 90–91
Louverture, Toussaint, 28, 29, 30, 128

Magloire, Clément, 45
Magloire, Danièle, 122
Magloire, Gérarde, 34
Maingot, Anthony, 58
Malengrez, Maude, 131
Mandelbrot, Benoit, 125
Manley, Michael, 67
Mannheim, Karl, 76
Marc, 89
Marcus, George E., 15
Martelly, Michel Joseph, 61, 144
Marx, Karl, 135
Mathieu, Frantz Junior, 86
Maximilien, Guy, 131
Mazama, Ama, 141
Mbembe, Achille, 119
Ménard, Nadève, 5–6, 145–146
Ménil, René, 127
Michel, 60
Mickael, 75, 77, 87
Midi, Francklin, 131
Mintz, Sidney, 103
Moïse, Jovenel, 135, 143–144
Monique, 121–122
Montas, Michèle, 49
Muscade, Hurbert, 131

Namphy, Henri, 58
Neal, Mark Anthony, 134
Neff, Jules, 36
Nesbitt, Nick, 128, 130
Nixon, Richard M., 54
noirisme, 45–46
N'Zengou-Tayo, Marie-José, 66

Parti Communiste Haïtien (PCH), 44
Paul, 96
Péralte, Charlemagne, 42, 133

Peter, 88
Pétion, Alexandre, 32
PetroCaribe scandal, 135
Philoctète, René, 140
Pierre, 71–72, 74–76, 87, 88
Pierre, Jemima, 84, 144
Pierre-Charles, Gérard, 62
Pierre-Louis, François, 55
Préval, René, 61, 72, 85
Price, Sally, 103
Price-Mars, Jean, 25, 38, 40–42, 48, 131, 141
Puebla, Carlos, 120

Rachelle, 12–13
rasanblaj: acts of, 130; decolonial praxis,
   147; places of belonging, 6; practices of
   Caribbean worldmaking, 103–104, 125;
   projects of decoloniality, 102; transfor-
   mative potential of, 101
Reagan, Ronald, 49
Regis, Guy, Jr., 122
Richard, 61, 94
Richardson, Laurie, 57
Ricoeur, Paul, 127
Rigaud, Georges, 44
Roberjot Lartigue, Arnaud André, 31
Robinson, Cedric J., 34, 39
Rodman, Martha, 14
Ronald, 94
Roosevelt, Franklin D., 44
Roumain, Jacques, 25, 41, 43–44, 47
Roumain, Nicole, 47
Roumer, Emile, 41
ruptures: colonial, 25–29; coloniality, 64;
   crisis, 3; displacements, 23–24; irrepa-
   rable, 50; in time, 54
Rush, Anne Spry, 38
Rushdie, Salman, 54

Said, Edward, 119
Saint-Lot, Marie-Jose Alcide, 124
Salome, Giovanna, 131
Salomon, Lysius Félicité, 36, 37–38
Sam, J. D., 44
Sam, Jean Vilburn Guillaume, 39
Samson, Jean Erian, 136–137, 144
Samuel, 86–87
Saunders, Prince, 32
Sautet, Marc, 115–116
Schermann, Carine, 131
Schmidt, Hans, 39
Schuller, Mark, 68
Scott, David, 10, 50, 77, 129
Senghor, Léopold Sédar, 41

INDEX

Sharpe, Christina, 5, 6
Smith, Matthew, 41–42, 46
Solange, 122
Solarz, Stephen, 39
Soulouque, Faustin, 35
Soup nan Kay Sonson, 104–112
Spivak, Gayatri, 119
Suffren, Samuel, 136
Sylvain, Bènito, 37
Sylvain, Madeleine, 25, 44
Sylvain, Normil, 41
Sylvester, Megan, 69

Tèt Kale Party (PHTK), 85, 135, 143–144
Trois/Cent/Soixante, 127, 130–136
Trouillot, Lyonel, 64–66, 114–115, 131
Trouillot, Michel-Rolph, 5, 59, 137
Trump, Donald, 136
Turner, Nat, 32
2010 earthquake: damages, 11, 70; decline of revues, 131; dehumanizing images of quake victims, 138; destroying bookstores, 122; fault lines, 17, 142; jenn doktè return after earthquake, 4, 66; post-earthquake recovery, 2, 12, 52; revues after earthquake, 142; scholars' analyses after earthquake, 129; social transformation, 14, 18; U.N. ramps up presence, 85

Ulysse, Gina Athena, 17, 102, 148
United Nations Stabilization Mission in Haiti (MINUSTAH), 84, 85, 86, 89, 91, 154n2
United States: aid to Haiti, 54–55; author's upbringing, 1; Black intellectuals, 46; Blacks in, 31; capitalism, 7; denial of Haitian diplomatic recognition, 32; dialogue between U.S. Blacks and Haitians, 134; financial interests in Haiti, 42; Haitian diaspora, 154n1;

Haitians living in, 154n4; imperialism, 24, 39, 49, 138; military occupation, 81; racist and paternalistic stance toward Haiti, 39; segregation, 39; suppression of intellectuals, 10
University of Haiti (UEH): academic standards, 74; autonomy from and dependence upon the state, 83, 85; crisis, 18–19, 79–80, 87–90, 146; eroded quality of education, 69; ethnographic fieldwork, 14; faculty, 15–16; habitus of improvisation, 97–98, 146; and jenn doktè, 71, 75–76; leaders, 85; shaped by jenerasyon 86, 52, 66; and state control, 58, 60; struggle for place, 18; students, 86–87, 94–97; yellow zone, 86, 146
U.S. Occupation: and anti-imperial nationalist movement, 40; Bélizaire undergraduate thesis, 132; Castor dissertation on, 62; end of, 101; and neocolonialism, 84; and Price-Mars, 48; resistance to, 42, 126; women organizing against, 43

Vaval, Dean, 97–98, 146
Vaval, Josué, 90
Vesey, Denmark, 32
Vincent, Sténio Joseph, 43–44, 101

Wêche, Evains, 139
Williams, Henry, 37
Williams, Raymond, 82
Williams, Saul, 133
Wilson, Woodrow, 39
Wolf-Meyer, Matthew, 52

Yusoff, Kathryn, 26

Zani, Leah, 112

About the Author

DARLÈNE ELIZABETH DUBUISSON is an assistant professor of cultural anthropology at the University of Pittsburgh. Her research spans sociocultural anthropology, activist research, Black intellectual histories, Black feminist ethnography, speculative fiction, and visual culture. Her publications focus primarily on the Caribbean and Latin America, weaving together analyses of Black radicalism, imagination, crises, and futures. In addition to being a scholar, she is a mother, partner, and educator.

Available titles in the Critical Caribbean Studies series:

Giselle Anatol, *The Things That Fly in the Night: Female Vampires in Literature of the Circum-Caribbean and African Diaspora*

Alaí Reyes-Santos, *Our Caribbean Kin: Race and Nation in the Neoliberal Antilles*

Milagros Ricourt, *The Dominican Racial Imaginary: Surveying the Landscape of Race and Nation in Hispaniola*

Katherine A. Zien, *Sovereign Acts: Performing Race, Space, and Belonging in Panama and the Canal Zone*

Frances R. Botkin, *Thieving Three-Fingered Jack: Transatlantic Tales of a Jamaican Outlaw, 1780–2015*

Melissa A. Johnson, *Becoming Creole: Nature and Race in Belize*

Carlos Garrido Castellano, *Beyond Representation in Contemporary Caribbean Art: Space, Politics, and the Public Sphere*

Njelle W. Hamilton, *Phonographic Memories: Popular Music and the Contemporary Caribbean Novel*

Lia T. Bascomb, *In Plenty and in Time of Need: Popular Culture and the Remapping of Barbadian Identity*

Aliyah Khan, *Far from Mecca: Globalizing the Muslim Caribbean*

Rafael Ocasio, *Race and Nation in Puerto Rican Folklore: Franz Boas and John Alden Mason in Porto Rico*

Ana-Maurine Lara, *Streetwalking: LGBTQ Lives and Protest in the Dominican Republic*

Anke Birkenmaier, ed., *Caribbean Migrations: The Legacies of Colonialism*

Sherina Feliciano-Santos, *A Contested Caribbean Indigeneity: Language, Social Practice, and Identity within Puerto Rican Taíno Activism*

H. Adlai Murdoch, ed., *The Struggle of Non-Sovereign Caribbean Territories: Neoliberalism since the French Antillean Uprisings of 2009*

Robert Fatton Jr., *The Guise of Exceptionalism: Unmasking the National Narratives of Haiti and the United States*

Rafael Ocasio, *Folk Stories from the Hills of Puerto Rico/Cuentos folklóricos de las montañas de Puerto Rico*

Yveline Alexis, *Haiti Fights Back: The Life and Legacy of Charlemagne Péralte*

Katerina Gonzalez Seligmann, *Writing the Caribbean in Magazine Time*

Jocelyn Fenton Stitt, *Dreams of Archives Unfolded: Absence and Caribbean Life Writing*

Alison Donnell, *Creolized Sexualities: Undoing Heteronormativity in the Literary Imagination of the Anglo-Caribbean*

Vincent Joos, *Urban Dwellings, Haitian Citizenships: Housing, Memory, and Daily Life in Haiti*

Krystal Nandini Ghisyawan, *Erotic Cartographies: Decolonization and the Queer Caribbean Imagination*

Yvon van der Pijl and Francio Guadeloupe, eds., *Equaliberty in the Dutch Caribbean: Ways of Being Non/Sovereign*

Patricia Joan Saunders, *Buyers Beware: Insurgency and Consumption in Caribbean Popular Culture*

Atreyee Phukan, *Contradictory Indianness: Indenture, Creolization, and Literary Imaginary*

Nikoli A. Attai, *Defiant Bodies: Making Queer Community in the Anglophone Caribbean*

Samuel Ginsburg, *The Cyborg Caribbean: Techno-Dominance in Twenty-First-Century Cuban, Dominican, and Puerto Rican Science Fiction*

Linden F. Lewis, *Forbes Burnham: The Life and Times of the Comrade Leader*

Keja L. Valens, *Culinary Colonialism, Caribbean Cookbooks, and Recipes for National Independence*

Kim Williams-Pulfer, *Get Involved! Stories of Bahamian Civil Society*

Preity R. Kumar, *An Ordinary Landscape of Violence: Women Loving Women in Guyana*

Kezia Page, *Inside Tenement Time: Suss, Spirit, and Surveillance*

Natalie Lauren Belisle, *Caribbean Inhospitality: The Poetics of Strangers at Home*

Darlène Elizabeth Dubuisson, *Reclaiming Haiti's Futures: Returned Intellectuals, Placemaking, and Radical Imagination*